FAR CATHAY AND FARTHER INDIA.

FAR CATHAY
AND FARTHER INDIA

FAR CATHAY AND FARTHER INDIA

A. RUXTON MAC MAHON

GYAN

Published by

Gyan Publishing House
5, Ansari Road
Daryaganj, New Delhi-110002
Phone: 011-47034999, 9811692060
E-mail: books@gyanbooks.com

Distribution Network
gyanbooks.com
India, USA, Canada, UK, Australia

ISBN: 978-93-7447-505-8 (PB)

First Published, 1893

2nd Impression 2026

Printed at: Gyan Press, Delhi.

FAR CATHAY AND FARTHER INDIA
Author: A. RUXTON MAC MAHON

FAR CATHAY

AND

FARTHER INDIA

BY

MAJOR-GENERAL A. RUXTON MAC MAHON

FORMERLY H. M. POLITICAL AGENT AT THE COURT OF AVA

"..... the ship
From Ceylon, Inde, or far Cathay, unloads."
BYRON.

LONDON:
HURST AND BLACKETT, LIMITED.
13, GREAT MARLBOROUGH STREET.
1893.

Dedicated by Permission

TO

THE MOST NOBLE

THE MARQUIS OF DUFFERIN AND AVA,

K.P., G.C.B., G.C.S.I., G.C.M.G., G.C.I.E.,

LATE VICEROY OF INDIA

PREFACE.

A few years ago when the affairs of His Majesty of the Golden Foot arrived at a climax, necessitating the annexation of Upper Burma and its dependencies, the author contributed various articles to *Blackwood*, *Asiatic Quarterly*, and other periodicals, some extracts of which, through the courtesy of the editors thereof, he has now used to supplement other information compiled by him at odd corners of his leisure during a residence of more than twenty-five years in Farther India.

A. RUXTON MAC MAHON.

3, Whitehall Court, S.W.

CONTENTS.

CHAPTER I.

BORDER POLITICS 1

The *Times* Insists on the Necessity of a Decided Frontier Policy—Hysteric Desire to avoid Offending China—Lord Salisbury Influenced thereby—Chinese Envoy demands that England shall Acknowledge the Suzerainty of the Son of Heaven—Basis of Claim—Lord Salisbury Fences the Question successfully—Lord Rosebery Admits the Claim—His Lordship's Policy from Different Standpoints—China no longer Hopelessly Exclusive—Proof of a Great Wave of Change—Tso-Tsung-Tang's Curious Legacy—Soundness of the Conclusions of the *Times*.

CHAPTER II.

FORMER INTERCOURSE BETWEEN FAR CATHAY AND FARTHER INDIA 15

Lord Dufferin's Proclamation—Dacoity, or Gang-robbery—Ancient Intercourse with China—Embassies between India and China—Marco Polo employed as Ambassador by Kublai Khan—Prestige of China as a Maritime Power—Her Interest in Farther India—Friar Oderic's Marvellous Tales—Marco's Account of the Andamans—The Selungs, or Sea-Karens—Visit of King Solomon and Hiram's Navies to this Region—Kublai Khan's Craze for Universal Dominion—Burmese ever Refused to Acknowledge Chinese Suzerainty—Pathetic Death of Panthay King—Burma and China involved in Wars with European States.

CHAPTER III.

THE BURMESE 55

Distribution of Races—Various Degrees of Civilisation—Character of the Burman—Distinct Personality of the Burmese Woman—Barbarous Custom attending Childbirth—Success of Lady Dufferin's Scheme for Alleviating this Evil—Position of Woman according to the Buddhist Code—Red-Letter Day in a Burmese Girl's Almanac—Her Freedom—Simplicity of Marriage—Honeymoon Eccentricities—Wives fully Identify themselves with their Husbands—Women fully Protected by Laws—Female Dress—Burmese Origin.

CHAPTER IV.

THE BURMESE (*Continued*) 94

The Burmese Possess two Religions—Phôngyees or Monks—Education, Religious and Secular—How utilised by Sir Arthur Phayre—The Christian Missionary and the 'Heathen Chinee'—Opium—Intemperance—Drastic Method for Checking it—English and Indigenous Education Contrasted—Burmese and English Literature—Architecture—Burmese Contact with Europeans—Mr. Gladstone fell on the Beer Question—King Theebaw fell on the Shoe Question—The Latter Explained—Burmese Acceptance of Accomplished Facts—Eastern and Western Civilisation Contrasted.

CHAPTER V.

BURMESE EMBASSY TO THE QUEEN OF ENGLAND . 127

Lord Dalhousie's Annexation—Burmese Embassy to England—Audience of Her Majesty at Windsor—Its Reception by H.R.H. the Prince of Wales—Assist at State Ball, Concert, and Garden Fêtes—Real Aim of Mission—Anarchy anticipated on King Mengdon's Death—How averted Temporarily—No one could Name future King till Mengdon was *in extremis*—Theebaw 'Out of the Running'—His Collegiate Career—Intrigue of the Queen of the South in Theebaw's Favour—The Mengyee introduces Constitutional Government—Origin of this Innovation—Theebaw's Unhappy Fate—Massacre.

CHAPTER VI.

THE TALAINGS AND ARAKANESE 149

The Môns and Talaings within Recent Times enjoyed a Distinct Nationality—Now Practically the Same as the Burmese—Ancient City of Thahtun—Arrival thereat of Buddhist Missionaries—Marco Polo's reference to Talaings—Mythical Origin of the Arakanese—Nothing Notable in their Annals till the Twelfth Century—Beginning of Close Connection of Arakan with Bengal—Archers of the King's Body-Guard—Likened to the Pretorians—Sufferings of the Arakanese at the Hands of the Portuguese—The Great Mogul Determines to Abate the Scandal.

CHAPTER VII.

THE SHANS 161

Shans very Widely Dispersed—Antiquity of their Civilisation—Chequered Career—Origin of Name—Divided into Three Branches—Shan Records found at Manipur—Chinese Emperor's Expedition to India—Frustrated by Shans—Kingdom of Pong long Existed in great Splendour—Broken up by King Anawrahta—The Koh-Shan-Pyi—Their Inhabitants—Shan Politics plain in Mengdôn's Time—Complications under Theebaw's *régime*—British Sphere of Influence Undefined—Prospects of Shan States under a Strong and Friendly Government.

CHAPTER VIII.

THE KARENS 177

Karens Divided into Three Principal Tribes and Numerous Clans—Information as to Origin, Based on Tradition, Nevertheless Reliable—Migrated to Burma with the Chinese—Ancient Kingdom—Their Habits and Customs denote Central Asian Origin—Language Reduced to Writing—Bghai Dress and Ornaments—Karen Talent for Melody—Belief in a Supreme Being—Spiritualism—Fetish Stones—Augury by Fowls' Bones—Sorcery Compared with what used to Prevail in England—Notions Regarding the Future Life—Origin of Christian Mission.

CHAPTER IX.

CHINO-BURMESE BORDER TRIBES 211

Lord Dalhousie ignores the Teaching of an Aphorism—Result of Lord Dufferin's annexation—The *status* of the Border Tribes—Hilly regions between Burma and India successfully Negotiated by Burmese and Shans—Singpos badly treated by the English—Rule relating to Succession—Caterans with redeeming Characteristics—Tea (Cammellia Thea) found in this Region—Zardandan or Gold Teeth—Sorcery among Them—Dagroian Cannibalism—The Kaya or Red Karen—Kaya as Manufacturers—Conspicuous loyalty of Hill Karens—Marriages—Funerals of a Chief and Common Folk compared.

CHAPTER X.

CHINO-BURMESE BORDER TRIBES (*Continued*) . 240

Yindiline—Low Social Condition—Taru—Acute Sense of Shame Turbulence of Gaykho and Tsaw-Koo Tribes—Treaties—Ordeals—Gunpowder—Marriage—*Crim. Con.*—Sporting Proclivities—Khyen or Chin—Girl's Faces Tattooed—Marriage—A Game of Forfeits—Omniverous, barring Cannabalism—Oaths Pertaining to Border Tribes—A Karen Curse—Rice-Beer—A Barrel always on Tap—Bamboo Buckets—Great Capacity—Karen and Santal Legend—Redemption of Captives—A Karen Robin Hood.

CHAPTER XI.

INDO-BURMESE BORDER TRIBES 261

General Summary—People considered Impracticable even by the Imperial Dalhousie—Success of Sir Cecil Bendon's Departure—Language of this Region of a Broken and Infirm Type—All the Tribes understand a Common Language—Proverbial Philosophy—Bachelors' and Spinsters' Clubs—Courtship and Marriage—Women Valued in Ratio to Physical Capacity—High Prices demanded for Marriageable Girls—'Girls of the Period'—Clothing, from Figleaves to Elaborate Toilettes—Naga Delicacy—Toungya or Jum Cultivation—Manipur—Game of Polo—Origin of Name.

CHAPTER XII.

A FIELD FOR COMMERCIAL ENTERPRISE . . . 290

Ancient Fascination of Far Cathay—Vasco da Gama and his Successors—Mineral Wealth of Yunnan Proverbial—Ssu-ch'-uan Population Congested—Eastern Yunnan Trade Dominated by French—Persistence of Commercial Chambers for Construction of Railways to China—Railways in Burma Successful—Chinese Emigration should be Encouraged—Purchas and other Mediæval Travellers—Power of King of Pegu—Commissariat in Burmese Armies—M'Leod's Journey in 1839—Burmese Rubies in the Sixteenth Century—Statistics of Burmese Trade—The Great Drawback to Commerce—Want of Roads—Burmese and Chinese Customers—A well-known Fable Quoted.

APPENDIX 335

LETTER FROM THE KING OF BURMA TO THE QUEEN OF ENGLAND.

HER MAJESTY'S REPLY.

LETTER FROM THE KING OF BURMA TO THE PRINCE OF WALES.

ILLUSTRATIONS.

A BURMESE BAND . . . . *Frontispiece.*

BURMESE LADIES . . . . *To face page* 77

THE SHOWÉ DAGÔN PAGODA . . . . . ,, ,, 127

A SHAN FAMILY . . . . ,, ,, 161

A KAREN MARKET BOAT . . . . . . ,, ,, 177

KACHIN WOMEN . . . ,, ,, 220

CHIN GROUP . . . . ,, ,, 248

BURMESE COMMANDER-IN-CHIEF . . ,, ,, 323

FAR CATHAY AND FARTHER INDIA.

CHAPTER I.

BORDER POLITICS.

The *Times* Insists on the Necessity of a Decided Frontier Policy—Hysteric Desire to avoid Offending China—Lord Salisbury Influenced thereby—Chinese Envoy demands that England shall Acknowledge the Suzerainty of the Son of Heaven—Basis of Claim—Lord Salisbury Fences the Question successfully—Lord Rosebery Admits the Claim—His Lordship's Policy from Different Standpoints—China no longer Hopelessly Exclusive—Proof of a Great Wave of Change—Tso-Tsung-Tang's Curious Legacy—Soundness of the Conclusions of the *Times*.

REFERRING to our Indo-Chinese frontiers, the *Times*, last spring, declared that Burma had become the most interesting province in India, and indulged in the following remarks: 'The serious Kakhyen disturbances, telegraphed by our correspondent, are exactly what might have been expected to happen, and what, in one form or another, will continue to recur until the frontier policy is settled and the question of the border tribes is taken up with a firm hand. They form a striking justification of the necessity for the conference recently held in Calcutta to determine that policy. As we have already noted, the Chief Commissioner of Burma, who is the officer directly responsible to the Viceroy and to the nation for the peace of his frontier, has spoken with no ambiguous voice. He has declared against the cruel procrastination of half measures—that alternation of plunder and punishment which was long tried with the corresponding hill races of Eastern Bengal. Such a system was unsuccessful enough in itself; but in these days of telegraphs and special correspondents it has become impossible, for it outrages the conscience of the nation. When we annexed Upper Burma, in January, 1886, the necessity of a frontier delimitation was clearly foreseen. During six years it has been, perhaps unavoidably, postponed; but further delay is a wrong, alike to the frontier tribes who have been left without an acknowledged master, and to the brave troops who are kept continually exposed to the casualties arising out of such a state of things.'

The frontier question is comprised under three heads. The most simple, of course, is where the boundary resolves itself into a matter of administrative convenience between our territories of Assam and Burma. The next in order of difficulty is where it actually marches with those of China and Siam. The most embarrassing, strange to say, is where we are positively left to our own devices in regard to an unexplored zone of considerable dimensions lying between what is practically known as Burma and the confines of Tibet and China, which, with a light heart, cartographers have assigned to us in accordance with their notion of the fitness of things. So far as can be judged by the result of recent explorations in the vicinity of our frontier posts, disclosing the extremely turbulent character of its inhabitants, the probability of our taking possession of this *terra incognita* must be relegated to a very distant future; we shall, therefore, very likely, content ourselves with annexing only so much of it as may be necessary for the effective discharge of our duties as suzerain. When we succeed in making the Kakhyen, and other cognate tribes, more amenable to discipline than they are now, and are prepared to repeat this very troublesome process with other clans beyond them, we can move our real boundary farther north, and realise possession of that portion of our dominions which now only exists in the imagination.

We must take the inhabitants 'in hand and civilise them thoroughly, or leave them alone,' suggests a frontier officer; 'a savage with a veneer of civilisation being a most difficult individual to deal with.' And, being a sportsman as well as a diplomatist, he characteristically clinches his argument with the pungent and undeniable truth that 'it is of no use firing at a tiger with a pea-shooter.'

We may here appropriately make a passing allusion to a friendly passage of arms between the Chinese envoy at the Court of St. James and our Prime Minister some twelve years ago. When our relations with the Court of Ava were so strained that annexation was inevitable, there was such a hysteric desire to do anything rather than incur Chinese hostility, that the Celestials, had they been so minded, might have put considerable pressure upon us. Even a strong man, like Lord Salisbury, was evidently influenced by this quasi panic; for, at the Guildhall banquet in 1885, he informed his hearers that, in dealing with Upper Burma, we should act in the most complete recognition of the rights of China, who, convinced of the fact that she might have worse neighbours than the English, was looking, contrary to nature, to a sun in the west. This touching confidence in China's friendliness must have been rudely shaken when, shortly afterwards, the representative of the Flowery Land essayed to keep his lordship to the strict letter of his after-dinner speech, by demanding that England should acknowledge her vassalage to China by the payment of decennial tribute as—he alleged—did Burma, in whose relative position she now stands.

It may here be explained that the Chinese base their tribute claim on a convention made at the close of the war of 1769, whereby—they declare—the Burmese agreed to send them decennial presents, and they argue that, in taking possession of Burma, we became responsible for her obligations. The Burmese, on the other hand, indignantly repudiate this idea, and retort that there was a reciprocal arrangement, by which both sides bound themselves to despatch presents in token of amity. With a happy instinct, Lord Salisbury accepted the situation, agreeing to send presents from Burma every ten years and receive return gifts—a solution worthy of Columbus, the propounder of the egg problem. His successor Lord Rosebery, however, was cajoled into consenting to the despatch of presents from the Burmese side only, and, thereby unequivocally admitting China's claims to suzerainty, gratuitously tendered a most abject submission to the Son of Heaven, without obtaining apparently any tangible *quid pro quo.*

> '*Cymbeline.* Well,
> My peace we will begin; and, Caius Lucius,
> Although the victor, we submit to Cæsar,
> And to the Roman empire; promising
> To pay our wonted tribute.'

The envoy afterwards modified this demand by condescending to allow us to purchase exemption from the suggested indignity by territorial indemnity, in the shape of a huge slice of our territory, making the Showelee River, considerably south of Bhamó, its southern boundary.

This not a little exercised the British Government, as it meant the complete cession to China not only of a broad band of debatable territory, said to be inhabited by 'savage tribes,' but also several hundred square miles of what is, and always has been, Burmese territory. It was felt at the time that if we could have reconciled to our conscience the propriety of handing over any of our new fellow-subjects to the tender mercies of the Chinese, it was open to grave doubt whether the result would be satisfactory. It was plausibly argued that the turbulent tribes dominating the trade routes, having Chinese affinities, would be more easily managed by Chinamen than by us. It so happens, however, that it is almost certain that the Shans, who are the only people in this region to which this description can apply, would prefer our rule. The hitherto impracticable Kakhyens are as alien to the Chinese as to the English. Indeed, if the theory of affinity were pushed to its logical conclusion, these representatives of the archaic Mongoloid family ought to be readily amenable to the more civilised people of the same stock; whereas experience of Burmese rule proves the contrary. Hitherto, the Chinese have been as unfortunate in dealing with turbulent border tribes as the English have been successful,—a fact that materially tends to demolish the arguments of those who favour the former. The people most affected, again, might reasonably object to be bandied from pillar to post, from ruler to ruler, without reference to their feelings; while the notion of surrendering an important *entrepôt* of trade and a strategical position like Bhamó, which not only controls the whole of the Upper Irawadi valley, but is also the natural centre for railway and telegraph lines between India, Burma, and China, seems absolutely preposterous.

Even the most complaisant were of opinion that the demand was a very high price to pay for the goodwill of China, but comforted themselves with the reflection that our representative would insist on receiving adequate value for his concession. An elucidation of the mystery and confirmation of this theory were recently afforded by the publication, *quasi* simultaneously, of two interesting papers, one by an apparently inspired writer in the *North China Herald*, and another in the *Manchester Guardian* by an eminent authority in the person of Sir Charles Crossthwaite, Chief Commissioner of Burma in those troublous times.

According to the former, 'Lord Rosebery dealt with the demand in a manner which, under other circumstances, we should say was very Chinese. He continued talking with the Marquis Tsêng in London, and meantime telegraphed to Mr. O'Conor, then Chargé d'Affaires in Pekin, to ascertain how far the Marquis represented his Government in making this demand, and on what terms the Chinese were willing to adjourn the discussion of the subject. Mr. O'Conor found that the Yamên had never heard of the Showelee River nor anything of the Marquis's demand, and apparently were serenely indifferent about it. He found, however, they were profoundly concerned in two matters: one was the demand then before them to give passports to Mr. Colman Macaulay and his mission to go into Tibet, and the other was the quinquennial * complimentary mission from the Kings of Burma to Pekin. The Yamên wanted to know what provision Great Britain proposed to make for this "tributary" mission.

* Decennial.

The Ministers cared little and knew less about the frontier: the Showelee River and the Irawadi were terms of no meaning, but the tributary mission was a topic of the last importance. With this information in his possession, Lord Rosebery, still simulating great interest in his negotiations with the Marquis Tsêng, instructed Mr. O'Conor to do the best he could, but to secure the postponement of any question relating to the frontier; and Mr. O'Conor played his hand remarkably well. He concluded the convention of 1886 with a celerity which must have astonished the Yamên. He agreed to postpone for the present the awkward question about the Tibet passports; he agreed that some Burmese ecclesiastics, led by the Buddhist Archbishop of Mandalay or Rangoon, should go every five years to Pekin (we believe that the appointment of a Buddhist Archbishop was explained by the alleged fact that the Emperor of China was the head of the Buddhist Church in China!); and on their side the Chinese decided to defer the discussion of any question connected with the frontier for the present. It was understood at the time, and is, we believe, in formal documents, though not in the text of the convention, that no British official was to form any part of this quinquennial mission, and that the Archbishop was to arrange for himself who the members of his suite were to be. But the strangest part of this extraordinary transaction was that, if the Marquis Tsêng never informed his Government of what he was doing, his Government kept him in the dark as to what they were doing. The Yamên knew nothing of the Showelee, and the Marquis knew nothing of the Tibet passports or the quinquennial mission. We are informed that absolutely the first information the Chinese Minister in London received of any negotiations in Pekin was an official *communiqué* in the London *Times* from the Foreign Office containing the text of the convention.'

The delimitation of the frontier was accordingly postponed at the urgent solicitation of Lord Rosebery. It was not lost sight of, however, for only a few years ago the demands of the Chinese became so pressing that the late Mr. Baber was sent post-haste to Bhamó to stave off the question.

'When Mr. O'Conor made his slapdash arrangement,' says the same authority, 'his chief in Downing Street felt very much like the criminal who was sentenced to death by a Sultan, and who secured a temporary respite by undertaking within a given period to teach the Sultan's favourite ass to speak. He defended his undertaking the hopeless task on the ground that in the meantime the Sultan might die, or the ass might die, or he himself might die, and in the interval he had his life. Lord Rosebery wanted the frontier matter put off, and trusted to the chapter of accidents. He drew bills on futurity in the hope that they might not have to be met, and with the certainty that, even if they had, the price would be less than that he was then called upon to pay. It was hoped, no doubt, that in five years the

Chinese would see how absurd was the arrangement of a Buddhist Archbishop going to Pekin; but now the bills have reached maturity, and the Chinese want to know how they are to be met. Here we must do the Chinese the justice to say, we are given to understand they are quite indifferent whether the Archbishop ever goes to Pekin or not, but they know the distaste the British authorities will have for this mission, and they hope to employ it as a screw to extract better terms in regard to the delimitation of the frontier.'

Last spring, accordingly, it appears they urgently called attention to the boundary question on the ground that the country had been at peace for some years and that there was no longer any reason why this important matter should be postponed.

Now that Lord Rosebery is again at the Foreign Office, 'John Chinaman' is sure to present his little bill. It will be interesting to watch how his lordship will tackle the difficulty.

Up to the year 1866, says Sir Charles Crossthwaite, who thoroughly endorses Lord Rosebery's former policy, 'it was hardly necessary, so far as the peace of the Indian Empire was concerned, to consider the feelings of China or manage her susceptibilities. Now, however, circumstances are distinctly changed. Burma has become an important factor in the problem of our political relations with China. Whether we like it or not, we cannot afford entirely to disregard either the feelings of the Chinese in Burma or the disposition of the Chinese Government. Fortunately, the statesmen who were directing our policy recognised the changed conditions and appreciated the delicacy of the situation from the very outset. China had a claim to Burma. Her claim might be dim and ill-defined, and founded rather on the history of the past than the facts of the present time. Still, it was a claim to the suzerainty of the country, and one which had to be answered.'

'It is easy to conceive what trouble the Chinese inside and outside the province might have caused us if their Government had been hostile and made known its wish to throw obstacles in the way of the settlement of Burma. The troubles which after so many years still obstruct the progress of the French in Tonquin show what might easily have happened in our province. Burma, said a Chinese journal some time ago, may be likened to a beautiful ball of gold, which a man having found lying in his path has picked up and carried off. A little boy who had lost the ball stopped the man and said, "Man, that is my ball." "Very well, my boy," said the man; "it is yours, I know. All I want is to keep it safe for you. It was lying about, and you will lose it." The boy was quite content with this, and went on with his play. But had the man spoken roughly to the boy and denied his claim, the child would have thrown dirt and stones at the man and followed him with abuse, and he would have had no peace or enjoyment in his possession of the ball. The writer then went on to say that the English had acted with the wisdom shown by the man in this parable, and therefore had been left to perform their task in peace. The French, on the other hand, had repudiated China's claims and insulted her dignity, and therefore they had been annoyed incessantly by Black Flags and pirates, as the French term the dacoits. True wisdom, therefore, and, it may be added, true courage, were shown by the British Government in its decision to avoid all cause of offence to China by admitting the claim of the Emperor to the suzerainty of Burma. A Government less conscious of its power might have hesitated to make any concession to a claim so unsubstantial. It has been agreed to send an embassy or deputation to China from Burma every ten years, with some presents, in accordance with an old custom. To please the child, his wish to have the ball nominally recognised as his property has been so far gratified, and at this shadowy price the quiet possession of the substance has been secured. Enough perhaps has been said to show that our relations with the Chinese Empire have been changed materially and rendered closer and more important by the annexation of Upper Burma. While on the north-west frontier the British Indian Empire is in contact with Russia, on the east it is in close touch with China. It is of importance that this position should be more widely known and appreciated.'

The interests of both England and China demand that they shall mutually establish and maintain a good understanding, so as to counteract any malign influence that may be brought to bear on either or both by the insidious advances of their great rival in the Asian question. Single-handed we easily beat the French in the little game of diplomacy lately played in India beyond the Ganges, and in alliance with China we can checkmate Russia in the bigger game.

The Chinese, it is said, are ready to meet us half-way. Enlightened men among them have long ago come to the conclusion that they can no longer maintain with advantage their time-honoured policy of exclusiveness. A remarkable proof of the wave of change which has been passing over the Flowery Land was notably exemplified in a very curious political legacy left, a few years ago, to the Chinese Emperor and his people by the famous Viceroy Tso-Tsung-Tang—a Chinese of the Chinese, a man in whom the characteristic virtues and defects of his race were magnified. It seems only yesterday that the crass imperturbability of the people of the Middle Kingdom was so pronounced that one as much expected to see the Iron Horse as to meet a Celestial without a pigtail. But now they are as fully convinced of the importance of railways and telegraphs as, only a short time ago, they were persuaded to the contrary.

To sum up, the conclusions of the *Times* as to the interest and importance of the frontier policy and the proper handling of the border tribes may be accepted in their entirety. But, after all, they are only part of the far larger question comprised in China going hand-in-hand with England, so that each may do her respective duty in the interests of universal commerce, by fully developing these most promising regions.

CHAPTER II.

FORMER INTERCOURSE BETWEEN FAR CATHAY AND FARTHER INDIA.

Lord Dufferin's Proclamation—Dacoity, or Gang-robbery—Ancient Intercourse with China—Embassies between India and China—Marco Polo employed as Ambassador by Kublai Khan—Prestige of China as a Maritime Power—Her Interest in Farther India—Friar Oderic's Marvellous Tales—Marco's Account of the Andamans—The Selungs, or Sea-Karens—Visit of King Solomon and Hiram's Navies to this Region—Kublai Khan's Craze for Universal Dominion—Burmese ever Refused to Acknowledge Chinese Suzerainty—Pathetic Death of Panthay King—Burma and China involved in Wars with European States.

On the 1st of January, 1886, His Excellency, the Earl of Dufferin, issued the following notice:

'By command of the Queen-Empress, it is hereby notified that the territories formerly governed by King Theebaw will no longer be under his rule, but have become part of Her Majesty's dominions, and will, during Her Majesty's pleasure, be administered by such officers as the Viceroy and Governor-General of India may from time to time appoint.'

To the superficial observer, this notification meant merely the prolongation of our boundary between China and India, extending, with a break at Nepal, from the north of Kashmir to the eastern limit of Assam. The more thoughtful, however, knew that our political responsibilities were vastly increased thereby. For, whereas before the whole breadth of the Himalaya range intervened between our Indian provinces and the boundary separating us from the outlying dependencies of the Flowery Land, we can now, as it were, shake hands across the border. The situation also had materially changed from the Chinese standpoint, for while India, in days of yore, was the *Ultima Thule* of Celestial geography, it had been brought to their very doors.

It was generally admitted that the purely military operations necessary for the occupation of Burma might be simple enough, yet no one imagined that a territory which had been subject to anarchy for many years could be reorganised without patience, trouble, and sympathetic treatment by officers of experience. The campaign, as anticipated, proved to be a mere military promenade, and, for weeks after the arrival of our troops at Mandalay, the attitude of the people seemed all that could be desired. This lull after the storm seems to have taken our authorities off their guard, for they too long delayed the necessary precautions for the civil administration of the country which they had all along deemed inevitable. Apparently living in a fool's paradise, their inaction seemed to denote their trust in administrative affairs arranging themselves as simply as was the case with the military manœuvres—that they had inherited, in fact, an Arcadia in which the necessities of a police executive found no place.

Dacoity, or gang-robbery, was the natural result of revolution and anarchy. In its initial stage, and probably in its subsequent development, it never assumed a strictly political tendency. Many who, under ordinary circumstances, were law-abiding people took to the nefarious calling for the mere love of excitement, or to be considered men of spirit by their sweethearts; others adopted it to escape starvation. Thus inoculated, they became more or less reckless and demoralised, and in organised gangs even ventured to confront our troops. At last it came to such a pass that they found they must either make it their regular business to rob others, or be robbed themselves, for, excepting at our widely separated posts on the river Irrawadi, there was neither law nor dominant authority in the country. They were between Scylla and Charybdis, for they were a prey to professional dacoits on the one hand, and if found with arms required for protection they were harassed by our troops on the other. Over-zealous efforts to stamp out dacoity by shooting and flogging men and burning villages, coupled with a want of readiness to pardon offenders who repented the evil of their ways, hardened men of this stamp and aggravated the difficulty.

Brigandage may be said to have been normal in Upper Burma. The maladministration by King

Theebaw no doubt emphasised it, but it was also rife in his astute and respectable father's time. The late King Mengdôn, in his personal interest, preferred to pay his officials modest salaries rather than allow them to acquire enormous gains to the detriment of the Royal treasury which the farming out of appointments under the ordinary system entailed. In the same selfish spirit, but presumably to keep them out of harm's way, His Majesty only allowed his sons miserable pittances in the way of pocket-money. The consequence was that many of his Ministers and some of the Royal Princes did not consider it beneath their dignity to be hand-in-glove with notorious free-booters in order to share the proceeds of robbery. A dacoit gang was, in fact, as much a political necessity to a Burmese Minister as a newspaper organ is to Ministers in more civilised countries.

During the prevalence of revolution and anarchy in our new inheritance, the attitude of China was a potent factor in the situation which could not be ignored. Had she elected to be hostile, the British authorities might have been involved in very serious complications. Her friendship, or, at any rate, her neutrality was therefore well-nigh indispensable. The success of our diplomatists in securing the goodwill of the Son of Heaven was accordingly highly commendable.

Though Burma may be taken as the pivot on which this work turns, the title, 'Far Cathay and Farther India,' seems sufficiently appropriate, in-asmuch as the subject relates not only to the meeting of China with Burma, but also includes other countries of the fluviatile region influenced by the Irawadi, Salwin, and Mekhong rivers, either directly subject to Britain or within its sphere of influence—a territory which Sir William Hunter describes as the 'battle-ground and grave of strange races and kingdoms who appear and disappear with scarcely an echo from their existence penetrating to the outer world.'*

In the very dawn of history considerable intercourse existed between many notable countries on the face of our globe, and that spacious seat of archaic civilisation which in modern times has loomed so largely as China; in the middle ages as Cathay; and in ancient times as Seres. As far back as 'the reign of Taiwu (B.C. 1634) ambassadors accompanied by interpreters and belonging to seventy-six distinct kingdoms are reported to have arrived from remote regions at the Court of China.'† Representatives of India and Indo-China were doubtless included in this goodly company. The Chinese annals, however, do not aid us on this point, and make no direct reference to foreign countries till a century or so before the Christian era, when India appears to have exercised as great a fascination for the Celestial imagination as it did in Europe fifteen centuries afterwards. During the reign of Hsia-wu-ti of the Han dynasty, it is recorded that a military commander named Chang Kien, on returning to Pekin from duty in the

* Hunter's 'Gazetteer of India.'

† Yule's 'Cathay, and the Way Thither.' London, 1866.

region of the Oxus, reported that he had heard of a country, situated to the south-east of Bactria, called Shintu or India, which promised to be specially interesting to the Middle Kingdom from the fact that Ssu-ch-'uan goods imported from India had been seen in the Bactrian markets, giving colour to a well-founded belief that the south-western provinces of the Flowery Land were in touch with Shintu, and thus seemed within measurable distance of a trade beneficial to both.

The Son of Heaven was not a little impressed by Chang Kien's report, and, in the interests of commerce and a possible increase of imperial tribute, acted upon it at once by dispatching commissioners to report on the three routes, which, according to the commander's information, seemed the most promising. These were: (1) by the Yang-tse-Kiang, described as dangerous and difficult; (2) through the Hiungiu territory, inhabited by turbulent people continually giving trouble on the frontier;* and (3) *viâ* Ssu-ch-'uan, in a westerly direction, regarding which particulars had not then been ascertained. All the exploring parties, however, returned discomfited, chiefly by reason of the impracticability of the 'barbarians' encountered in every direction.

It is curious to notice how history repeats itself. In 1868, for instance, three attempts were made to penetrate the obscurities of this very region,

* Chang Kien had been imprisoned by this tribe, and therefore was able to report from personal experience.

and all were frustrated owing to identical misfortune. Mr. Cooper elected to explore Chang Kien's route No. 3. Arriving at Ssu-ch-'uan from the Chinese seaboard, he managed to reach the most westerly point attained by any traveller from the Flowery Land. Unfortunately, however, just as he fancied himself certain of being able to penetrate the 'iron wall' between Cathay and Shintu, his hopes were doomed by the prohibition of the Chinese authorities. Major Sladen's expedition from Bhamó was unable to proceed further than Momein or Teng-yueh-chou, the frontier town of Yunnan. The governor treated its members very courteously, but objected to their proceeding farther, on the professed ground of danger to themselves from the disturbed state of the country due to the Panthay rebellion. Its leader, hampered with instructions to avoid 'complications,'—the bane of the official mind—had therefore to return without having effected commercial results; and, by entering into friendly relations with the Panthays, unwittingly hatched further complications, which resulted in serious misunderstanding with the Chinese Government, and the complete discomfiture and ruin of his quondam friends. Another expedition was dispatched in 1874, under the guidance of Colonel Horace Browne, which ended in a complete *fiasco*, after having proceeded only a short distance from Bhamó. This mission is also notable for the untoward fate of Augustus Raymond Margery, its capable and distinguished pioneer.

The great effort of Captain Dondart de la Grée from Saigon *viâ* Kiang-hung, with the view of exploring the head waters of the Mekhong, was not so easily baffled, though similar tactics were tried to prevent his visiting Talifu. Captain Dondart, being too ill to attempt the feat (he subsequently died), entrusted its execution to Lieutenant Garnier, his second in command, who actually bearded the pseudo Emperor Suleiman in his capital. Suffice it to remark, the French were bitterly disappointed to find that the Mekhong was altogether impracticable as a means for developing commerce.

Hsia-wu-ti's immediate successors were not so sanguine as he, so the matter remained in abeyance for a long time. India, as a matter of fact, did not become known to the Chinese for two centuries afterwards, and then not by the short cut across the intervening regions, but by the Bactrian route, which was used up to the middle of the seventeenth century, when it was stopped by the King of Great Tibet in retaliation for the Great Mogul's invasion of his country.

Chang Kien's idea of a more direct communication between the Flowery Land and Shintu, though long shelved, was not abandoned. Indeed, it was revived with the pertinacity for which the Celestials are famous when vital interests are at stake. Tentative measures to this end were initiated so successfully, that they were encouraged to extend their operations, and eventually established an important trade *entrepôt* at Bhamó, with which India is in touch *viâ* the Irawadi and the

Bay of Bengal. It is interesting to note that Bhamó is marked on Fra Mauro's famous world map, published in the middle of the fifteenth century, and 'on the upper part of the river of Ava is a rubric which runs: *Qui le marchatantie se translata da fuime a fuime per andar in Chataio.* "Here goods are transferred from river to river and so pass on to Cathay."'*

During the Woo dynasty, or in the third century of our era, the King of Foonan—now Tonquin and Cambodia—sent an embassy to India, which arrived by the mouth of the Irawadi *viâ* the Bay of Bengal, to the great astonishment of the king of the country, who gave the envoys Scythian horses to take back to their sovereign. A perusal of curious details, placed on record by these and other Chinese travellers, proves that the Celestials were then better informed about India than might be expected. At a very early period, China exercised such an influence in Hindustan that several ambassadors came therefrom charged with friendly letters and presents, which by Celestial euphony—as is the case to this day—were termed tribute. There was some excuse for this arrogance, for at a remote age China achieved a position entitling her to be considered the most powerful nation among the States of Central Asia; and it is very possible Indian Princes, who had been conquered and oppressed by Scythian hordes, may have hoped

* Yule's 'Geographical Introduction to Gill's River of Golden Sand.' London, 1883.

to rid themselves of the yoke by endeavouring to ingratiate themselves with the paramount Power, which had already extended its conquests beyond the Caspian Sea and as far as Bengal.

From very remote times embassies very frequently passed between the Middle Kingdom and Hindustan, when such diplomatic amenities were not even dreamt of, much less in vogue, in Europe. The first on record* is in the middle of the seventh century, A.D., when the King of Magadha or Behar sent an ambassador to Tai-tsung of the T'ang dynasty, probably the greatest monarch in Chinese history, who in return was graciously pleased to send one of his officers to the Indian king, with an imperial patent inviting his submission. The latter, fully impressed with the honour of being selected as the first recipient of such condescension, complied with the imperial requisition, and in recognition of his obsequiousness the Emperor accredited an ambassador to the Court of Magadha, 'in order that the principles of humanity and justice which had been diffused in that country might have a permanent protector and representative there.' This amicable arrangement existed for some years, or till the conduct of the King's successor provoked the Emperor to invade India and punish his refractory feudatory, a feat His Majesty performed by the aid of the sovereigns of Tibet and Nepal so effectually, that the Kings of the Five Indies sent ambassadors to offer homage to the Son of Heaven, and five hun-

* Yule's 'Cathay, and the Way Thither.'

dred and eighty-one cities surrendered to the arms of China, adding greatly to her prestige.

After Buddhism was introduced into the Middle Kingdom, the Princes of all the Buddhist countries in this region also joyfully despatched missions to the Emperor, who often condescended to return the compliment by imperial missions to keep up his prestige.

Marco Polo was often employed in various embassies by Kublai Khan, when he ascertained that his zeal, courage, and discretion could be relied on, and that his reports, instead of being confined to the four corners of his instructions—as was the case with the despatches submitted by his own subjects—were replete with interesting particulars of the countries and peoples he exploited. In his first important mission he visited and gave most interesting particulars regarding various places in Yunnan and Burma, which have become familiar in recent discussions on the subject of trade routes between the Flowery Land and the Golden Chersonese. Difficulties, however, arise as to the exact extent of the great traveller's journey; in other words, to determine where his narrative is founded on personal knowledge and where on hearsay merely.

Not the least interesting of his adventures was when, with his father Niccolo and his uncle Maffeo, he was commissioned by the Great Khan to return with three barons sent to his Court as ambassadors from Argon, Lord of the Levant,*

* Yule's 'Marco Polo.'

to fetch as his bride a lady belonging to the family of Queen Bologna, his late consort. It appears that the Khan called the Italians into his presence, and intrusted them with golden tablets of authority, which gave them the right of passage through all his dominions, and secured them facilities for procuring all that they might require. Thirteen ships were commissioned for the use of the embassy, escorting Queen Coachin, Lord Argon's bride-elect, and her companion, the daughter of the King of Manu. The capacity of these vessels may be imagined when they are described as having had four masts, and often hoisting as many as twelve sails, with some sixty or seventy private cabins, provided with closets and other conveniences, as well as public rooms for the use of merchants and other first-class passengers, besides ample accommodation for two hundred or more sailors, who sometimes had their families with them, and also managed to find space for small kitchen-gardens in spare ship's buckets. These arks, though larger than any ships afloat in Europe, and containing as many water-tight compartments as the largest American liner of the present day, were, according to Marco, smaller than the Chinese possessed before that period. The fleet put forth to sea with the envoys and a goodly company, and first touched at Java, and, loosing thence, it proceeded to the different ports in the Indian seas, the voyage lasting about two years, thus enabling our Venetians to give most interesting accounts of their novel experiences, as well as an idea of the extent of Chinese influence at that time in Farther India. Suffice it to say, the envoys arrived at their destination in due course, and handed over the ladies to Casan, who, owing to the death of his father Argon, had not only become Lord of the Levant, but, in accordance with the custom of the country, had also inherited his father's right to the young lady in Marco's charge.

Animated with the same spirit of enterprise that stimulated Drake, Frobisher, and other English worthies, the Great Khan was not a little aggressive, for he sent numerous expeditions against Japan and Java, which, though not always successful, prove that he had vast resources at his disposal, in the shape of ships, mariners, troops of various kinds, as well as abundance of war *matériel.* No wonder, then, that he insisted on all intercourse with the Flowery Land resolving itself into the form of homage; for he had learned from the annals of his country that, for several centuries previously, the Kings of India and the Golden Chersonese had been in the habit of sending embassies to China for the payment of tribute. At the time of Marco Polo's voyage, the prestige of China as a maritime Power seems to have arrived at its zenith. It subsequently waned, and in the beginning of the fifteenth century the Emperor felt himself constrained to send a large fleet with a military force to India and the Golden Chersonese, to coerce those that wavered in their allegiance, and encourage the loyal by the bestowal of honours and imperial gifts.

Some of the great traveller's experience in this region may appropriately be mentioned here, as they show that Cathay had then very many material interests in Farther India. He first notes Chamba or Cochin China, which he describes as peopled by 'idolaters' subject to Kublai Khan, to whom they paid yearly a tribute 'of elephants, and nothing but elephants.' Judging rightly that this very curious subsidy needed explanation, he enters into particulars in his own quaint fashion, to the effect that the imbecile king of the country, finding himself unequal to cope with the great force of horse and foot, commanded by a great baron, whom the Khan sent to annex Chamba, dispatched envoys with a piteous petition, offering that potentate an annual tribute of as many elephants as he pleased if he would order his baron 'to desist from harrowing his kingdom and quit his territories.'* Kublai, 'moved with pity,' complied with this prayer, and coolly directed his officer to 'carry his arms to the conquest of some other country.' The Great Khan impressed on his lieutenants the necessity of coercing all who declined to submit to his jurisdiction—the order in which they were exploited being a mere matter of detail with which he did not condescend to concern himself. He might have exclaimed with Pistol, 'The world's my oyster, which I with sword will open.'

Excepting an extraordinary number of pachyderms, almost the only other fact Polo considers

* Yule's 'Marco Polo.'

worthy of remark was the Solomon-like proclivities of the King, who was blessed with three hundred and twenty-six olive-branches, and approved a rather arbitrary mode of selecting his wives. 'You must know,' Marco says, 'that in that kingdom no woman is allowed to marry until the King shall have seen her; if the woman pleases him, then he takes her to wife; if she does not, then he gives her a dowry, to get her a husband withal.'* Strange to say, Marco Polo does not even incidentally allude to the 'really wonderful thing' described by his countryman Friar Oderic when in Cochin China.† The worthy padre gravely informs us that the fish of that country are remarkable for a most accommodating spirit of self-sacrifice in leaping on shore at certain seasons of the year, and thus, most considerately, sparing the people the trouble of catching them in the sea. In the ordinary course of things they knew they were destined to die, and practically warned the fishermen not to let down their nets; just as the historical racoon, in like predicament, called out from a tree-top to his would-be murderer—a crack shot—'Don't shoot. I'll come down.'

Another strange omission in one so observant as our traveller is the absence of any allusion to the abnormal size of the tortoise tribe in that portion of Farther India. Dominie Sampson would certainly have pronounced them 'prodi-

* Yule's 'Marco Polo.'

† Yule's 'Cathay, and the Way Thither.'

gious,' judging by the size of the shell seen by the friar, which he assures us was bigger than the dome of the cathedral church of St. Antonio in Padua.

Before bidding a final farewell to trans-Gangetic countries subject to his master, the Great Khan, Marco Polo visited the Andaman and Nicobar groups of islands, which, though situated so close to the highly civilised Indo-China, are inhabited by Mincopies, or Oriental negroes, in the lowest stage of barbarism. He describes these peoples—as, in his opinion, 'indeed it was highly proper to do in this our book'—rather in the highly sensational method approved in sailors' yarns, than in his own quaintly matter-of-fact way. After premising that the inhabitants have no semblance of any form of government, 'are no better than wild beasts,' as well as being 'idolaters,' he records that they 'are a most cruel generation, and eat every body that they can catch, if not of their own raee,' and also that 'the men have heads like dogs, and teeth and eyes likewise; in fact, in the face they are just like big mastiff dogs.'

Purchas, who visited the islands in the sixteenth century, confirms all that Polo says of the cannibalism of their people.

'If by evill chance any ship bee lost on those islands, as many have beene, there is not one man of those ships lost that escapeth uneaten or unslain . . . They would trucke for olde shirts or pieces of old linnen breeches. These ragges they let downe with a rope into their Barke unto them and looke what they thought those things to be worth, so much fruit they would make fast to the rope and let us hale it in; and it was told me that at some times a man shall have for an olde Shirt a good piece of Amber.' *

The shock to Marco's delicacy at the absence of clothing on the part of the Nicobar people is thus commented on:

'I tell you they go all naked, both men and women, and do not use the slightest covering of any kind.'

Though in compliance with the arbitrary decrees of fashion near the English settlements, the men now submit to a compromise in the shape of a very narrow cloth, and the women of a grass girdle, others beyond this zone remain naked and are not ashamed. Till comparatively late times, all the islanders were more or less partial to the highly objectionable practice of killing and eating their fellow-creatures. In fact, it was owing to frightful disclosures of massacres of crews of vessels visiting the islands that led to their being periodically visited by Her Majesty's men-of-war, and eventually occupied by the British Government. The inhabitants are still 'idolaters'; still prefer nudity to the encumbrance of clothing, and would not object to Dean Swift's suggestion of 'cold missionary on their sideboards'; nevertheless, the dog face description decidedly comes under the head of libel.

* Purchas' 'Pilgrimes.' London, 1625.

This unique and primitive race, which for centuries has been estranged from the outer world, is threatened in the near future with complete extinction. Like the Pacific islanders, they are unable to survive contact with European civilisation.

Not far from the Andamans, in the Mergui Archipelago, and therefore British subjects, Marco Polo would have found in the Selungs or Sea-Karens of Burmo-Malay type a race of islanders differing materially in mental as well as physical characteristics from the negroes he condemns so severely. For though he would doubtless have classed them as 'idolaters,' with merely a traditional belief in a beneficent God, he would also have found them naturally kind and confiding, though timid, owing to long-endured oppression at the hands of Malays, Chinese, and Burmese, of whose slave-hunting expeditions they give accounts which 'bear melancholy marks of truthfulness.' As a rule, they live in their boats, which they cleverly construct with rude tools, aided by fire, and obtain rice by the barter of sea-slugs, turtles, beeswax, and other natural products of their islands. Some success has been achieved by the English in encouraging cultivation and village settlements; but so spasmodically that the white man is chiefly known by vague report as a beneficent being whose visits, as Blair has it, are 'like those of angels, few and far between.'

The inevitable absorption by China of the trans-Gangetic peoples, checked as it is, and indefinitely delayed though it may be, by the predominance of Western civilisation, must needs be a potent factor in the question of immigration from the over-crowded provinces of Cathay to the sparsely populated regions of the Golden Chersonese. Before venturing to offer a few suggestions on a subject of such paramount importance to our future prospects, we propose, by way of preface, to indulge in a brief retrospect of the relations that have for centuries existed between our recent inheritance and the great empire of China. To begin with their rulers—the happy possessors of numerous titles indicative of their great glory and power, but who for all practical purposes may be referred to as the 'Great Chief of Righteousness' and 'Son of Heaven'—the distinctions they both affected—condescended to address each other as 'Younger Brother' and 'Elder Brother' respectively. And as is the case with other brothers we wot of, who, though they may occasionally quarrel, are nevertheless the best of friends, so these brethren of the Golden Chersonese and Far Cathay, notwithstanding many a sharp tussle and stand-up fight, on the whole cordially fraternised. Their people never allowed the wars, in which they were occasionally plunged by their rulers, to disturb for any length of time their reciprocal feelings of goodwill.

Though the Burmese consider themselves ineffably superior to all other peoples, next in the scale of humanity they admit the Chinese, whom they honour with a distinguishing cognomen, while they rather superciliously dispose of all other nations, excepting themselves, under a single generic title. With prodigious indifference to ethnic diagnosis, a well-read Burman, who, according to Dr. Mason, 'has a mind like a schoolman of the middle ages, a repository of obsolete metaphysics and exploded science,' is content to divide the inhabitants of the world into three great families: themselves, including cognate races in Farther India, they call Bumá; those west of them, such as Europeans, Americans, Africans, Indians, &c., they designate Kulá; and the Chinese and all east of them they style Tarop or Taruk—an appellative given to the peoples of the Flowery Land after the Mongol invasion of Burma in the thirteenth century, apparently equivalent, says Sir Arthur Phayre, to Turk, as probably Nusruddin, the commander, and certainly several of the soldiers of the invading army were Turks.*

Perhaps the Burmese inherit their indifference to ethnology from the Chinese. To quote Mr. Baber: 'It must not for a moment be supposed that the natives of Western China draw any distinction between one foreign nation and another;

* So the Lolo tribes of China—who, some say, have affinity with the Karens—'compare the world to an open hand: the thumb, stretched out far from the digits, represents foreigners; the forefinger themselves; the middle finger indicates Mahommedans; the third the Chinese; and the little finger the Tartars. (Perhaps the thumb was for the occasion transferred from Tibet to Europe.) The great Emperor of China is imagined to sit enthroned in the middle of the palm.'—Colborne Baber's 'Journey of Exploration in Western Ssŭch-uan,' Royal Geographical Society Supplementary Papers, vol. i.

so far from that, they are apt to include Japanese and Nipalese, and even Manchus and Mongols, in the same category with Europeans. One very soon discovers that any discrimination of so minute a character is far beyond the range of native intellect. I was therefore obliged to accept the position of a foreigner in general, without distinction of race or religion, nationality, language, or business.'

From the very earliest times the Chinese visited Burma and other parts of the Golden Chersonese, both by sea and by land, and received a cordial welcome from their inhabitants. The practical results of this intercourse have not, however, been so pronounced as might have been expected. Yet the civilisation that existed on the seaboard of Farther India in ancient times was no doubt partly influenced by the Chinese—famous for maritime enterprise—and also by the Phœnicians and King Solomon's servants, who went thither in search of gold and precious stones, apes, peacocks, ivory, and almug-trees.

China may be termed rather a congeries of States than a single homogeneous empire, as some of the viceroys of her distant provinces are practically independent; but railways and the telegraph will soon remedy this, and support her claim to be considered a nation, and not merely an agglomeration of peoples. History proves that some three thousand years ago the true Chinese occupied only a fractional part of what is now known as the Celestial Empire, and were surrounded by indigenous tribes whose external characteristics they effaced by their superior energy and civilisation. The same influence is still progressing in Farther India, a process of absorption defining the movement, which is fast removing differences between peoples who have hitherto played as prominent a part in its history as the English, French, and Germans have done in the history of Europe, and who will eventually become as much Chinese as the inhabitants of Yunnan, Ss-ch'-uan, and other border provinces now are, were it not for the counteracting influence of Western civilisation already referred to.

While the greater part of Europe was in a state of barbarous ignorance, this enterprising people, probably navigating by the magnet, are known to have pushed their explorations and carried on an extensive commerce throughout the Eastern hemisphere; and, judging by their annals, their historians and geographers of the early part of the Christian era spoke of the Irawadi and the Ganges as naturally as a Fellow of the Royal Geographical Society does now. When Vasco da Gama, after his discovery of the route to India by the Cape, first encountered the Arabs, they had their charts, astrolabes, and astronomical tables, but as yet no compass. The Chinese, however, had, centuries before this, acquired a maritime influence in the East which put the vaunted supremacy of the Arabs into the shade.

History records the Phœnician feat of having sailed round Africa B.C. 604, and the still more wonderful exploit achieved by them four hundred years before, when, with King Solomon's stewards, they went to the Golden Chersonese to fetch him materials for building, enriching, and beautifying the Temple. We can well imagine that the navies of Solomon and Hiram, manned by the mariners of Zidon and Arphad, and piloted by the wise men of Tyre, freighted with embroidered fine linen from Egypt; blue and purple from the isles of Elishu; emeralds, corals, and agates from Syria; oil and palm from Judah; rich wares, wine of Helbon, and white wool from Damascus; iron, cassia, and calamus from Dan and Javan, visited this region—for Ezekiel, speaking of the Tyre which was of perfect beauty and glorious in the midst of the seas, says, 'Thy wares went forth out of the seas, thou filledst many peoples; thou didst enrich the kings of the earth with the multitude of thy riches and thy merchandise.' But none of these ancient mariners, so far as we know, were aided in any way by scientific appliances. It will be seen, therefore, that the Chinese, by their knowledge and application of the magnet, possessed advantages long denied to the rest of the world.

From Marco Polo we learn that, in the thirteenth century, during the reign of the famous Emperor, Kublai Khan, the Chinese—far from exhibiting their traditional characteristics of exclusiveness—not infrequently asserted themselves in a very pronounced fashion. Graphic accounts handed down to us by the celebrated traveller prove that the physical difficulties of intercourse between China and Farther India, which modern travellers assure us are so appalling, were of no account with the Great Khan, who practically proved his faith in being able to remove mountains, by dispatching across the alleged almost impracticable alpine barriers efficiently equipped armies, powerful enough to overrun and completely conquer Burma. The reports of the celebrated Venetian further demonstrate the great capacity for ship-building, as well as the aptitude for maritime enterprise, which distinguished the Chinese of his time—worthy of Fohi or Noah, their reputed founder, the first and most eminent shipbuilder ever known.

Kublai Khan was as enterprising by land as by sea. Far from being content with his own enormous territory, he had, as already explained, an inveterate craze to be acknowledged suzerain of all the States on his borders; hence arose endless difficulties with Burma, which may conveniently be referred to now. With the political sagacity which used to distinguish Chinese statesmen in connection with the administration of the south-western provinces of the Empire, he determined first to conquer Yunnan; for, holding it, he knew he could dominate the trade as well as political affairs pertaining to the peoples who have their habitat on or near the rivers flowing to the south. Kublai first made his reputation as lieutenant of his brother Mangu, who reigned at Karakoram as the Great Khan in the thirteenth century. He had command of the Mongol armies, which for thirty years had been fighting to subdue the Chinese Empire, and in person directed the preliminary arrangements for the conquest of Yunnan, leaving them to be carried out by his second in command. According to Burmese history, this officer, adopting his master's policy, sent a deputation to Mien or Burma, and demanded recognition of the Khan's suzerainty in the shape of tribute. The Burmese king scouted the notion, and caused the envoys to be decapitated for alleged insolence. Kublai Khan was not slow to avenge this outrage, and sent a vast army to attack Mien. A Burmese force for three months successfully resisted the invaders, but was then obliged to retreat to Malè, where they made a creditable stand, but were eventually routed, and forced to retreat on the capital, which they found had already been abandoned. It appears that preparations had been begun for the defence of the city, in the shape of a huge wall composed of the *débris* of numerous pagodas which had been demolished for the purpose, but were arrested owing to the verification of an ominous prediction, setting forth that the city would be captured by the Chinese, which was found inscribed on a copper plate discovered in the process of dilapidation. The superstitious king lost all heart when he read the inscription, and, collecting his valuables, fled in all haste to Bassein. The Mongol army pursued the king and his retinue as far as a place some thirty miles below Prome, known to this day as Taruk-hmaw —Turk or Chinese point. Straitened by want of provisions, they here abandoned the pursuit, and, after returning again to the capital, plundered it, and went back to their own country. The Burmese, thoroughly disgusted with the cowardice of their king, nicknamed him Taruk-pyè-men—the king who fled from the Chinese—a title which has stuck to him ever since.

There is no allusion in Burmese history to collisions on the frontier at this time; and their improbability is evidenced by the pusillanimous disposition of the Burmese monarch, who was very unlikely to have attacked a more powerful country than his own. Yet, according to Marco Polo, the Great Khan sent an army into the kingdoms of Carajan (Yunnan) and Vochan (Yung Chang), to protect his subjects from the attacks of unruly people. The King of Mien, 'a very puissant prince, with much territory, treasure, and people,'* taking umbrage, it is said, at this manœuvre, considered it incumbent on him to give the Khan such a lesson, that he would never again dare to molest his frontier. He accordingly prepared a force consisting of two thousand elephants, each carrying from twelve to sixteen well-armed warriors, besides cavalry and infantry amounting to sixty thousand men, and caused it to march against the Tartars. The commander of the Tartar host naturally 'waxed uneasy' when he considered he had only twelve thousand

* Yule's 'Marco Polo,' 1871.

horsemen to encounter this vast army. 'Nevertheless, he was a most valiant and able soldier, of great experience in arms, and an excellent captain;' and having troops on which he could implicitly rely, as well as confidence in himself, he felt equal to the occasion, and made his dispositions accordingly. To this end he advanced his troops to meet the enemy, and halted them in the plains of Vochan, hard by a forest. The Burmese king made a counter demonstration with skill, and advanced to the attack. The Tartar horses could not be made to face the elephants, to the dismay of their riders. Their commander had, however, foreseen this dilemma and ordered his men to dismount, fasten their horses to the trees of the forest to which they had retreated, and ply their bows and arrows. This they did so deftly and strenuously as to cause the elephants to turn tail and fly with the fighting men on their backs. 'They sped with a noise and uproar that you would have trowed the world was coming to an end! and then, too, they plunged into the wood, and rushed this way and that, dashing their castles against the trees, bursting their harness, and smashing and destroying everything that was on them.'* Suffice it to add, the Burmese, in spite of a gallant resistance, were routed with great slaughter.

The fame and glories of Mien, with its gold and silver towers, or Pugân, as it was subsequently known, extended far beyond the limits of

* Yule's 'Marco Polo.'

the Golden Chersonese, and even reached Kara-koram, the Court of Kublai Khan. The Great Khan, foiled in his ambitious attempts to conquer the comparatively war-like Japanese on the east of his dominions, was fain to turn his attention to his western neighbours, on hearing marvellous accounts of the richness of their country and the probabilities of its easy conquest. The splendours of Pugân have departed, and yet it is one of the most interesting places in Burma, though now it does not contain more than a dozen inhabited houses.

> '"A jolly place," he said, "in times of old,
> But something ails it now: the spot is cursed."'

The fall of the Pugân monarchy inevitably followed the Mongol invasion; yet it appears Burma stubbornly refused to acknowledge Celestial suzerainty, though many attempts were made to make her bow her neck to the yoke. One of these, in 1416, might have been critical to her destiny, as the time chosen for attacking her was when her hands were full with Pegu. It appears some Shan chiefs revolted, and a few of them were sent as prisoners to Ava. The others invoked the aid of China, which responded willingly by sending an army, and demanding the release of the prisoners. The point as to whether they were to be surrendered or not was left to be decided by the result of single combat between champions. Suffice it to say, the Burmese representative slew his antagonist, and, according to agreement, the Chinese army retired. The Celestials did not, however, remain quiescent very long, and in 1444, backed by an army, revived the demand for tribute from Taruk-pyè-men in 1281. The Burmese refused to acknowledge the claim, which was not pressed; but later on, in lieu thereof, the Chinese insisted on the surrender of the chief of Mogoung, who had taken refuge at the Burmese capital. The Burmans accepted battle rather than give up the man, and completely defeated the invaders. They were again threatened with serious trouble in the seventeenth century, when a certain Yunhli, who had assumed the title of the Emperor of China, when driven from his capital, Nankin, established himself in Yunnan, and, not content with levying taxes from the people of that province, attempted to do likewise with tribes subject to Burmese suzerainty. The Burmese resented this assumption by force of arms; but sundry awful portents, such as earthquakes, storms, and the appearance of two suns in the sky, caused the superstitious monarch, in abject terror, to fancy that he had no alternative excepting to acquiesce in Yunhli's pretensions. Accordingly, in compliance with an ancient custom, he built for him a temporary palace, wherein he placed his eldest marriageable daughter, in the hope of appeasing the wrath of the conqueror. It so fell out, however, that the pseudo-Emperor was driven out of Yunnan by the Tartars, and took refuge in Burma, where he became a naturalised subject. To the lasting disgrace of the Burmese, this adventurer was surrendered on the demand of a Manchu general.

Leaving collateral, though doubtless important, issues, aside,—such as anarchy, which paralysed our trade and injuriously affected our administration, French intrigues, the Shoe question, and other matters of high politics,—the final dismemberment of the Burmese Empire was primarily due to the impracticability of King Theebaw, in the matter of complaints on the part of an English commercial company. So, just twelve decades ago, the inevitable would have been precipitated by similar perversity on the part of one of His Majesty's predecessors, in connection with the remonstrances of a Chinese trader, were it not for the infinite resource, strategic knowledge, and determined spirit evinced by the Burmese generals, confronted though they were by apparently overwhelming numbers.

In consequence of a series of misunderstandings in matters connected with the frontier between Burma and China, the Emperor Kienlung in 1766–69 invaded Burma four times.* Though a competent civil administrator, he was no warrior, and owing to his selection of incompetent commanders, who grossly mismanaged the campaigns, his army was twice obliged to retreat to China. In no way discouraged, the Emperor was determined not to allow what he considered a petty barbarian Power to successfully defy the 'Son of Heaven,' and in 1767 dispatched a strong

* See Phayre's 'History of Burma.' London, 1883.

force, which also had to retire precipitately from Burmese territory. Notwithstanding all these reverses, he determined, two years afterwards, to invade the country again with even a more powerful army than before, selecting a time when the Burmese monarch was distracted by omens in the shape of earthquakes, which rent the great national temples, and seemed to portend coming disaster. His Majesty was, however, quite equal to the occasion, for he dispatched troops commanded by capable officers to encounter the invaders, whose success so discouraged the Chinese general that he was constrained to solicit permission to return unmolested to his own country, when he found his forces surrounded 'like cows in a pond,' and entirely at the mercy of the Burmese. The Burmese commander summoned a council of war, the members of which unanimously gave it as their opinion that no quarter should be given to the Celestials. He overruled this advice, on the ground that undue severity would only perpetuate ill feelings, to the mutual and lasting disadvantage of both countries; and that therefore it was more politic to arrive at a friendly settlement, rather than exasperate a very powerful nation. Accordingly it was arranged that peace and friendship should be established between the two great countries as of yore; and that the 'gold and silver road' of commerce should remain open. Presents were exchanged between the parties to the settlement, and it was agreed that envoys bearing friendly letters and gifts should be sent every ten years by each sovereign to the other. The Chinese claim for decennial tribute is based apparently on what took place at the end of this war. Logically it would tell against the suppliant Celestials; but, as a matter of fact, owing to the tact of the Burmese general, both sides were satisfied, and marched off, as it were, with drums beating and colours flying.

In the recent controversy regarding the alleged suzerain rights of China in Burma, this incident, as related in Sir Arthur Phayre's carefully authenticated 'History of Burma,' was relied on by those opposed to the Chinese claims, their opponents ridiculing it as the fond imaginings of the Burmese Court historiographer, differing from the account given by Crawfurd and by Chinese historians. Crawfurd's version is certainly not in accord with most of the recognised authorities on Burmese affairs; but it was admittedly founded on Court gossip, while the *dicta* of Celestial historians is not quoted. The truth probably is, as Sir Arthur Phayre suggests, that the campaigns of Chinese armies in Burma from 1765 to 1769 are noticed very briefly in the histories of China, Gutzlaff alone telling the truth without disguise of the discomfiture of the Chinese armies. Gutzlaff's account, by the way, is almost word for word identical with that given by the despised Burmese historian, excepting that he merely contents himself with recording that a treaty was made, without entering into particulars with regard to its details.

The most amicable relations have ever since existed between the two countries, in spite of not a little provocation to misunderstanding, owing to overtures made by the pseudo-King Suleiman of Talifu to His Majesty of the Golden Foot. The late King Mengdôn, staunch in his loyalty to his 'Elder Brother,' denounced Suleiman as a rebel. Not so the English, who, according a warm reception to Panthay envoys in 1872–73, in defiance of their obligations to China, incensed the latter against England, and caused her, by measures short, sharp, and decisive, to re-assert her power and make a clean sweep of the Panthays.* Thus, by British intrigues, China was awakened to a sense of her responsibilities as regards Yunnan, just as French intrigues influenced England in precipitating the inevitable as to Upper Burma.

Mr. Colborne Baber's interesting remarks in connection with the Panthay rising may conveniently be quoted here.

'The word Panthay has received such complete recognition as the national name of the Mahommedan revolutionaries in Yunnan that I fear it will be almost useless to assert that the term is utterly unknown in the country which was temporarily under the denomination of Sultan Sulei-

* When the Panthays surrendered, their king, coming into the presence of his victorious rival, said, 'I have nothing to ask but this —spare the people.' He then took poison, and immediately expired. His head was immediately cut off and exposed, and heedless of his prayer—probably the most impressive and pathetic ever uttered by a dying patriot—the victors proceeded to massacre the helpless garrison and townsfolk.—Baber's 'Notes on Mr. Grosvenor's Mission.'

man, otherwise Tu-wen-hsiu. The rebels were and are known to themselves and to the Imperialists by the name of Hui-hui, or Hui-tzu (Mahommedans), the latter expression being slightly derogatory. The name of "Sultan," utterly foreign to the ordinary Chinese, was never applied to their ruler, except perhaps by the two or three hadjis among them. The name "Suleiman" is equally unknown. The Mahommedans of Yunnan are precisely the same race as their Confucian or Buddhist countrymen; and it is even doubtful if they were Mahommedans except so far as they professed an abhorrence for pork . . . That they were intelligent, courageous, honest, and liberal to strangers, is as certain as their ignorance of the law and the prophets. All honour to their good qualities, but let us cease to cite their short-lived rule as an instance of the "Great Mahommedan Revival." The rebellion was first a question of pork and nothing else, beginning with jealousies and bickerings between pig-butchers and the fleshers of Islam in the market-places. The officials who were appealed to invariably decided against the Mussulmans. Great discontent ensued, and soon burst into a flame.' *

Though a profound peace has characterised the relations between the Burmese and Chinese since 1769, they were both involved in various wars with powerful European States, with results affecting the fortunes of both very differently; for 'Younger Brother' was dismayed to find his

* Baber's 'Notes on Route of Grosvenor's Mission.'

patrimony wrested from him and himself an exiled prisoner, while 'Elder Brother' was elated at the notion that he had successfully withstood, and actually defeated, the flower of an army belonging to one of the most war-like nations in Christendom. The Chinese were satisfied with the results of their encounters with a European foe, especially as they were not to blame for the disturbance of the peace in that portion of the Golden Chersonese belonging to the 'Son of Heaven.' Really they were the victims of an insatiable earth-hunger, as well as a morbid political ambition, which, of late years, has distinguished the French, whose twofold object—as they cynically admit—was to acquire a new colony in Tonquin and supplant the English as the dominant power in Farther India. So long as France confined herself to Cochin-China and Annam, China contented herself with a policy which she found convenient in the case of the British annexation in Burma, remaining quiet while the latter absorbed the maritime provinces, but asserting her alleged suzerain rights when they approached nearer to her. When the French, however, under the flimsiest of pretexts, ventured to occupy Tonquin, China very naturally demurred to part with a province which undoubtedly belonged to the Celestial Empire, and, in support of her contention, was obliged to appeal to arms—a challenge accepted by France with a light heart. After a weary campaign, which taxed the resources of both sides to the utmost, and caused a terrible loss of life, each side emerged from the conflict, loudly asserting itself the victor. It is unnecessary to our present purpose to decide this knotty point; but the fact that raw levies, consisting of peasants, robbers, and ragamuffins of all kinds, armed, it is true, partly with weapons of precision, but which were worse than useless owing to the want of proper cartridges; cheated by commissariat officials and paymasters, and with commanders who, considering discretion the better part of valour, took up their position a day's march or so from the front—should more or less be able to hold their own against well-disciplined French troops, commanded by experienced officers, offers food for serious reflection. For if the Chinese should take the lesson to heart, and utilise the enormous rough material they possess, by subjecting it to proper discipline and organisation, as well as centralised administration and control, by the aid of railways and the telegraph—there is no reason why they should not be able to defy the world. Baron Hubner, in his very interesting work,* declares he is frightened at the results of Chinese emigration, which in a comparatively short space of time has flooded three-quarters of the globe, and indulges in the following commentary: 'Two enormous reservoirs; two rivers are issuing from them, the white river and the yellow river—the one fertilising the lands through which it runs with the seeds of Christian civilisation, and the other threatening to destroy

* 'Through the British Empire.'

them. Already at several points these rivers are meeting and contending for the mastery. What will be the final issue? The twentieth century will determine it in its annals.' If there be substantial ground for the Baron's misgivings, how truly appalling would be the prospect if the Celestials should take it into their heads to carry fire and sword into some of the countries they now overrun in the interests of peaceful industry! In our concluding chapter, however, it will be shown that, as regards Farther India, they will be welcomed rather as ministering angels than as destroying demons.

Agreeably to the convention entered into at the close of the war of 1769—already noticed—embassies have since been dispatched by both countries at irregular intervals. Judging by the light brought to bear on these events by persons behind the scenes, both sides have practised the most glaring deceptions on each other in the matter of the ambassadorial *personnel* and the treatment of the envoys accredited to their Courts. Laughing in their sleeves, as it were, at their own knavish tricks, they never dreamed that they themselves were hoodwinked by precisely similar tactics. Neither, for instance, deemed it incumbent on them to select men of high rank to represent them. Anomalous as it may also appear, no effort was spared on either side to welcome envoys with becoming honour, and to make their official reception as brilliant and imposing as the requirements of ancient custom demanded. The traditionary canons as to the barbaric pomp inevitable on such occasions were adhered to most religiously. Yet, with all this, the officials of both Courts seemed to take a childish pleasure in offering every conceivable slight to their seemingly highly-honoured guests, endeavouring to mortify them in every possible way, under the mistaken impression that by so doing they exalted themselves at the expense of their friends. What is now known as the Shoe Question was, as an engine of oppression, a never-failing source of delight to the Burmese, for the process of unbooting within the palace precincts was as abhorrent to the Chinese as to Europeans. This infatuation would have caused the loss of their country in the thirteenth century, had Kublai Khan chosen to take it, and doubtless had not a little to do with the final catastrophe. Causing misguided foreigners to perform unnecessary obeisance was a practical joke of perennial flavour, the most stiff-necked being unwittingly forced to become victims thereto by being led through doorways so low that they necessarily bowed their heads. But the plan of all others for humbling strangers which pleased them most was to induce them to attend the great annual *kadaw*, or levée, held at the end of the Buddhist Lent, when all the officials and great men of the country, as well as the tributary chiefs, were bound to do homage at the Golden Foot, presenting gifts as tokens of allegiance to the Lord of the White Elephant.

Burmese envoys deputed to Pekin were apparently paid back in their own coin by the Chinese, who, by way of relieving the monotonous existence of the former, caused them to stand in the streets with the gaping crowds, and dance attendance on the Emperor, when he chose to go out for an airing, to visit monasteries and tea-gardens, or besport himself on the ice. With exquisite, though mayhap unconscious irony, they also insisted on their putting in an appearance at the Emperor's annual levée, identical with the Burmese *kadaw*.

The probability of having to deal with France —a cloud which loomed large on our political horizon before Upper Burma became part of the British Empire—no longer exists. Though the political history of the French in this region comprises events which happened more than a hundred years ago, it is only within comparatively recent times we have had occasion to be exercised by their doings. At one time, France had reasonable hopes of founding an empire rivalling the British Empire in India proper. In 1774, a revolution in Cochin China deprived the reigning monarch, Gia Loung, of his throne; but in 1790, assisted by French adventurers, he not only re-established his power in Cochin China, but added Tonquin to his dominions. Three years before, His Majesty, assisted by Bishop Adran, a French missionary in whom he had implicit confidence, concluded a treaty with Louis XVI. of France, who agreed to afford military assistance in lieu of a considerable cession of territory. Several French men-of-war and a large contingent of troops were actually despatched, but only went as far as Pondicherry; had they reached their destination, a rich appanage would undoubtedly have accrued to the French crown. On the plea of troubles in France requiring their presence at home, but really by reason of ignoble intrigues inspired by a spiteful woman, the enterprise was abandoned, and France thus lost a splendid chance of becoming a great Asiatic power like her insular rival. It was in the hope of securing to themselves the great advantages their predecessors allowed to escape when almost within their grasp, that the French have been so active of late in Cochin China and Tonquin, and have indulged in the hope of taking possession of Siam and the Shan States, and of assuming a protectorate over Upper Burma. Their too pronounced intrigues, however, only hastened the annexation of the latter country, while the judicious policy of the British Government in dealing with the Shan States, combined with the tendency of Siam to seek the protection of England in the event of her being coerced in any way by her Gallic neighbours, have doubtless, ere now, convinced the French that there is little probability of their dreams being realised.

With France satisfactorily disposed of, and with Siam friendly, the great expectations hoped for consequent on the meeting of Far Cathay with Farther India seem within measurable distance of fulfilment.

CHAPTER III.

THE BURMESE.

Distribution of Races—Various Degrees of Civilisation—Character of the Burman—Distinct Personality of the Burmese Woman—Barbarous Custom attending Childbirth—Success of Lady Dufferin's Scheme for Alleviating this Evil—Position of Woman according to the Buddhist Code—Red-Letter Day in a Burmese Girl's Almanac—Her Freedom—Simplicity of Marriage—Honeymoon Eccentricities—Wives fully Identify themselves with their Husbands—Women fully Protected by Laws—Female Dress—Burmese Origin.

THERE are reasonable grounds for supposing that a comparatively advanced maritime civilisation existed on the seaboard of Burma from the most ancient times, and that a few tribes favourably placed became considerable nations. These races were exposed at intervals to the irruption of inland Mongoloid peoples impelled by the pressure of others behind them. Thus the Môns or Talaings have, as it were, been obliterated by the Burmese, to whose stronger individuality the Arakanese have also succumbed. The Burmese in turn have been enveloped and pressed forward by the Shans or Tais, who have occupied the upper basins of the Salwen and the Mekhong, the former taking the whole of the Irawadi basin. The Karens again have either dispersed into the more or less inaccessible mountain systems, or have been content to become subjects of plain-dwelling peoples, though not amalgamating with them.

Besides these prominent, if not historic races, there are a number of tribes whose civilisation varies through every degree excepting the highest, constituting a ragged fringe to the region between our own territories in Bengal, the Empire of China, and the Kingdom of Siam.

'The Burmese are probably the gayest and most light-hearted people in the world; their neighbours the dullest and least impressionable. Blessed with a happy temperament, a contented disposition, and jocund spirits, which make light of the inevitable ills to which mankind is liable, they defy dull care. The latter, on the contrary, prone to morose discontent, and often a prey to melancholy, speedily succumb to the frowns of Fortune. Partly owing to their natural temperament, and partly to the influence of their literature, fundamentally of Hindu origin, the former are somewhat proud, arrogant, and conceited—a weakness from which the others are exempt. Their religious writings, moreover, impress on their minds the fact that they, as Buddhists, are infinitely superior to all other races who have not been baptised in this faith, and are, therefore, outside the pale of salvation.

'For many reasons combined, we witness in Burma a practical example of the reign of

Liberty, Equality, and Fraternity, which might serve as an ideal to the most advanced of modern theorists;'* still we find that with the extraordinary self-complaisance that characterises them, the Burmese are fully under the impression that owing to the inexorable rule of *Kan*, or destiny, they are ineffably superior to other mortals. They are further happy in the firm conviction that they are wiser, better, and braver than any other people.

The 'Maharajah Weng,' or national history, teaches them—indeed, their very name implies—that they are lineal descendants of celestial beings called Brahmas, who were tempted to visit this earth from the seventh heaven, but who, overcome by the allurements of 'sin, the world, and the devil,' were unable to return to their former abodes. These annals are further replete with records of events very flattering to their pride, which their *poays* or plays continually recall to their memory. No wonder, then, they have an exceedingly good opinion of themselves. Nevertheless, they possess a manly independence of character, combined with *bonhomie*, very refreshing to those accustomed to Oriental obsequiousness or stolid reserve. Though they have many faults, and are full of eccentricities and contradictions, they have also many admirable qualities; so that Englishmen thrown into daily contact with them entertain for them and inspire them in return with a kindly feeling which seems

* Mr. Hordern's paper in *Fraser*, July, 1875.

impossible in the case of the neighbouring races. Naturally idle, and having neither fixity of purpose nor perseverance, discipline or regular employment is most irksome to them. Nevertheless, the soldiers of a Burmese army thrive in regions where those of other armies would starve; in a spirit truly accommodating, every beast of the field, every fowl of the air, every fish of the sea, everything that creepeth on the face of the earth, and every herb not actually poisonous, is accepted by them as food.

With all his deficiencies, the Burmese soldier has one advantage over disciplined troops. He requires no commissariat, and is ready for service at a few minutes' notice. A few pounds of rice and a little *gnapi* or fish-paste carried on his person sufficing for his very modest requirements. Not deficient in pluck, cheerful, obedient, and patient under physical hardship, it is found that for sudden and short expeditions, to chase rebels or punish freebooters, he is second to none. There were reasonable hopes, therefore, of making him thoroughly efficient; but, in spite of every effort, the experiment had to be abandoned. The Burman is impracticable as regards routine and discipline. Drill is simply odious to him after the novelty wears off; an incorrigible sloven, he cannot understand the necessity of keeping his arms and accoutrements clean and in a serviceable condition. Marching to and fro on sentry is to him simply ridiculous; he cannot be reconciled to the loss of his cheroot, even when guarding a powder-magazine; and night, as he sagely remarks, being allotted by an all-wise Providence as the time for sleep, he does not understand why he should then remain awake. As soldiers, therefore, they are thoroughly out of the question.

These defects of character are also prejudicial to their success in mechanical arts. A Burman will often try his hand at various trades, and not infrequently at the wane of life adopt the medical profession, which in Burma requires neither diploma nor training. He may accordingly be styled 'Jack of all trades and master of none,' excepting in the case of those passed masters of Art, such as carving and jewellers' work, which require a long apprenticeship and steady application. Inveterate gamblers, the Burmese are ready to stake everything they possess on chance, and, under the native *régime*, even their wives, childdren, and their own liberty were thus hazarded. Hence the lottery mania, due, it is said, to Italian teaching, which more or less ruined the country in Theebaw's time.

In spite of these shortcomings, the Burmese possess many admirable qualities, which enlist the sympathy and interest of all who are brought into contact with them. Entirely free from all prejudices of caste, they make no difference between the despised Pariah from the coast of Coromandel and the twice-born Brahmin of Benares. All men with them are equal, excepting the King, his ministers, and the priests. Fraternising readily with Europeans, 'Jack Burman' is a prime favourite with 'Tommy Atkins' and Englishmen of all classes. Strictly tolerant in matters of religion, Christians, Jews, Mahommedans and Hindus are allowed to practise the rites of their several religions without let or hindrance. With surprising candour, their teachers allow that Christianity is almost as good as Buddhism, but opine that the former suits Europeans and Americans and the latter the people of Indo-China; therefore, while on the one hand they do not care to attempt the conversion of the Christians, on the other, they cannot understand why Christian missionaries should not also let them alone.

No calamity is so overwhelming as to cause the Burman to despond. Buoyant and elastic, he soon recovers from personal or domestic disaster. His cattle may die of murrain, his crops may be destroyed, his house and all his belongings may be burned, without putting him out very much. Like Mark Tapley, he is 'jolly' under all circumstances. Few Burmans care to amass much wealth, and when one does so he spends most of it building pagodas, monasteries, caravansaries, or other works for the public benefit, so as to acquire thereby religious merit for himself and his future transmigrations. But, though riches have no charm for them, they are great dabblers in small mercantile ventures. They are also distinguished for their great public spirit, often shown at much personal sacrifice. Were it not for this admirable trait in their character, the general community would be put to intolerable inconvenience. For the Burmese Government never provided in any way for public works, leaving it to the people to construct roads, bridges, wells, ponds, caravansaries, and the like, for the public utility. Vanity, or ambition, or charity, or perhaps all three combined, inspire the people, as they inspire many public-spirited people with ourselves, when they desire to be public benefactors. But, whatever their motives, the public certainly profits by the results, and expresses its sense of benefits received by conferring on the donors honorary titles much esteemed by the recipients.

The Burman has an amazing aptitude for adapting himself to circumstances; so much so, that it is hardly too much to say that, if the humblest coolie were suddenly made a grandee, he would comport himself in his new sphere as if to the manner born. He is generally free from care. A bountiful soil supplies all his modest wants with little labour; ambition has no charms for him, and he jogs through life merrily, lazily, and aimlessly. If he has not actually found the philosopher's stone, he has perhaps more nearly succeeded in achieving that feat than any other member of the human race.

To sum up, the Burman, with his numerous faults, has many virtues. Given to braggadocio, he is withal the very pink of courtesy; cruel under excitement, he evinces the tenderest compassion for the meanest of God's creatures; though bigoted, he is extremely tolerant: apathetic and lazy when he has no need for exertion, he is vivacious and energetic on occasion; partial to much exaggeration, yet generally truthful; sober and abstemious, yet prone to excessive indulgence under temptation; devoid of ambition or sordid desire for wealth, yet keenly anxious for power and the fruits thereof; full of eccentricities and contradictions though he be, Englishmen thrown into daily contact with the Burman entertain for him, and in turn inspire him with, a kindly feeling rarely met with where natives of India are concerned. Centralisation and other results of what is termed Progress tend, alas! to blunt this reciprocal sympathy, which serves to prevent friction in the working of the administrative machine. Absolutely free from care as is the Burman, blessed with a happy and contented disposition as well as a buoyant temperament which makes light of the ills to which flesh is heir, enjoying as he does a life of great tranquillity, the most ardent reformer cannot help feeling a pang at the thought that this Arcadian existence must be pushed aside in the hurry of an advancing civilisation, whose teachings will necessarily dissipate the fond imaginings inspired by their drama and national history. The matter-of-fact prose of every-day life must usurp the place of the romantic idylls of the past. Whether the result be the increased happiness and real welfare of the people depends much on whether, alive to our vast responsibilities, we are willing to learn a lesson from the past, and prove that the benefit of living under a settled government may not be too dearly purchased if it tends, directly or indirectly, to the social, moral, and physical ruin of a nation which deserves our liveliest interest and keenest sympathy.

The Burmese woman enjoys a personality so distinct that she is entitled to be treated separately. Though theoretically inferior to her male prototype as regards progress towards Nirvana, Nei-ban, or Everlasting Rest, to which all good Buddhists aspire, practically she is his equal in everything connected with present mundane affairs. She enjoys an incomparably higher position than do women of other Eastern countries, and vies even with her Western sisters in this respect, inasmuch as she has voluntarily conceded to her, by custom as well as by law, all that is clamoured for by the most zealous advocates of women's rights. Her *status*, in fact, is precisely similar to that of the Hindu woman in the heroic days of Indian history, before that great blight on Hindu national life, in the shape of the enforced exclusion of women, was caused by Mahommedan oppression after the conquest of India. There was then, as there is now in Burma, perfect freedom between the sexes, and the influence of women was as powerful as it is now weak.

An unbending policy of non-interference with the religions of the people of India has, to the lasting and ineffable reproach of the British Government, entailed intolerable misery and humiliation on many millions of Hindu women.

Amid the plaudits of Christendom, it abolished the diabolical practices of female infanticide and self-immolation of widows on the funeral pyres of their husbands, after having been—in slavish adherence to this policy—for several decades, accessories, before and after the fact, to many murders. But it still permits infant marriages, which are the cause of untold misery in India, and consigns to a living death of infamous slavery the unfortunate widows it has rescued by its well-intentioned, but, in a Hindu sense, abortive philanthropy. When the scandal of condoning such a demoniacal practice as *Satí* became so pronounced that its suppression in the interests of ordinary morality was admitted as a foregone conclusion by those charged with the administration of the country, many learned and complaisant Pundits were found capable of proving that this course was justifiable according to Hindu law. So if infant marriages were declared unlawful, and adequate relief and protection afforded to Hindu widows, equally learned and equally accommodating Pundits would doubtless be forthcoming, and able to quote precedents in favour of the new departure.

In dealing with the women of Burma, fortunately, we are not, as was the case with Hindu women, obliged to carry out legacies devised by the cruelty or the heartlessness of man. We possess a *tabula rasa* in this respect, and it will be greatly to our discredit if we do not prove ourselves equal to the occasion.

Long before we ever dreamt of instructing the masses in Great Britain, a system of secular and religious education obtained in Burma, which from old association's sake was endeared to the people, and entwined itself with their national life. Monastery schools exist in almost every village. To these custom and religion demand that every boy shall go, in order that he may receive gratis a rudimentary education in the 'three R's,' as well as in the tenets of his religion. Girls, however, are denied this privilege. The celibate teachers would be scandalised at the very notion of conducting a girls' school. The Vini or code for the guidance of Buddhist monks is very strict as regards their conduct towards females, insisting on their hiding their faces behind fans when preaching, lest the charms of the ladies listening to them when expounding the Law should cause them to succumb to the lust of the eye. A member of the Sacred Order is not allowed to sleep under the same roof, travel in the same carriage or boat, much less to touch a female; the last prohibition including the monk's mother, even if she be in danger of drowning, unless there be no other aid available, and then he must not hold out his hand, but only offer her his habit or his staff to cling to, and thus save her. He durst not even allow his natural feelings to affect him, but must school himself into imagining that he is merely pulling out a log of wood!

Girls have the option, it is true, of attending

lay schools which favour the monastic curriculum, yet this boon is taken advantage of but sparingly. Practically, therefore, so far as elementary education of males is concerned, Burma compares favourably with even Western countries, while that of females is backward. Illiterate though the latter be, they in a measure compensate themselves for this deficiency by their remarkable astuteness, *savoir-faire*, industry, and common-sense, which enables them to transact business of every kind most efficiently. Girls very early develop the trading talent for which their mothers are proverbial, and those of the poorer classes are utilised in this way long before boys exhibit a specialité for anything more practical for making their way in the world than football or nine-pins. They cannot, however, in defiance of public opinion as it now exists, and in the absence of a demand for female labour, compete successfully for clerkships or other employments of which males now enjoy the monopoly. Hence they deem there is no need that they should qualify therefor; so their brothers distance them in purely literary efforts, though the girls more than hold their own in all that concerns the ordinary affairs of life.

Owing to the interest taken in the instruction of girls and women by missionaries of all denominations, and the hearty encouragement and support accorded thereto by Government, female education has made considerable progress under British rule. It must necessarily, however, be a plant of slow growth. Time must elapse before the fossilised notion of its inutility can be exploded, and women brought to value learning for its own sake. Barring the utilitarian view, there is absolutely no prejudice against the education of women, so we may hope that the impetus already given thereto will be productive of the happiest results.

Important as the subject of their mental culture undoubtedly is, attention to the physical well-being of actual and possible mothers in a country whose chief want is population is a far more imperative duty. The exquisite suffering which at child-birth is the natural heritage of women is intensely aggravated at a critical time in their lives by the practice prevalent in Burma, whereby the patient is subject to torture by fire for seven days, and drenched with drastic and powerfully-scented drinks, with the professed object of eliminating noxious humours, but resulting in prematurely aging the victim. This barbarous custom, though universal in places unaffected by Western civilisation, is happily becoming obsolete in the larger towns under the influence and example of women of other nationalities.

The National Association for supplying Female Medical Aid to the Women of India, so successfully inaugurated by the Countess of Dufferin, has a most promising field for its operations in Burma, where exist none of the caste prejudices which in India are often so fatal to schemes intended to ameliorate the condition of the natives.

Lady Dufferin's reflections on what obtains in India, and her remedy therefor, might, *mutatis mutandis*, be applied to Farther India.

'I found,' she remarks, 'that even in cases where Nature, if left to herself, would be the best doctor, the ignorant practice of the so-called midwife led to infinite mischief, and might often be characterised as abominably cruel. It seemed to me, then, that, if only the people of India could be made to realise that their women have to bear more than their necessary share of human suffering, and that it rests with the men of this country and with the women of other nationalities to relieve them of that unnecessary burden, then surely the men would put their shoulders to the wheel and would determine that the wives and mothers and sisters and daughters dependent upon them should, in time of sickness and pain, have every relief that human skill and tender nursing can afford them.'* Suffice it to say, this appeal did not fall on barren ground in Burma, when the scheme was properly brought home to the comprehension of its eminently charitable people.

In spite of what matter-of-fact Western theologists may say to the contrary, the Burman knows that, by the inexorable fiat of Buddhist law, he cannot claim to be more than a mere animal, unless he submits to the ordeal of Buddhist baptism, which entails shaving the head, abandoning the world, donning the mendicant's dress, and becoming a monk —even if it be only for twenty-four hours. The

* *Asiatic Quarterly Review*, April, 1886.

Burmese woman is also aware, alas! that by the canons of the same code, her sex alone offers an insuperable barrier to her attaining this exalted state of humanity. They tell her, with uncompromising plainness, that her only hope of salvation is that, by great piety in this life, she may become a man in the next transmigration, and, as such, joining the privileged ranks of the yellow-robed fraternity, become a candidate for baptism.

The greatest event in the career of a Buddhist youth is when he enters a monastery as a probationer for the priesthood; though some irreverent lads have a notion that the occasion of having a pair of inexpressibles tattooed on their persons—a mark of manhood—is a far more notable episode. The ceremony known as *Natwin Mengala*, or ear-boring, is the great red-letter day in the Burmese girl's almanac. It is quite as important an incident in her career as putting on the yellow robe or being tattooed is to her brother. Though not claiming the religious character pertaining to Buddhist baptism, it is her nearest equivalent thereof, and is an event of such importance that all relatives and friends are bound to put in an appearance when summoned to the festival held in honour of the occasion, conventional excuses for absence being adjudged almost tantamount to insult.*

When the English young lady is presented at Court, or for the first time appears at a public ball, all the world knows she has been launched into

* 'The Burman.' Shway Yeo.

society, or 'come out,' as the saying is; so, in the case of the Burmese maiden of high or low degree, the ear-boring ceremonial proves conclusively that she is no longer a child. She now puts away her dolls and other playthings, and only surreptitiously sucks the sweeties or chews the sugar-cane, in which her soul openly delighted before; while in society she assumes a gravity of demeanour beyond her years—befitting, she imagines, her new condition. 'Nothing,' says Shway Yeo, 'like getting the ears bored to set a girl thinking about the wave of the hair that falls down in lappets by her ears, or the best recipe for the fragrant, straw-coloured thanakah, with which she tints her face and charms half the senses of the gallants . . . In a word, the *Natwin Mengala* transforms the girl into a woman, just as much as admission to the monastery makes the boy a man. This is her baptism, and is the distinctive mark of her race.'* After this she frequently holds levées, to which all her bachelor friends have the *entrée.* Some three hours or so after the shades of eve have fallen, or at what is popularly known as 'bachelor's roving time,' she may be seen arrayed in all her very best, with her jetty locks ornamented by a single orchid or other flower coquettishly arranged therein, and her little oil-lamp properly trimmed and lighted—seated, either alone or with one or two girl-friends, in the verandah of her home, after the elders have retired or gone to bed. In the mean-

* 'The Burman,' by Shway Yeo. London, 1882.

time, the various youths of her acquaintance who may be sauntering about know by the glimmer of her lamp-signal that they are welcome to improve the occasion if they can; for Burmese etiquette forbids lonely walks, or other pronounced ways for effecting this object, in vogue with Western lovers. The Burmese maiden, so far as this custom is concerned, has as much latitude given her as trans-Atlantic fashion awards to the American belle and her admirers, and, if rumour be consistent, repays the confidence placed in her by an equally strict attention to decorum. Amorous swains are fully aware that they run the risk of being taken up by the police if they happen to be abroad at night-time without being able to give a satisfactory account of themselves. But it would be a very hard-hearted constable indeed who would 'run in' a youth reasonably supposed to be abroad on courting thoughts intent.

Those who hold marriage to be a sacrament are scandalised at the free-and-easy notions held by the Burmese on the subject. With them it is a simple contract, having nothing of a religious character about it. The fact of both appearing together in public at a bridal feast given by the bridegroom and his parents, has even superseded the traditionally simple ordeal of eating out of the same dish, which, being tantamount to the irrevocable 'I will' in the marriage service of the Church of England, is as binding with them as having the knot tied by a bishop, or the agreement ratified by a marriage registrar, with us.

The actual ceremony is a humdrum affair, but its subsequent development, as expressed by the boisterous conduct of youths on the occasion of the beginning of the honeymoon, is decidedly of a more pronounced character. We throw rice and old slippers after the happy pair when they start on their first journey together, while they adopt a very objectionable equivalent to this harmless custom. For, on the night of the wedding, a number of young bachelors are accustomed to surround the house occupied by the newly-married couple, and, unless bought off by the payment of blackmail, pelt the thatched or wooden shingled roof with stones, brickbats, and other missiles, which causes a din that would wake the Seven Sleepers, and occasionally does injury to the inmates. We have ever been under the impression that the practice was a senseless and impudent system of extortion. But Shway Yeo (in his very interesting book) declares the learned in Burmese folk-lore assign it a much more romantic origin. These authorities assert, he tells us, that nine celestial beings, called Brahmas, already referred to, elected to remain on earth, instead of returning to their abode in heavenly regions; and owing to contenting themselves with earthly food, instead of celestial manna, degenerated from their pristine angelic forms, and, taking the shape of mortals, five became men and four women. 'The fifth man naturally resented being left compulsorily single, and pelted the happy couples with stones on their marriage night. Sympathy with the feelings of this archetypal bachelor has perpetuated the stone-throwing by the Loo-byos (bachelors) to the present day.'*

In the 'good old times,' when the law of *Tonzan* or custom was paramount, the newly-wedded pair submitted to the infliction more or less complaisantly, or relieved their injured feelings by vociferating uncomplimentary expletives connected with the female relatives of their persecutors to the third or fourth generation. But, in these degenerate days of so-called Progress, the perpetrators of high jinks of this kind often find themselves arraigned before a police-court, and punished under the provisions of a code which has superseded Menoo.

Though there was no provision for divorce in the Hindu creed from which Buddhism revolted, it is allowed under the reformed religion, and is almost as simple a process as marriage. Anomalous as it may seem, however, the ties of consanguinity are as much respected and family affection as pronounced in Burma as in communities where it is more difficult. In no other country do wives identify themselves so fully in all that concerns their husbands. The better half of a magistrate, police-officer, tax-collector, or merchant, in the good man's absence, not only accepts, but acts on his responsibility; while, still stranger to relate, the people affected by this eccentricity, far from demurring, accept it as a matter of course.

* 'The Burman,' by Shway Yeo. London, 1882.

According to the laws of Menoo,* the property possessed by husband and wife on marriage, that earned by either or both after marriage, by ingenuity and skill, as well as any gifts they may have received from the king, are shared equally, if the quotas contributed by each are equal. If either should have been the sole bread-winner, he or she takes two-thirds and the other one-third. The clothes and ornaments of both are also valued, and a similar system of give and take adopted, while the debts incurred during cohabitation are shared equally. If there be male children by the marriage, the man takes them; if female children, the woman. When one or other desires to separate, and the wish is not reciprocated, while no fault can be attributed to either further than the fact of their 'destinies not having been cast together,' the former can only retain royal gifts and a single suit of clothes, while the latter is entitled to the rest of the property. If the person wanting a divorce has no property, he or she must give the price of his or her body, in other words, pay damages. Either husband or wife can claim a divorce if certain indiscretions enumerated in the Code are proved against the other; and in some cases the wife can not only take the whole of the joint property, but has also the privilege, if she pleases, of turning her husband out of doors with but a single garment to cover his nakedness.

The sage Menoo, while making due allowances for the weakness of human nature, and affording

* Richardson's 'Laws of Menoo.' Maulmain, 1847.

relief to the victims of unhappy and ill-assorted unions, strongly insists on the religious obligations of marriage. He tells us that wives may be divided into seven classes: namely, 'a wife like a mother, a wife like a slave, a wife like a sister, a wife like a friend, a wife like a master, a wife like a thief, and a wife like an enemy.' Of these he further explains, the first four 'ought not to be put away by any man, but should be lived with for life;' the remaining three, 'even if they have borne ten children, may be put away, they need not be lived with for one day; and of the seven, the wife like a slave, if she pray to be a man in the next life, will not be disappointed, her prayer will be heard, and before others she will attain *Neiban* or *Nirvana*.' In Burma, therefore, the weaker vessel is amply protected by law.

It says much for the naturally pleasant ways, gracious manners, and general attractiveness of the Burmese woman that one forgets she does not exactly conform to the classic type of beauty. She steadily holds her own in spite of being heavily handicapped by prejudiced male opinion, which has the hardihood to assert that the dress worn by the daughters of Eve in Burma is ill-calculated to enhance any beauty of form they may possess. The inherent simplicity of the initial female garment baffles the descriptive powers of ordinary men, who, devoid of æsthetic propriety, declare that it merely consists of an oblong petticoat and 'body' combined, called a *tamein*, shapeless as a bathing-towel, and merely hitched on to the figure under one armpit and at the waist in some mysterious fashion. Fitch, as quoted by Purchas, perhaps gives the best notion of the *tamein.* 'It was also ordayned,' according to his account, 'that the women should not have past three cubites of cloth in their nether clothes, which they bind about them; which are so straight that when they goe in the streets they show one side of the legge bare above the knee.'*

Padre Sangermano, following Purchas, is sponsor to an abominable story in which a certain queen set the fashion in view to adding piquancy to the beauty of the women and increasing the number of marriages. We prefer to pin our faith on Captain Lewin's pleasanter notion that the *tamein* is of ancient origin, 'for it is recorded in Plutarch's "Lives," in his comparison between Numa and Licurgus with reference to the Spartan women, that "the skirts of the habit which the virgins wore were not sewn to the bottom, but open at the side as they walked and discovered the thigh." '†

Only men incompetent to form a sound opinion on this important subject have hitherto essayed to describe the costume of a Burmese belle. The results have been unsatisfactory and ludicrous. With profound shame the present writer is obliged to confess that he distinctly shirks the responsibility of attempting a feat which has disconcerted so many of his predecessors, and thereby allows

* Purchas' 'Pilgrimes.' London, 1625.

† Lewin's 'Wild Races of South-Eastern India.' London, 1876

BURMESE LADIES

his name to be added to the list of male incapables. In atonement for this remissness, he humbly quotes and fully endorses the opinion of a very competent authority in the person of Lady Violet Greville writing in a number of the *Nineteenth Century*.

'The feminine dress of all classes,' says this lady, 'consists of a plain loose white jacket reaching to below the waist, narrow sleeves (fashionable again), and a tight petticoat of silk clasped round their hips with a pin, and managed when they walk with inimitable grace. From the back depends another piece, which trails a little on the ground and resembles a scanty drawing-room train. These pieces of silk are of the daintiest and most artistic hues, generally of pale peach colour, shot with pink or yellow or pale gold . . . Add to this a scarf of silk of some contrasting colour, and you have the Burmese costume complete, simple, pretty, and nice to look at. Flowers seem to be their ideal, and they themselves are like flowers to look at.'

Even a casual traveller like the authoress of this fascinating description notices that 'the independence of Burmese women is remarkable. They manage their own affairs, hold stalls in the bazaar, with which no one interferes, marry when they choose, and divorce their husbands as soon as they please. No jealous veils cover their faces, no melancholy *purdah* seclusion prevents them from mixing with the male sex. They flirt, dance, and laugh with as many admirers as they choose, and, last of all, they smoke—not dainty little cigarettes on the sly, taking a whiff as they read a naughty French novel, as their European sisters do; no, but cigars! cigars longer than men use in Europe; cigars a foot long, and two inches in circumference . . . There, ladies, unemancipated creatures, though you call yourselves civilized, what do you think of that?' Taking all this into consideration, this writer opines that Burma 'is the paradise of women. From the wicked Queen of Theebaw who murdered seventy relations in a single day because they were in the way . . . to the pretty girls who hold stalls in the bazaars in order to maintain their independence, Burma is the land of women *par excellence*.'

Whatever may have been the shortcomings of the Government we have supplanted, or the faults of our fellow-subjects, unsympathetic treatment of women was certainly not one of them. Let us hope, therefore, that not only may we possess as blameless a record, but also that we may do our duty by the genial women of Burma, so as to fit them for the high position to which their virtues, their natural genius, their cleverness, and their many other admirable qualities entitle them.

At one time, apparently, the Burmese were as uncouth, boorish, and truculent as any of the surrounding tribes. But by various influences, which will be dealt with hereafter, they had already attained a fairly high degree of civilisation, and not a little culture, when first encountered by Europeans.

From Sir Arthur Phayre* we learn that they, ages ago, were formed into a nation by the union of Mongoloid tribes, who then occupied the land which is still the home of their race. This union, he goes on to say, 'was accomplished very gradually under the influence of Aryan immigrants, chiefly, if we may trust the national traditions, Kshatriyas from Gangetic India, who introduced the softening influences of Buddhism, and probably the simple handicrafts of weaving, the acquirement of which is, next to agriculture, of the greatest importance to a rude people.' Professor Max Müller, by the evidence of Burmese language, classifies them under the head of a Lohitic subdivision of the Bhotia family, now known as Tibeto Burman. Sir Arthur Phayre, Mr. Bryan Hodgson, and other authorities, judging both by physical characteristics and affinities of language, concur with the professor, and further tell us that the Singphos on the north of Burma, and the equally uncivilised tribes on the Arakan and Manipur frontiers, are their true kinsmen. They classify them among the numerous races which, at a remote period, left their ancient habitat beyond the snowy range, passed through some of 'the hundred gates of the Himalaya,' and after having sojourned for a while in the country now known as Assam, arrived in due course at the upper basin of the Irawadi. The Burmese indignantly repudiate this kinship, and quote the 'Maharajah Weng,' or national history, to prove

* Phayre's 'History of Burma.' London, 1883.

that the Kshatriyas referred to by Sir Arthur Phayre, who accompanied an army led across the frontier by a prince named Abhi Rajah, were their progenitors. This prince, they declare, formed Hindu settlements in the region indicated above, and built the city of Tagoung, which Colonel Yule says may be identified with the Tugma metropolis of Ptolemy. The existing ruins of this city certainly give support to the general truth of their tradition, as Buddhist images, bricks stamped with the image of Buddha, and Pali inscriptions in the ancient Devanagiri character, have been found therein.

Professor Lassen, whose authority in matters connected with this region is undoubted, sides with the Burmese view. Colonel Yule, on the other hand, considers that the Burmese legend 'is manifestly of equal value and like invention to that which deduced the Romans from the emigration of the pious Æneas, the ancient Britons from Brut the Trojan, and the Gael from Scota, the daughter of Pharaoh.'* There is no ethnic proof at present of Hindu settlements having existed in the upper valley of the Irrawadi, probably because the Aryans were physically weaker and comparatively fewer than the indigenous inhabitants, and thus lost their identity in the course of three or four generations. The same may be said of the Dravidian immigrants, who long played a very important part in the maritime provinces of Burma. Though the scientists have

* Yule's 'Mission to the Court of Ava.' London, 1858.

probably arrived at sound conclusions regarding the origin of the Burmese, they fail to satisfy non-scientific observers acquainted with the border tribes and the people who ought to claim cousinship with them, but, as already explained, will not. Some centuries ago, the Burmese were doubtless in a state of barbarism; but they have now achieved a unique position in the civilisation of Farther India. The aim of the present writer is to endeavour to interest his readers by furnishing a few particulars regarding the chief influences, more or less subtle, as well as more or less tangible, which have contributed to this result.

Ethnical influences may appropriately be considered first. The Mongoloid tribes, by whose amalgamation the Burmese were formed into a nation, differed materially in one respect from their reputed congeners, who are essentially highlanders; for they had already become dwellers in the plains, and consequently far more amenable to the teachings of a higher civilisation brought to bear on them by Indian immigrants than they otherwise would have been. The savage and chronically turbulent border tribes were then probably very much the same as we now find them; the Burmese a little more civilised. The latter have since changed so much that it seems ridiculous to speak of both as belonging to the same race. For the Burmese reside in settled communities, thoroughly at peace with one another; whereas the others hide in secluded villages, in a perpetual state of warfare, and are distinguished for vendettas of such long standing that the original cause of offence has been forgotten. The typical mountain Mongoloid is very matter-of-fact, and absolutely devoid of humour; the Burman, on the contrary, has a keen sense of the ridiculous. The former rarely exhibits feelings of surprise, joy, gratitude, or admiration. Nor is he endowed with a feeling for art like the latter, who decorates his carts, boats, agricultural implements, articles for domestic use, rest-houses for travellers, monasteries, and other religious buildings, etc., with bold and elaborate carving, unique of its kind.

The difference between the Malay and the Papuan, as described by Mr. Wallace, might, *mutatis mutandis*, be applied to the people we are comparing. 'The Malay,' he says, 'is bashful, cold, undemonstrative, and quiet: the Papuan is bold, impetuous, excitable, and noisy: the former is grave, and seldom laughs; the latter is joyous and laughter-loving; the one conceals his emotions, the other displays them.'* These mountaineers, in common with other border tribes, were subject to the most harsh and unsympathetic treatment at the hands of the late *régime*; while their fellow Burmese subjects, actuated by feelings of contemptuous dislike, were only too willing to accept the cue given them by their rulers. They treated with disdain the notion of having any social relations with a people whom they considered little better than brutes, and naturally

* 'Transactions of the Ethnological Society of London,' vol. iii.

had little intercourse with them. It is reasonable to suppose, therefore, that for a very long period they have not been indebted to these tribes, nor to other branches of the parent stock, for any infusion of new blood. Hence we must seek elsewhere for the ethnical influences which have made them physically different to their Turanian brethren. We must also do this in the cases of the Aryans and Dravidians, as well as various alien races who have contracted unions with them, but who, when compared with the total population, are an insignificant factor in the problem. It is unnecessary to revert to prehistoric times, or even to go far afield, when its solution is patent to all who have compared the Burmese with the various peoples who have intercourse with them. The face of the Burman has his Tartar genealogy stamped upon it in characters that cannot be mistaken. The least observant cannot fail to notice the predominating infusion of Chinese and Shan blood with the Tibeto-Mongoloid, especially in Upper Burma, where the people are much fairer than they are farther south. The Chinese, again, who have for centuries been influencing the Burmese in many ways, have been gradually gravitating towards the Irawadi Valley, and, as the more energetic and intelligent, will sooner or later absorb them.

The Aryans, who reached Burma overland, caught the Mongoloid tribes on the bound, after they had emerged from barbarism, and gave them an impetus towards a higher civilisation. Dravidian settlers who arrived by sea triumphed in like manner, in spite of having to deal with a people of such savage habits that they were only known to the outer world as Bhilu, or ogres. But the crowning glory is rightly awardable to other Aryan visitors who also came by sea, for they gave them religion, a written language, and literature.

Burmese history, whether we take what Western people would deem the purely mythical, the prehistoric, or the legendary periods, is essentially Hindu. Their comparatively modern annals also unmistakably betray the original Hindu influence. This is even the case where historiographers give the rein to fervid imagination, and embellish their exceedingly dry record of facts with highly-coloured results. Like the Holy Bible, their 'Maharajah Weng,' or national history, has its Genesis, and gives a description of the creation of the world, and of its first inhabitant. It also records what happened after that great event, in the minutest detail. It affects, for instance, to trace the ancestors of the deposed King Theebaw, in regular sequence, to Maha Thumadâ, the first emperor of the world, and even ventures to include Gaudama Buddha in the royal line. In spite of being disfigured with many similar blemishes, calculated to overstrain the credulity of the most indulgent reader, the 'Maharajah Weng' has earned high encomiums from very competent judges.

Sir Arthur Phayre says: 'The general fulness of the national historical records of the countries which comprised the Burmese Empire is remarkable. They present a marked contrast to the scantiness or total absence of such writings among the ancient Hindu kingdoms.'* Professor Lassen confirms these views, and states that they 'deserve on the whole the praise of credibility, as their authors relate not only the favourable events of their history, but also the unfavourable.'† Shway Yeo, on the other hand, accepts them in the light of fairy-tales, declaring that 'no defects are recorded in those courtly pages; reverses are charmed into acts of clemency; armies vast as those that people dreamland march through its chapters; its heroes are of the old ballad type; its treasures such as might have been the produce of Aladdin's lamp.'‡

These differences of opinion are easily reconciled; for it is evident that the favourable commentators did not even condescend to notice their puerile eccentricities; while the hostile critic fastened on them, and ignored really trustworthy information. It is unfortunate that the great standard work of the country should be tarnished by the absurd interpolations of persons bound to flatter the Court circle to which they were attached, and thus be furnished with an excuse for going beyond the record. Possibly, however, they were constrained by a laudable desire to make it more interesting and acceptable to the

* Phayre's 'History of Burma.' London, 1883.

† 'Indische Alterthumskunde.'

‡ 'The Burman,' by Shway Yeo. London, 1882.

general reader; just as the playwrights, who, following their example, unblushingly plagiarize from the works of Indian authors, but, recognising the extreme dulness of the borrowed literature, improvise situations suitable to Burmese taste, and indicate where 'gag' may be introduced with effect. Burma has not yet introduced a Macaulay or a Thiers to make history more interesting than fiction; and so we must accept with indulgence the Court historiographer's efforts to enliven what would otherwise be an exceedingly prosaic record. Their flights of fancy, it is true, might seriously invalidate the trustworthiness of the national annals, were they not, very fortunately, counterbalanced by *thamaings*, or histories found in the principal monasteries, which, while recording particulars regarding their founders and other benefactors to their inmates, also include notices of secular events. These are well-supplemented by inscriptions on stone slabs, and on bells cast for religious purposes, and suspended within the precincts of the pagodas. Although one naturally resents the notion of pranks being played with history, the student's regard for truth must indeed be keen if he can read the 'Maharajah Weng,' with interest, shorn of the compiler's embellishments.

Burmese ideas regarding history and cosmography are, it need hardly be said, very different from ours. Nevertheless, the people have a general, if superficial, knowledge of these subjects, based on traditional records learned from earliest infancy by means of their dramatical performances, which have for them a wonderful fascination, and also considerable influence in forming and developing the national character. Maha Thumadâ, and other immortal heroes whose exploits are glorified in their dramas, have a lasting hold on their imagination. With us the names of Odin and Thor, Trigga and Iduna, are names only, though their deeds of potency remain to cast a spell on all the nurseries of northern Europe. All the witch and dragon lore which Odin and the Asur brought from the East exist under new names in the nursery lore of our infancy; in 'Jack the Giant Killer,' 'Cinderella,' 'Blue Beard,' 'The Giant who smelt the blood of an Englishman,' 'Puss in Boots,' etc. We matter-of-fact Westerns, it is true, discard these tales when we leave the nursery; but to the more romantic Easterns they show themselves ever in a renewed and immortal bloom.

This idiosyncrasy, weakness, or whatever it may be termed, which, like our remote ancestors, the Burmese possess, cannot be disposed of casually as a trivial psychological truism; but must be accepted as an important factor in enabling us to decide the weighty problem of governing an independent, impulsive, high-spirited, and naturally proud people, the guidance of whose destinies, for good or evil, we have assumed.

A generally accepted law in their cosmogony, is that a revolution in nature, termed Lawka, meaning destruction and reproduction, causes one world to succeed another. The remote and moral causes of the world's destruction are said to be lust, anger, and ignorance, from which spring three other immediate and physical causes, fire, water, and wind. When the world was last created, a substance of delicious taste and perfume, like the food of the Nats or demigods, and in appearance like the soft skin which forms on boiled milk, came first on the surface of the water, and then gave a pungent aroma to the earth. Its savour ascended to the heavenly abodes of the Bramas, who, not satisfied with heavenly manna and the exquisite enjoyment of flying about in heavens lit by the effulgence of their own bodies, came down to earth to taste the creamlike substance that had formed thereon. The result was disastrous; for by eating it their bodies became heavy, dull, and opaque, and their hearts full of envy, hatred, malice, and all uncharitableness. Then, in punishment for their misdeeds, this upper crust disappeared, and was gradually replaced by coarser foods, the acquisition of which caused 'theft, lying, railing, and punishment to become rife.' The Bramas, finding affairs had come to this pass, took counsel together, and agreed to select a ruler, who should be a judge over all matters, with power to reward the good and to punish the wicked. They accordingly chose a man who, like Saul, excelled all other men in stature and symmetry, an embryo Budh, of great wisdom, piety, and force of character, agreeing to submit to his rule and allot him one-tenth of their produce. His name was Maha Thumadâ, and from him, if we are to believe the 'Maharajah Weng,' Theebaw can claim descent in regular sequence.

Even in an age distinguished for the encouragement given to the study of geography, the fellows of all the geographical societies in Europe would probably be sadly at a loss if asked to indicate on any of their maps the kingdoms of Thoonaparanta and Tumpadeepa; much more so if called on to furnish a local habitation and a name for even one of the great umbrella-bearing chiefs of Eastern countries referred to in the King of Burma's numerous titles.

An elucidation of the mystery is, however, to be found in Burmese cosmography, which appears to be fundamentally that of the Hindus; but the imaginations of its teachers have developed the immensities of the latter with variations.

In the centre of our present mundane system is, they say, the Mount Myenmo of fabulous height, surrounded by seven concentric ranges. Round these the sun, moon, and stars revolve—somewhat like the heaven of Dante, which begins from the Mount Purgatory, and rises upward through the seven planetary spheres. At its four cardinal points are four great islands, each having five hundred dependent islets. One of these is Zampoodeepa (erroneously called Tumpadeepa), so named from a gigantic and sacred Eugenia tree thereon, twelve hundred miles in length, one hundred and eighty-six miles in circumference, with five principal branches, each six hundred miles long. This Zampoodeepa, or great southern island, is held to have been under the beneficent sway of his Great, Glorious, and most Excellent Majesty, their most Gracious Sovereign recently deposed.

Burmese authorities differ as to the exact position of Thoonaparanta, while there is a general concensus of opinion among Western geographers that it is identical with the Auria Regio of Ptolemy, or Indo-China. We must content ourselves, therefore, with knowing that Thoonaparanta must, at any rate, be situated in that part of the world called Zampoodeepa and its surrounding five hundred islets. To this knowledge Burmese cosmography helps us by forbidding all communication between the four great islands, owing to the tempestuous seas of Thamodra, or the great midocean, whose waves are often mountains high, wherein fearful whirlpools are apt to engulph adventurous mariners; not to speak of the Leviathans, leagues in length, that sport therein. But the English and other Europeans, who are said to inhabit some of the small islands, are able to visit Burma, China, and India, owing to the comparative tranquillity of the seas which encompass these dependencies of Zampoodeepa.

The inhabitants of the other three islands live, it is said, from five hundred to one thousand years without care of any kind, and die tranquilly at the end of their allotted time, to be born again in the same island. They neither ascend into the superior heavens, nor descend into hell, and have neither aspirations nor fears. Burmese divines, however, teach that their lot ought not be envied by the people of Zampoodeepa, who, by the merit of pious deeds, can not only win for themselves exalted seats in the realms of the Nats or demigods, but can attain to the perfect state of Neiban or Nirvana.

Though there is no necessity for giving even a brief outline of the national history, it is interesting to note the frequency with which the capital of the country was changed, as on these incidents much more was involved than meets the eye in the record. Many of the Burmese kings, swayed by gross superstition, were at the mercy of Hindu astrologers, who recklessly counselled them to alter the sites of the royal cities, by interpreting natural phenomena and trivial incidents in proof of its necessity. Thus in several instances the appearance of wild beasts within the environs of the capital was declared to be tantamount to its speedy relapse into jungle; while on one occasion the alighting of a vulture on the palace spire was declared to bode dire misfortune to the king unless he planted the royal residence elsewhere. Ava, by reason of foolish counsels of this kind, became the capital no less than four times; Amerapura twice; and as often were they allowed to lapse into decay. Changing the site of a capital meant the total demolition of the abandoned city; but neither this nor its reconstruction was, after all, so serious a matter as it might appear at first sight. Masonry buildings were the exception in

Burmese royal cities. Even the king's palaces were made of wood, while a few of the citizens' dwellings were of the same material, and the rest of bamboos and thatch. When the royal order came for removal, all that the people had to do was to mark the component parts of their habitations, and set them up again in the fresh sites allotted them. The springing up of a new capital might therefore be compared to mushroom growth. Though the actual changing was thus a comparatively simple matter, the inevitable concomitants were well-nigh appalling, inasmuch as they consisted in the burying alive at the city gates and in the palace environs a certain number of human beings, under the impression that the ghosts of the victims hovered near the sites of their sepulture, and kept watch and ward against people entering with evil intent. It was well-known in Burma that such immolations occurred when the city of Mandalay was founded.

On this occasion, says Shway Yeo, 'fifty-two persons of both sexes, of various ages and rank, were consigned to a living tomb.'* He was of opinion that this terrible catastrophe was due to the advice tendered by the Brahmin astrologers already referred to, especially as its necessity chimed in with the popular superstition regarding the propriety of propitiating Nats or demons, in order to counteract misfortune. It would be as fair, however, to saddle the people with even so much responsibility, as it would be to fasten on

* 'The Burman,' by Shway Yeo. London, 1882.

them the onus of the massacres which took place when a scion of the house of Aloungpra (Alompra) ascended the throne. It is true that they cling somewhat to the demonology practised by their Tartar ancestors; but this particular phase of it they are content to relegate to their superiors, disposing of it as 'royal custom,' in which the laity have no right to interfere. Some say the Burmese borrowed the idea of human sacrifices from the Chinese, among whom the practice has been prevalent from times immemorial; but there seem to be no valid grounds for adding to the responsibilities of the Celestials by charging them with the demoralisation of their neighbours. Others declare that it originated with the Chaldeans, from whom it passed to other Eastern nations. The superstition has further been prevalent among many Western peoples, the English not excepted. In fact, our ceremony of burying coins under foundation-stones, graciously accepted as a duty by royal personages, and esteemed an honour by people of the highest rank, is, after all, probably only the lingering on, in a feeble, eviscerated form, of the old sacrifice. Money is now substituted for a living animal, as was the latter for a human being. As the proof, therefore, of any external influence having operated on the Burmese is not forthcoming, the blame for the awful custom which has existed among them within the present generation can only be attributed to the innate natural depravity which they share with unregenerate mankind.

CHAPTER IV.

THE BURMESE *(Continued)*.

The Burmese Possess two Religions—Phôngyees or Monks—Education, Religious and Secular—How utilised by Sir Arthur Phayre—The Christian Missionary and the 'Heathen Chinee'—Opium—Intemperance—Drastic Method for Checking it—English and Indigenous Education Contrasted—Burmese and English Literature—Architecture—Burmese Contact with Europeans—Mr. Gladstone fell on the Beer Question—King Thsebaw fell on the Shoe Question—The Latter Explained—Burmese Acceptance of Accomplished Facts—Eastern and Western Civilisation Contrasted.

THE Burmese endeavour to serve God and Mammon. They apparently consider it necessary to their happiness to possess two religions, the imported and the indigenous; one for high days and holy days, to further their spiritual welfare; the other for every-day use, to promote their worldly interests. Though Buddhism, the imported faith, is purer in Burma than in any other Buddhist country, and harmoniously binds together the civil, religious, and social life of the people, it is in some instances merely a veneering on geniolatry, their ancient cult. Many still regard the spirit world with an awe not countenanced by the Buddhist creed; but as this venerable religion, while it denounces the superstition, does not afford them any help out of their dilemma, as professed Buddhists they deem it highly judicious as well as expedient to be on good terms with both the good and evil genii, so as to make things go smoothly in this life.

They regard the spirit world with an awe not countenanced by the Buddhist creed, in spite of the denunciations of their more orthodox brethren and the edicts fulminated by the late King Meng-dôn, an eminent and consistent Defender of the Faith. The Pharisaical section of the community, which inveighs the most bitterly against the weaknesses of the vulgar, is not, however, altogether free from the taint of this superstition. Even they are prone to attribute misfortunes to the malignant influence of evil Nats or demons, and when a physician, for instance, is at his wits' end in a case of severe illness, he gravely informs the patient that, all the resources of the medical art having been exhausted, a sorcerer must be called in to exorcise the spirit which has caused the complaint. Atheist though he be, when sudden mishap or dire calamity overtakes the Burman, he involuntarily cries aloud, *Phra kaiba!* 'God help me!' but it is to the unknown God, to whom the Athenians raised an altar, that his supplication goes forth—a cry indicative of the pent-up yearnings of unregenerate human nature for superior aid when subordinate agency is found to be of no avail.

The Burmese comply, it is true, with the requirements of their professed religion, but in a decidedly perfunctory manner, consisting, for the most part, of weekly visits to the pagodas, which, to uninitiated Western observers, appear more like pleasant picnics than religious solemnities. Any form of religion is certainly preferable to demonology, and it behoves us to beware lest, by our irreligious education, we scrape off this veneering, and lay bare, in all its hideous nakedness, the heathenism concealed beneath.

With the Burman Buddhists, no doubt, the religious and moral residuum is still considerable. Their faith, in spite of the veneering, is a great reality. The labours of their Phôngyees or monks, in the religious instruction of the young, posing, as they do, as living exemplars of their Great Master, greatly enhance this feeling. From authentic Buddhist records, we learn that India, at a very early period, took a keen and very sympathetic interest in the spiritual condition of the Burmese, the Great Master himself having given two natives of Burma eight hairs from his head, which they reverently carried home, and enshrined in a pagoda near the present site of Rangoon, now known as Showé Dagōn. From its first introduction, Buddhism favoured the general extension of education, and appealed to the masses through the vernacular tongues; and thus, in spite of its tenets as to the worthlessness of worldly objects and the inherent misery of being, induced a general interest in the affairs of life.*

* Phayre's 'History of Burma.' London, 1883.

By no more outward and visible sign do the Burmese prove their faith in the teachings of Buddha, than in their devotion to their religious teachers or monks, whom they consider living exemplars of their Great Master, and as such reverentially term Phôngyee or 'Great Glory.'

The Phôngyees, when ordained, vow, in the words of the English Church Catechism, 'to renounce the devil and all his works, the pomps and vanities of this wicked world, and the sinful desires of the flesh,' as well as to keep their bodies 'in temperance, soberness, and chastity.' They, as a body, act consistently with these professions, and are deeply reverenced accordingly. By a harmless fiction, they are supposed to be mendicants; but they are mendicants only in so far as mendicity implies poverty. The *Thathanabein*, or Archbishop of Mandalay, and the humblest Phôngyee of an obscure village, as regards disposable worldly possessions, are, in fact, on a par. By the rules of their order, the Phôngyees are allowed to have only food enough for their bodily wants, raiment sufficient to cover their nakedness, and shelter from the heat of the sun or the inclemency of the weather. Their supporters or disciples, however, interpret these conditions very liberally. In the first two, their generosity is naturally circumscribed; in the last, it has full scope. The pious, therefore, gladly avail themselves of the opportunity for acquiring religious merit in a manner approved by the Lord Buddha himself. The first monks probably lived in huts or under the shade of trees—like the Indian jogis or hermits; but it was never the intention of the Great Master that members of the Buddhist order should take example from these selfish and useless ascetics, in living far from, and depriving themselves of the satisfaction of doing good to their fellow-creatures. Consequently, very early in his teaching, the laity were encouraged to build commodious buildings for himself and his disciples. They responded to the Master's suggestion with the utmost enthusiasm. The Burmese have worthily followed suit. The laity, in short, do all in their power to make the members of the yellow-robed fraternity comfortable, happy, and contented. It may well then be asked, what do the Phôngyees do in return for all the attention bestowed on them? In reply it can be said that they are assiduous in the duty of teaching the principles of religion to the young, as well as imparting to them a rudimentary education in reading, writing, arithmetic, and sometimes geography, according to their cosmogony. As before noted, it is essential that every boy, whether poor or rich, gentle or simple, shall attend the monastic schools. Compulsory education, it will be seen, is accordingly in full force; and, thanks to the Phôngyees, the Burmese, so far as elementary education is concerned, are far ahead of the Indians, from whom their knowledge of letters is derived. To their teachers they are further indebted for model instruction in the humanities, including their duty towards their neighbours;

especially—to quote the Church Catechism again —'in submitting themselves to all their governors spiritual pastors and masters, and to order themselves lowly and reverently to all their betters' —practical lessons not sufficiently attended to in the English Government schools.

The Phôngyees possess no sacerdotal functions, and cannot impart ghostly comfort to erring sinners; for every Buddhist believes he must stand or fall by the state of his account of religious merits and demerits, as recorded in the book of Fate. They are invited to the house of mourning, not for the purpose of offering consolation to the unhappy or the bereaved, but in subservience to the prevalent superstition that the presence of holy persons scares away malignant spirits. Social gatherings on joyful occasions or for amusement are seldom, if ever, honoured by their presence. As celibates, they would be much exercised if asked to assist at a marriage. In short, judged by a Western standard, it would appear that they fail to sympathise with the people and to do their duty by them. But, after all, if we make up a debtor account between the clergy and the laity, the balance seems decidedly in favour of the former; for much that is good in the Burmese character is no doubt due to the instruction imbibed in the Phôngyee Kyoung or monastery, and the wholesome influence exercised therein.

The question of religious and secular education in Burma presents an entirely novel and extremely interesting aspect, not only to the philanthropist and administrator, but also to the specialist and doctrinaire. European travellers, more than a century ago, recorded with admiration and astonishment that the Burmese had, long before, satisfactorily solved the vexed problem of bringing elementary education within reach of the humblest members of the community, without the risk of friction of any kind—a question which has hitherto baffled the ingenuity of the wisest European and American statesmen. They found existing a system of clerical and lay education, based upon religion and embracing the quaintest ideas regarding a fabulous cosmogony and history, eminently suited to the wants of a simple and credulous people, with whom it found favour from the impress of ancient tradition and custom. First of all, there was the monastery school, found in almost every village, which then, as now, was freely open to all classes, rich or poor, high or low, where every boy received gratuitously the rudiments of education. Secondly, there was the lay seminary, modelled on the monastic institution, open to girls as well as boys, conducted by pious persons who, in the afternoon of life, elected to occupy themselves in the essentially meritorious work of teaching, instead of wearying themselves, to no purpose—so far as the acquisition of religious merit is concerned—in the sordid pursuit of gain. These schools, both clerical and lay, exist to the present day. There is no anomaly in the curriculum. While strict discipline is enforced by both monks and laymen in essentials, indulgence is otherwise the rule, so that learning is not so irksome as in more pretentious establishments. The lessons imbibed in both, being identical with the grand precepts handed down to them by the founder of their religion, have a lasting hold on their imaginations, and have 'impressed on the national life such precepts as self-denial, honesty, truthfulness, obedience to parents, tenderness to animals, and faithfulness to the marriage tie.'*

With the generous sympathy felt by the late Sir Arthur Phayre in all that concerned Burma and the Burmese, that able administrator hesitated long before he meddled in any way with a fabric which had so successfully stood the test of time; for he had learned, by our sad experience in India, to eschew the craze which had sapped the foundations of the more ancient Hindu edifice, without taking reasonable precautions to minimise, if he could not forestall, the inevitable catastrophe. But at last he was constrained to admit that the exigencies of the case brooked no further delay, for he could no longer blind himself to the fact that the Burman, living in a fool's paradise, must be engulphed or carried away in the rapidly advancing tide of Western civilisation, unless a safety-plank were improvised in his behalf, or a life-buoy thrown out to him.

With a breadth of view and statesmanlike conception of the situation truly admirable, Sir Arthur elected to preserve intact, as best he could, the

* Mr. Hordern in *Fraser's Magazine*, November, 1877.

venerable institution which owed its very existence to the conservatism of national opinion, which, like the clinging ivy on an ancient building crumbling to decay, tends to retard, if it does not actually obviate, its ultimate ruin. In other words, guided by a true interpretation of the rules of political economy, and imbued with a happy instinct as to what constitutes the legitimate goal of a sympathetic Government, acting also in harmony with the practical as well as sentimental aspirations of the people, he resolved to support the existing educational machinery, and utilise it as a means of introducing, by degrees, Western habits of thought and methods of instruction. He accordingly took the most influential monks and lay teachers into his confidence; and the genuine frankness with which they responded to his appeal showed a wide tolerance and enlightened spirit truly admirable. Their attitude was abundantly justified so long as this officer controlled the destinies of Burma. In course of time, however, Sir Arthur Phayre was no longer at the helm of the educational bark, while his successors who had won their spurs in other provinces took command. Though loyally adopting the system of navigation favoured by the first commander, they endeavoured to improve upon it. They were evidently dissatisfied with the travelling powers of the old vessel, and anxious to enable her to compete successfully with other ships, as well as to keep up their own prestige as smart commanders, they had her fitted with the newest and most approved machinery, and, putting on full pressure, essayed to drive her at greater speed than the ancient hull could stand. In other words, they applied to Burma the system which guided them in Bengal, 'the weakness of which is that it ignores religion as the basis of both Hindu and Mohammedan society, and in its schools and colleges confines its efforts to secular education.'*

The Burmese system of secular and religious education, which had developed in the people a moral standard so high and social qualities so estimable, encouraged the English to formulate projects for the higher education of a people who had done so much for themselves. But these schemes, alas! were far in advance of their aspirations or requirements. Our agnostic policy, in which religion forms no part of the curriculum, has replaced a system based on religion, which has produced such admirable results. The consequence is that the Burman, unable to bear the strain of purely intellectual teaching, becomes a sceptic in matters of religion; arrogant, overbearing, and indifferent to the amenities of social life, which used not to be the case under different handling.

'English education'—as Sir Lepel Griffin pithily puts it—'is an excellent thing, but, like a powerful medicine, it should be administered with discretion, and we must be careful that we do not invite a destructive demon, in-

* Sir Lepel Griffin. *Asiatic Quarterly Review.*

stead of a healing angel, to trouble the still pool '* of Burmese society.

The bitter cry from India is that by our agnostic teaching we have made the Hindu sceptical of the merits of the comfortable religion which satisfied his ancestors for ages, and, landing him on the strands of unbelief, have given him nothing to guide him in his search for truth, excepting the broad light of intellectual knowledge. 'But the English embroidery,' says Sir Lepel Griffin, 'is only on the hem of the mysterious garment of Indian life, and the great mass of the people are unaffected by the struggles of the young men of our schools and colleges to obtain a share in the offices at the disposal of Government.' The orthodox Hindu, bound hand and foot by the trammels of caste, cannot move one hair's-breadth from the groove of its canons without incurring social ostracism—to him a living death. At the same time, it must be admitted, it intervenes as a real friend in saving the weak from oppression, and, when slavery was rife, to protect the servants and their families from the evil passions of their masters. It also deters the Hindu from succumbing to the allurements of drink and opium, so freely offered under the ægis of a Christian Government. The unfortunate Burman, however, has no such safeguard, and experience unhappily proves that the civil and religious institutions which have developed in him the high moral standard and the estimable social qualities

* *Asiatic Quarterly Review*, April, 1886.

which enlist the keen sympathy of Europeans are unable to bear the strain of some of the evil effects of Western civilisation.

The native Government, fully alive to the failings of their countrymen, long ago came to the conclusion that ordinary deterrents, such as fines, imprisonment, and fear of public opinion, were ineffectual to cope with intemperance. It was therefore accustomed, with not a little success, to check the evil by employing measures of a decidedly drastic character in the case of a confirmed drunkard, such as flogging round the town and naked exposure to the sun, with stones piled upon the offender's chest and stomach. The Burmese authorities certainly achieved satisfactory results, which we, backed by all the powers of our vaunted Penal Code, are unable to accomplish. Drunkenness, the elders complain, is very prevalent and on the increase; debauchery and license have ruined naturally strong constitutions; the gambling propensities of the people have been encouraged rather than checked; and they also note with dismay the terrible consequences of the consumption of opium on their countrymen, who, unfortunately, cannot—like the Chinamen—exercise moderation in its use, but, owing to excessive indulgence, become ruined, morally and physically, taking to theft and brigandage in order to obtain the means of satisfying their cravings for the drug. When brought in contact with the customs introduced by us, the straightforward and manly truthfulness, which was one of the most pleasing characteristics of the people, has too often given way, they aver, to fraud, trickery, and falsehood; while obedience to parents, reverence for age, and the innate natural kindliness and consideration for others, which used to be their distinguishing traits, are now conspicuous by their absence. Instead of being trained in the monastic schools from early boyhood, where they were well grounded in their own language, and taught lessons of high morality, which tended to make them good citizens, amenable to all properly-constituted authority, lads are now kept in the monasteries, they say, for as long only as the requirements of religion and custom exact, whence they are drafted, as soon as possible, either to the purely secular seminaries or to the Christian missionary schools, with the avowed object of fitting them for Government or mercantile employment, carrying away from both only worldly-minded or sceptical convictions. In these establishments they acquire more or less a knowledge, or perhaps only a smattering, of English, to the practical exclusion of their mother tongue, flippant and disrespectful behaviour, instead of the courteous manners inculcated in the monasteries, and a decided proclivity to scoff at religious and moral obligations, which used not to be their wont.

Not the least of the boons received by Burma from India is that of a written language with a grammatical instruction which gives it a concrete and permanent shape; the result being that the homogeneity of the tribes, now amalgamated under the designation of Burmese, is preserved, and thus forms a contrast to the disintegration that characterises their northern congeners, owing to the great diversity of dialects prevailing in the region they occupy. The construction of the Burmese alphabet distinctly proves its Indian origin; while the rounded form of its letters indicates the influence of Southern Indian languages, inscribed with the stylus on palm-leaves. Burmese literature, partly influenced though it has been by Western civilisation, is essentially what it was when the Hindus first taught the people a knowledge of letters. As much of it has a religious tendency, and serves to flatter the exalted opinion they have of themselves, it naturally makes a very decided impression on a proud, high-spirited people, who, though fond of gaiety and amusement, decidedly recognise a religious element in the secular affairs of life. Whatever may be its fault, it is decidedly pure, and singularly free from offences against sound morality which too often debase the literature of more advanced nationalities. Besides the 'Pitika' or Buddhist scriptures, and the 'Maharajah Weng' or the great history of kings, they have numerous commentaries on both, as well as treatises on medicine, astronomy, astrology, cosmography, arithmetic, and grammar. All have a religious tinge, grammar not excepted; for even that work contains a dissertation on the sacred Pali language.* The royal library at Mandalay, which probably is still preserved, contained a valuable collection of Pali and Burmese works, and in some of the principal monasteries there are excellent libraries of which the abbots are justly proud. The public have access to them by making interest with the custodians. But as they only consist of manuscripts on palm-leaves, which have to be copied if their contents are to be utilised beyond the precincts of the monasteries, the diffusion of literature among the people is not very great. What there is consists chiefly of extracts from the national history, and Zats or short stories describing the experiences of the founder of their religion, in his numerous transmigrations till he became Buddha. All the scenes of these Zats are laid in India, as is the case with most of their religious and secular works.

The printing-press—which must be placed to the credit of Western civilisation—has been utilised in greatly increasing the number of these historical gleanings and semi-religious narratives. The American missionaries have given the people an excellent translation of the Holy Bible, and have also published many religious books and tracts with the avowed object of converting them.

* The famous Pali grammar of Kachayano, supposed to have been written five hundred years before Christ, and to be the oldest grammar in India, was discovered in Burma by Dr. Mason in 1853, after it had been given up as lost. Other copies have since been found in Ceylon.

As the Burmese have absolutely nothing in the way of popular literature, in our acceptation of the word, they have also aided the endeavours of the English Government to supply this want by bringing within reach of the people several useful and interesting works, intended to wean them from their childish pleasure in fabulous tales. The Burmese, though so many of them can read, do not either for interest or instruction study their books very much, and an effort to promote this taste in favour of literature of an elevating tendency deserves much sympathy and encouragement. But they have so long been nourished on a *pabulum* far from appetising, that they shrink from the more wholesome food which would be so much better for them if they could digest it. From a lack of sympathy, however, with a somewhat romantic people, who require to be judiciously humoured and not driven, we, expecting them to run before they can walk, have as yet to learn the secret of success in this as well as in other matters of education.

Before adjudging a nation's place in the scale of civilisation, the progress it has achieved in the knowledge of architecture is a pertinent subject for inquiry. It must be confessed that the Burmese in this respect are comparatively backward, and that the results of purely indigenous effort, as now exemplified, are not very creditable either to their inventive genius or constructive ability—unless, indeed, the three principal temples at Pugân, erected between 1057 and 1227 A.D., be the work of a Burmese architect. In this case, the latter must have been a veritable Triton among minnows, when we compare his productions with those of his contemporaries and successors. Their pagodas, monasteries, and dwelling-houses severally follow the same plans so religiously that they appear to have been built after sealed patterns. This idiosyncrasy is partly due to an absurd social prejudice, which forbids the idea of anyone walking overhead; hence human habitations of all kinds have but one story, and consequently there is little opportunity for architectural display. It is therefore somewhat anomalous to find that in the aforementioned temples they have buildings of exceptional interest and beauty of which any nation might well be proud. It has not inaptly been remarked that all of them suggest memories of Southern Catholic Europe, and possess 'an actual sublimity of architectural effect which excites wonder and almost awe.'* One of these, the Ananda, built by Kyinsitha, King of Burma in the eleventh century, or about the period of the Norman conquest of England, having 'marked peculiarities and felicities of its own' which tend to enhance this exceptional influence. The other two buildings were also erected probably under the auspices of Burmese kings; but how the architects were inspired remains an unsolved archæological problem to this day—complicated not a little by the prevalence therein of the pointed arch, which was

* Yule's 'Mission to the Court of Ava.'

almost universally adopted in the Burmese style of that period.

Having briefly disposed of some of the results of Eastern civilisation, we may now take into consideration what Western civilisation has done for the people. Several European travellers have visited Burma. But apparently only the Dutch, French, Portuguese, and English have resided in the country long enough and in sufficient numbers to affect the indigenous civilisation. Let us briefly glance at what history records of their achievements.

Early in the seventeenth century the Dutch had possession of the island of Negrais, and the English had factories at Syriam, Prome, Ava, and probably at Bhamó. A dispute between the governor of Pegu and the Dutch commandant caused the expulsion of both the Dutch and the English—the Burmese then, as now, taking little trouble to distinguish one European nationality from another. The results of their occupation were not sufficiently tangible, apparently, to induce the Dutch to try their fortunes again, for we hear no more of them. The English were more adventurous; for in the eighteenth century, when Aloungpra (Alompra), the founder of the last Burmese dynasty, was at war with the Talaings, we find them again at Syriam, where they as well as the French had settlements. The policy of these settlers was, to say the least, vacillating, as it was guided merely by the fluctuating fortunes of the contending nations. The English were the first to get into difficulties thereby, owing to their treacherous behaviour towards the Burmese; yet Aloungpra, in the most magnanimous spirit, not only forgave them, but also allowed them to establish factories at Rangoon and Bassein. Some time afterwards, it appears the French were guilty of similar reprehensible conduct; but the king was then implacable, and in a fit of rage put to death the agent of their factory as well as the captain and officers of a French ship which then happened to be at anchor in the river near Syriam. The subordinates of the factory were sent as prisoners to Ava, where their descendants, known as native Christians, are now to be found. Their compatriots neither resented this ignominy, nor tried their fortunes again in Burma till very lately, when by their pronounced intrigues, antagonistic to English claims, they precipitated events which led to the recent war and annexation of King Theebaw's dominions. Neither the Dutch nor the French, therefore, seem to have exercised much influence on the Burmese. The Portuguese and English, however, have made their mark on Burmese history. Very soon after Vasco di Gama discovered the Cape route to India, the Portuguese began to take advantage of this splendid field, and in 1498, under the guidance of the celebrated Albuquerque, arrived on the Malabar coast, and, from thence sweeping the Indian and Chinese seas with their ships, created for themselves a great prestige, and gave a vast impetus to trade in all the surrounding regions.

Albuquerque, soon after his arrival in India, deputed an envoy for the purpose of making a commercial treaty with the Viceroy of Martaban, now an insignificant village opposite Maulmaui, but then a great trading emporium. The Viceroy, much impressed by the Portuguese power and promises, actually defied his sovereign, who promptly made arrangements for investing Martaban and bringing his rebellious vassal to his senses. The latter, trusting to his own troops, but chiefly to his Portuguese allies, nothing daunted, persisted in his defiance. When the actual tug of war arrived, however, he found himself the victim of misplaced confidence in the foreigners, for they deserted in a body when they found their employer was getting the worst of the struggle. They thus precipitated the capture of the town, with the attendant horrors of a successful Asiatic siege. This incident not a little damaged their reputation for courage and trustworthiness.

Early in the seventeenth century, swarms of Portuguese pirates infested the Burmese seas, and adventurers of that nation had much to do in influencing the course of events in Arakan and the adjacent countries, as well as the Irawadi delta.* The King of Arakan was a notable dupe of their intrigues. His Majesty was very anxious to retain Syriam occupied by his victorious army, wherein a detachment of Ara-

* For details regarding the exploits of the Portuguese during this period, see Phayre's 'History of Burma.' London, 1883.

kanese troops had been left with the main body returned to Arakan. But knowing he could not do so without the concurrence of the Portuguese, and too proud to solicit their aid openly, he endeavoured to secure their good offices by indirect means. Impelled by a very common weakness of Oriental diplomacy, he selected as his agent at Syriam a young Portuguese, named Philip de Brito, a menial of his palace, who began life as a ship-boy. De Brito shamefully abused this confidence in his integrity, and, aided by the boldness of a Portuguese officer named Salvador Ribeyro, expelled the Arkanese garrison from the fort, and assumed the governorship of the settlement. He then proceeded to Goa, and obtained the sanction of the Portuguese Viceroy of India to represent him at Syriam. De Brito further played his cards so well that the Viceroy was induced to give him his niece in marriage, to send him back to Pegu with the title of Captain-General, and to give him six Portuguese ships to support his authority. Ribeyro, who acted as governor during his chief's absence, not only maintained strict discipline among his somewhat turbulent and discontented countrymen, under very aggravating circumstances, but in a commendable spirit of loyalty, took such prudent measures to conciliate the Talaing chiefs and secure their confidence, that when De Brito returned as the Portuguese Viceroy's representative, they offered to accept him as King of Pegu. Had De Brito been as prudent and judicious as his lieutenant, he might easily have secured a rich appanage to the throne of Portugal. But, intoxicated by his rapid rise to power and fortune, he not only wantonly outraged the religious feelings of his subjects, thus exciting their bitterest hatred to his person, but was recklessly aggressive towards the King of Burma, failing at the same time to make adequate provision against inevitable retaliation. The opportunity for his complete discomfiture offered before long. For the King of Burma, aided by the King of Arakan—who was only too anxious to punish his former servant—taking advantage of the disaffection in Pegu caused by De Brito's unwise rule, and noting the want of proper preparation for such a contingency, regularly invested Syriam and captured it without much difficulty. Most of the native garrison managed to effect their escape before the final crisis, but De Brito and the Portuguese were made prisoners. The commander was impaled on a high stake in front of his own house, many of the leading officers were executed, and the rest, as well as De Brito's wife and several persons of mixed race, were—like the French in the same predicament a century before—sent as slaves to Ava. Nothing now remains to tell that the Portuguese have been in the country, excepting a few brick ruins, the descendants of those slaves many of whom were drafted into the Burmese artillery, and a brief reference in the 'Maharajah Weng' to De Brito, denounced as the 'sacrilegious wretch who destroyed pagodas.'

Half a century before De Brito's time, the

country was visited by his compatriot Ferdinand Mendes Pinto, a man of very different calibre. His narrative of travels in Burma, though written under a certain glamour that affected other travellers as observant and self-possessed as he, are verified by the native chronicles so far as they relate to historical events. Though his adventures do not find space in the 'Maharajah Weng,' his book caused quite a sensation in the Western literary world, where De Brito's name was unknown; for, as was the case with Marco Polo, it became a byword for untruthfulness. Congreve, in his 'Love for Love,' makes one of his characters say, 'Ferdinand Mendes Pinto was but a type of thee, thou liar of the first magnitude.'

British influence was initiated in 1824–25 by an appeal to arms, resulting in forcing the Burmese to surrender the seaboard provinces of Arakan and Tenasserim, thus cutting off the pinions of the bird with outstretched wings to which, in the extreme flight of fancy of an English historian, the Burmese Empire has been likened. It was emphasised in like manner in 1852–53, when its body was taken away by the annexation of Pegu, thus depriving Burma proper of maritime intercourse with the outer world, excepting through English territory. The Burmese Government neglected to take these lessons to heart, and so in 1885–86 it culminated by the same process, and the bird's tail, or, in other words, all that was left of the Burmese Empire, disappeared. The British declare that these several annexations were inevitable owing to the crass impracticability of the Burmese, while the latter retort that the truth is aptly illustrated in the ancient fable of the wolf and the lamb. A decision on this knotty point fortunately does not come within the scope of this work.

Mr. Gladstone, the most powerful minister of modern times, after surviving charges of having brought England within measurable distance of war with France, Russia, and the Boers; of causing Austria, Turkey, and Egypt to be hostile, and Ireland more impracticable than ever; of deliberately betraying Gordon to his death, and in being too late in all his negotiations and expeditions, fell on an insignificant issue—the beer question. So his Great, Glorious, and most Excellent Majesty, who reigned over the kingdoms of Thoonaparanta, Zampoodeepa, and all the Great Umbrella-wearing Chiefs of the Eastern countries, the King of the Rising Sun, Lord of the Celestial Elephant, Master of many White Elephants, and Great Chief of Righteousness, author of the atrocious massacres which appalled Christendom a few years ago, whose subsequent barbarous eccentricities are notorious, whose reign was characterised throughout by a violation of treaties, by acts of aggression on the British frontier, by outrages on British subjects and injustice to British trade, fell on an equally contemptible issue—the 'Shoe Question'!

Matter-of-fact people may assert that the perverse impracticability of King Theebaw brought on the war. But, on the other hand, it may be answered that the many grievous sins preferred against the Great Chief of Righteousness had been practically condoned, and no novel features presented themselves to explain the necessity of waging war with him, when we complaisantly accepted the situation at a time the relations between the two countries were apparently much more strained. Deep-laid schemes, however, of Franco-Burman diplomacy, challenging our right of interference and calculated to undermine our legitimate power of controlling political affairs connected with Upper Burma, made intervention absolutely imperative. And so it came to pass that the arch-apostle of non-intervention, after his great forbearance had been taxed to the utmost, was at last constrained to issue an ultimatum, which, though studiously moderate in tone and non-aggressive to ordinary readers, is identical with a declaration of war to those who can read between the lines. A notable clause thereof provided that a diplomatic agent of the Indian Viceroy, who was to reside at Mandalay, should receive becoming treatment at the hands of the Burmese Government. To this the Burmese replied that representatives of the British would be treated, as hitherto, with becoming honour and respect. If King Theebaw had been accustomed to treat European envoys in European fashion, this reply would be unanswerable; for it may be assumed that the bare insinuation that an envoy may not be properly received is outside the pale of civilised diplomacy. In other respects the Burmese rejoinder was doubtless evasive, emphasised by the fulmination of a hostile proclamation as a counterblast to our warlike preparations. Still the same things happened often enough before, without impressing on the English Government the necessity or expediency of carrying fire and sword into King Theebaw's dominions. But His Majesty did not so govern, nor was he in the least inclined to treat European envoys as they were wont to be treated at civilised Courts. Indeed, representatives of the most powerful sovereign in the world were not vouchsafed an audience with the Lord of the Rising Sun unless they removed their boots, or, in diplomatic language, submitted to the 'humiliating circumstances,' whose abolition was the real *fons et origo* of the ultimatum.

The Burmese, if pressed home, would probably have declared that they had not the slightest notion what the English meant by the term to which they took exception. They might have urged with a semblance of truth that our envoys had hitherto expressed themselves satisfied with the treatment accorded them by the Burmese Court, and that, as no objection had ever been made by the English Government, to take that opportunity of doing so was a palpable *ruse* for picking a quarrel. Stern, uncompromising, and precise as the ultimatum undoubtedly was in other respects, it did not define what was meant by the phrase 'humiliating circumstances.' But the Burmese knew perfectly well that the allusion could only apply to what was known as the 'Shoe Question,' whose favourable settlement, from a European standpoint, had frequently been pressed on their notice by both English officials and others, though the British Government had never before properly asserted itself in the matter. Finding, however, they had lost the substance, they clung to this shadow of assumed superiority with insane infatuation; so much so that many were fully convinced that this absurd pretension had become such an integral part of the constitution that the King's concession would have been tantamount to his own instant abdication. And Theebaw's defiant attitude certainly favoured this idea, if it did not actually confirm it.

Unfortunately for the Lord of the Rising Sun, our Government cut the Gordian knot, by insisting in effect, though not actually in words, that its representative should be received by the King as is customary at civilised Courts, not crouching on the floor as a suppliant, divested of his sword and boots. To modify an ancient and ridiculous custom, held to be degrading by all Europeans, was more than the King of Zampoodeepa, with all his boasted power, could concede with impunity; and so, probably very much against his own will, Theebaw was obliged to fight.

If Burmese historians may be believed, the custom of removing boots before appearing in the royal presence dates from the very earliest times. They significantly refer to a precedent which occurred A.D. 1281, when ten Chinese envoys are said to have been beheaded because they insisted on wearing their boots when granted a royal audience. But Burmese courtiers are discreetly silent as to the terrible retribution which followed. The Emperor of China despatched a vast army, which took possession of Pugân, in those days the capital of Burma, routed the Burmese troops, and pursued them to a place which to this day is called Tarophmaw, or Chinese Point. The conduct of some of our envoys, and of the Government which dispatched them, does not, it must be owned, compare favourably with the firmness displayed by the redoubtable and independent Chinese and their resolute Emperor. Indeed, the records of the slights, indignities, and impositions our representatives have been made to suffer at the hands of the Burmese, and the scant support and protection vouchsafed them by their own Government, is anything but pleasant reading for an Englishman.

Of these, perhaps, the 'Shoe Question' was the most intolerable. The physical discomfort of having to mount the filthy palace steps, and traverse dusty and roughly-boarded corridors unshod, was bad enough; but the unpleasant necessity was undoubtedly aggravated by the knowledge that our outwardly polite conductors inwardly chuckled at the mortification of the Kulas, or Western foreigners.

Unsophisticated Burmans, prone to grovel before even a palm-leaf inscribed with a royal order, and to make humble obeisance not only to the King, but also to the spire that marks the centre of the palace of the City of Gems, of Burma, of Zampoodeepa, and, therefore, of the world, cannot in the least realise why we should cavil at the simple act of removing our boots, which the highest in the land accept as a matter of course, and even deem a privilege. But others, who have travelled in civilised countries, and are well acquainted with European customs, though distinguished for their courtesy in ordinary intercourse with Europeans, seemed to take a fiendish delight in carrying out this absurd etiquette of the most arrogant Court in the world, whose code was to humble all who resorted thereto, by way of impressing on them a due sense of the exalted dignity, glory, honour, and power of the sovereign. The British Government calmly acquiesced in the unutterable humiliation thus suffered by its servants, so long as it favoured a policy of 'masterly inactivity,' but gladly took advantage of this weakness when its prestige was absolutely imperilled.

The Burmese, by the inexorable logic of fact, have now come to the conclusion that British influence, whether backed by British soldiers and breechloaders, or supported by British spirits and opium, is a real and tangible thing. But they are by no means convinced that they have derived as much benefit therefrom as evil. They rebelliously refuse to kiss the rod, or to admit that what the British have done for them or their country is calculated to inspire feelings of gratitude, respect, and affection, as the exponents of their policy would have them believe. On the contrary, with considerable cogency they argue that, if the assumptions of the latter be correct, by parity of reasoning the provinces longest under British control ought to show the greatest progress, and their inhabitants be the happiest and best, the most prosperous and contented; whereas the reverse is the case, as even the present administrators of Burma would not venture to deny. The policy of the Government of India, though paved with the best intentions, was for many years cursed with a moral obliquity of vision which saw no harm in depriving Lower Burma of the whole of her surplus revenue. And it is now blind to its own advantage by hesitating to advance the necessary outlay for the development of Upper Burma, though, as Sir Richard Temple says, the investment would 'fructify a hundred-fold.' This attitude—well understood and discussed by those who have received an English education, or are interested in the prosperity of the country—has a bad effect on English influence. When we first took possession of Burma, the blessings of British rule in the cause of order were palpable and tangible, when compared with the evils of disorder and anarchy which characterised the old *régime*. 'Everyone had a standard whereby to measure the merits of that rule compared with what had gone before. This merit, like Aaron's rod, swallowed up all other considerations.'* But, with the proverbial short memory

* Sir R. Temple. *Fortnightly Review*, January, 1883.

of Asiatics, they have forgotten their former troubles, and, freed from chronic anxieties, now take advantage of the leisure thus given them to take umbrage at the faults and failings of their deliverers.

To sum up—Eastern civilisation found the nation now known as Burmese a barbarous race, split up into numerous tribes, isolated from each other by feuds, jealousies, and differences of dialect, and induced them to abandon their savage habits and become a civilised and united people. It then gradually introduced the arts of love and peace by teaching them simple handicrafts and the rudiments of agriculture and commerce, satisfied that the tender influences of a pure religion would, in their own good time, reclaim them from demonology, which distinguishes the neighbouring cognate tribes to this day. Thus prepared for stronger intellectual food, it initiated them into the mysteries of the Buddhist religion, which, as Edwin Arnold says, 'has in it the eternity of a universal hope, the immortality of a boundless love, an indestructible element of boundless faith in final good, and the proudest assertion ever made of human freedom.'* It further reduced their language to writing, and furnished them with a grammar. It then gave them a fairly copious and singularly pure literature, religious, historical, pseudo-scientific and dramatical, which, with religion, has done much in forming and accentuating the national character. It granted them

* Preface to 'Light of Asia.'

as well a system of free elementary education, accessible to youths of high and low degree. Finally, it made them happy in the thought that, by reason of all these inestimable privileges, they are incomparably more fortunate than other people. Western civilisation, unfortunately, too often inaugurated its advent by ravaging the country with fire and sword, and, after taking possession, introducing customs which demoralised the people. The English, its most recent representatives, found the Burmese absolutely free from care, leading a happy, contented, and tranquil Arcadian existence, which, alas! cannot be said of them since they have eaten of the fruit of the tree of knowledge of good and evil tendered them by their conquerors. Though, as Sir John Gorst has said, the Government of India 'is, on the whole, more truly administered for the benefit of the governed than any that has ever been witnessed; that it is, on the whole, one of the justest and most equitable of which history gives any account;' yet it is hampered by a want of sympathy which endeavours to apply to Burma the policy that obtains in India, unmindful of the diametrically opposite conditions existing in each country. It has not yet, therefore, learned the secret of governing the Burmese as wisely as it might. Western civilisation has given them a literature consisting of the best of all books—the Holy Bible—and many works of great merit, interest, and usefulness; but the 'Pitika' or Buddhist bible, and the Zats, still hold their own. It also diligently promotes education, but its efforts in this direction have not as yet been universally appreciated. Justice is promptly and equitably administered; life and property are comparatively safe; in fact, the Burmese possess all the advantages of the *pax Britannica.* All these blessings are now only accepted as a matter of course by a people who formerly were the victims of gross injustice and misrule. A revolution was inevitable at the clashing of the two civilisations, and in due course the fitter will survive. The Burmese believe that Eastern civilisation has ever been a blessing to Burma, Western civilisation sometimes a curse. Whatever mistakes the English, or the present exponents of the latter, may have made, they are now earnestly striving to do their duty by the people, who, it is hoped, will before long reconsider their judgment, and give it in favour of Western civilisation.

THE SHOWÉ DAGÓN PAGODA.

CHAPTER V.

BURMESE EMBASSY TO THE QUEEN OF ENGLAND.

Lord Dalhousie's Annexation—Burmese Embassy to England—Its Reception by Her Majesty at Windsor—Its Reception by H.R.H. the Prince of Wales—Assist at State Ball, Concert, and Garden Fêtes—Real Aim of Mission—Anarchy anticipated on King Mengdon's Death—How averted Temporarily—No one could Name future King till Mengdon was *in extremis*—Theebaw 'Out of the Running'—His Collegiate Career—Intrigue of the Queen of the South in Theebaw's Favour—The Mengyee introduces Constitutional Government—Origin of this Innovation—Theebaw's Unhappy Fate—Massacre.

The Marquis of Dalhousie, when carrying out the annexations with which his rule as Governor-General of India is identified, did not mince matters when he dealt with Indian potentates, for he took possession of the whole of their territories. In the case of Burma, however, where a like policy seemed inevitable, the great Proconsul stayed his hand, contenting himself with a moiety. Various motives, more or less plausible, have been adduced for what Sir Henry Durand termed taking two bites of the cherry, without convincing anyone. The real reasons will probably not be known to the public, if ever, till the breaking of the seals of his lordship's papers, which is not to take place till the year 1910, or half-a-century after his death.

As regards the Indian Sovereign, born and bred in the purple, to whom 'the pomps and vanities of this wicked world' were all in all, such a deprivation of territory would have been tantamount to the more drastic treatment meted out to him. To the Buddhist monk, however—as King Mengdon was when called to the throne—who sought nothing but the fulfilment of the Law and eventual delivery from the misery of metempsychosis, the discarding of the yellow robe of a celibate of the Sacred Order for the purple of royalty was at first looked upon as merely a trivial incident, a single rung in the Ladder of Existence, by one who gave out that he was the coming Buddha and Convener of the Fifth Synod. As time went on, however, this ecstatic Buddhist philosophy was unable to bear the strain of counteracting influences incidental to his new position, so different to the serene tranquillity of monastic life, and soon it became simply a veneer to a polygamy worthy of King Solomon, coupled with a very pronounced astuteness in furthering his material interests.

Naturally deeply concerned at the loss of the valuable province of Pegu, His Majesty, as best he could, resigned himself to his fate, but very naturally refused to put a seal to his degradation either by word or deed. The Marquis solved the difficulty by drawing a straight line across the map where Pegu ended, and ordering his boundary Commissioner to conform thereto. The King, however, had his revenge when it came to the turn of his lordship to ask a favour by not only successfully posing as an independent sovereign in the remnant of territory left him, but also by refusing to receive an envoy from his conqueror unless he divested himself of his boots in the royal presence. In so acting, His Majesty was no doubt strictly within his rights according to former precedent. But, even allowing for the compassionate indulgence a victor might reasonably extend to a fallen foe, Lord Dalhousie, with his intimate knowledge of Oriental Courts, must have known that, by allowing his envoy to conform to a ridiculous etiquette, which in Theebaw's time was properly styled 'humiliating circumstances,' he unequivocally acquiesced in the assumption of independence put forward by the Lord of the White Elephant. At the same time, he certainly paid an exorbitant price for the treaty he negotiated, but never secured, besides giving a handle to an insignificant potentate to indulge in the luxury of flouting the ruler of two hundred and fifty millions,—an opportunity of which he at once took advantage.

By way of apology for this complaisance, the secretary of the mission records the following note: 'Our old envoys used to give in to this practice. Thus Mr. Edward Fleetwood, who went as envoy from the Governor of Fort St. George in 1695, says: "When the palace gates were opened, we fell down upon our knees, and made three bows; which done, we entered the garden, the presents following; and, having gone about halfway from the gate to the place where the King was seated, we made three bows again as before. When we got within fifteen yards of the King, we made three bows again, as we had done before, and were ordered to sit down." (Dalrymple's 'Or. Repertory, I.') Exactly the same did Captain George Baker in 1775. But Fleetwood is not ashamed; Baker is, and apologises, so there was some advance. Colonel Symes, in 1795, did not go on his knees, but he was bullied into taking his hat off to the palace. So did Captain Hiram Cox two years later, and even dropped on one knee and bowed his head to "pay respects to the throne before the King's entrance."'*

There is, it is true, this much analogy between what the servants of a struggling company did in the seventeenth and eighteenth centuries and envoys of the Queen of England in the nineteenth, that both must act in strict accordance with the wishes and intentions of their employers, expressed or implied, whatever be their private feelings in the matter, leaving the onus of wrong-doing, if any, to the latter. Captain Baker's explanation of his conduct, which furnished material for difference of opinion, is straightforward and sensible. 'The custom of the country,' he remarks, 'is well known; that some such ceremony has always been paid, and they that would reform the manners of a jealous prince or bigoted people, need

* Yule's 'Mission to the Court of Ava.' London, 1858.

much force or eloquence; I was master of neither. Moreover, I was possessed of no instructions on that head, and I could not justify myself to those who had an authority to examine me for interrupting that friendship and good understanding which we might expect to ensue from this journey on a punctilio, which in a little time, by prudent management, I believe may in a great measure be got over.'

The Government of India, not only in correspondence with the Court of Ava, but by 'humiliating circumstances,' fully acquiesced in the independent attitude taken up by His Majesty of the Golden Foot, but at the same time somewhat inconsistently took umbrage at the latter exercising the privileges conceded him, though, under the circumstances, it could not very well take His Majesty to task.

It must be said that the Court of Ava carried on its official correspondence with the Governor-General of India through the recognised channel, beyond which it never dreamed of going till it was goaded into another line of conduct. A positively insignificant incident, which the immediate successor of Sir Arthur Phayre looked on in the light of 'high politics,' had much to do in tempting the Arbiter of Existence to adopt this change of front. It happened that His Majesty decided to send two intelligent Burmese gentlemen, graduates of the Calcutta college, to Paris and London to finish their education, and asked the present writer, as Political Agent, to obtain for them the necessary letters of introduction. The royal *protegés*, when calling for these documents, confessed they were much exercised by the Prime Minister entrusting them with stars roughly made in the bazaar from a European pattern, with instructions that they were to be given to the Prime Ministers of England and France respectively. The students, having some knowledge of the outer world, recognised the absurdity of the affair, and besought the political agent to extricate them from their dilemma. He essayed to do so in an interview with the minister, but failed, as the brilliant idea of pleasing foreign ministers with what he himself considered childish baubles was a happy thought of his own. And so the young men departed, their joyous anticipations of the delights of London and Paris considerably discounted by the ordeal in store for them. Suffice it to say, they executed their commission without setting the Thames on fire or creating a revolution in France. In fact, the result was eminently prosaic. Mr. Gladstone privately expressed his acknowledgments, and the minister of the 'politest nation' probably did likewise.

King Mengdôn, from the Burmese point of view, possessed literary attainments of a high order. He was a ripe Pali scholar and an eminent authority on the 'Maharajah Weng,' or Great History of Kings, which is the only history recognised in the Burmese educational curriculum. With a wonderfully retentive memory, which was never at a loss in the ramifications of abstruse

FACSIMILE OF KING MENGDÔN'S HANDWRITING.

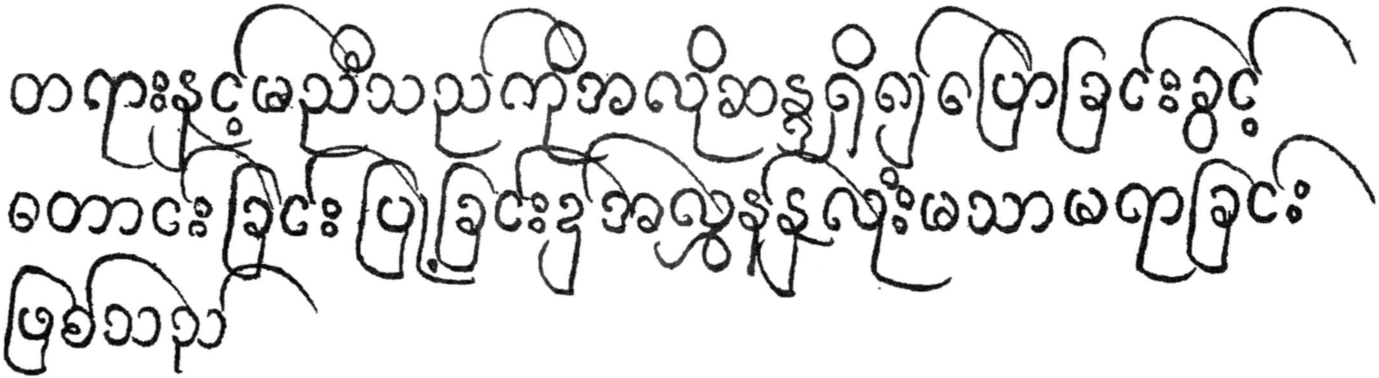

FREE TRANSLATION.

'I trust inconvenient requests won't be preferred.'

metaphysical dogmas, in dates and events of ancient historic lore, or in the delivery of sonorous moral platitudes, of which he possessed a copious repertory derived from his monastic studies, the Possessor of Supreme Wisdom had the utmost contempt for what we consider a liberal education, and deemed it sheer waste of time to concern himself with the history, manners and customs, schools of thought and methods of government pertaining to people who have the misfortune to live beyond the limits of the kingdoms of Zampoodeepa and Thoonaparanta. If he troubled himself in the matter at all, the Great Chief of Righteousness may have dismissed the subject with the comfortable reflection that some of the more enlightened peoples beyond the pale might be privileged so far as to take a leaf out of His Majesty's book. The British idea of posing as exemplars to even the umbrella-bearing chiefs, much less to the more highly-favoured inhabitants of Zampoodeepa and Thoonaparanta, the Ruler of the Sea and Land considered as the very acme of effrontery. Did he not know from the reports of his officers who had resided in England that the British had nothing to teach his faithful subjects, and merely endeavoured to copy all the latter did in the most slavish manner. The notion of our system of administration reflected in the contemplative mind of His Majesty may be gauged from an extract from Shway Yeo:

'When Miudohn Min heard in 1874 that the elections had gone against the Ministry, and that

Disraeli was to be Premier, he sighed, and said: "Then poor Ga-la-sa-tong" (Gladstone) "is in prison, I suppose. I am sorry for him. I don't think he was a bad fellow, and I gave him the fifteen-string salue" (the Burmese order of knighthood) "a year or two ago." That is the Burmese notion of how to settle the Opposition.'

The owner of the Sekya, or Indra's weapon, long failed to assert himself as became the heir of such a glorious prerogative. He was no doubt influenced by his antecedents. As a member of the sacred order, he was satisfied with the small world comprised within the limits of his monastery; so when he succeeded to the throne of his ancestors, with its usual concomitants of bloodshed, in which he had no share, and therefore incurred no responsibility, he preferred to adopt the *rôle* of the Great Chief of Righteousness rather than merit such a belligerent title, or do anything, in fact, which would spoil his chance of becoming Areemadehya or the expected Buddha, on obtaining the deliverance. His Majesty's ministers, however, were by no means satisfied with aspirations confined within the walls of the City of Gems, and therefore suggested that it was quite compatible with his undoubted future great destiny, in a Buddhist sense, that the fervent hopes of foreign peoples of being kept within touch of the Arbiter of Existence should be satisfied, instead of their being cruelly debarred this high privilege by the machinations of the English. The Supporter of Religion, therefore, in the exercise of supreme benevolence, determined to prove to the whole world that he was an independent sovereign by sending his envoys to European States and acquainting them of the new departure.

The only mission of any importance was the embassy accredited to Her Majesty the Queen in 1872, to which the present writer had the honour of being appointed Political Officer in charge. The embassy consisted of Mengyee Maha Saythoo Kenwon Mengyee, Envoy Extraordinary and Minister Plenipotentiary; Maha Menhla Kyaw-den Paden Wondouk, Attaché; Maha Mengyaw Rajah Pangyet Wondouk, Attaché; Menhla Zayathoo Saraydawgyee, Secretary. They were accompanied by Mr. Edmund Jones, agent to His Majesty the King of Burma. The envoy possessed literary attainments of a high order. He was undoubtedly one of the most talented and most trusted of the King's advisers. He served in each executive and judicial grade, and in every special work demanding prudence, sagacity, and administrative capacity he was invariably employed. Thus the task of receiving envoys and other matters requiring tact, discretion, and judgment naturally devolved on one who, in all these attributes, as well as in gentlemanly feeling and courteous bearing, was particularly distinguished. His wide experience of many subjects, acquired by long practice under various conditions, pointed him out as a fit leader for a mission of this kind. The Paden Wondouk and the Pangyet Wondouk were the *protegés* of the late heir-apparent popularly known as the

'War Prince,' who, with liberal views on the subject of education, selected several youths of approved talent, and sent them to Calcutta and elsewhere, to enable them to secure advantages denied to them in Burma. The Paden Wondouk, after acting as the King's agent at Rangoon for some time, was sent to England in a semi-official capacity. He has a good knowledge of English, and is possessed of considerable ability. The Pangyet Wondouk, from having resided several years in Paris, speaks French with fluency and precision, and is distinguished by polished and winning manners. He acted for some time as Judge of the Mixed Court at Mandalay; he also holds a French diploma as civil engineer, and is a man of considerable ability and scholarly attainments. The secretary of the embassy, though ignorant of English, was a great literary authority among the savans of Mandalay. Hearty and genial, with intelligence and good-humour beaming in his expressive countenance, which served as an index to his generous and candid nature, he was a general favourite everywhere, and a considerable share of the popularity of the embassy was due to his influence.*

* Finding the secretary a *persona grata* with Englishmen, he was frequently employed in missions to the Indian Government, after the return of the embassy to Burma, and acquitted himself so satisfactorily that he was promoted to the rank of Wondouk. But on one occasion he was unsuccessful, and was obliged to return after a long absence to report accordingly. Over his meeting with the enraged Theebaw we may draw the veil. Next day he died of 'official cholic!' 'Verily the lines of statesmen in the royal City of Gems are not cast in pleasant places. If they rise rapidly, they come down with as

On the 21st of June the embassy was received by the Queen at Windsor Castle, on which occasion the envoy delivered a letter from the King of Burma which the present writer had the honour of translating and reading to Her Majesty. On that occasion His Excellency also laid at Her Majesty's feet a casket containing presents from his royal master. The Queen having accepted these, and, through the political officer, entered into friendly conversation with the Envoy, the embassy withdrew and returned to London.

The Prince of Wales received the embassy the same evening, and was presented with the Order of the Salway of twenty-one strands from His Majesty the King of Burma. On the following day, by command of the Queen, a *levée* was held at St. James's Palace by the Prince of Wales. The envoys, in the charge of the present writer as Political Officer, and, attended by Mr. Jones, formed part of the diplomatic circle, and were introduced by the Duke of Argyll, Her Majesty's Secretary of State for India. They were also present at a state ball and concert given by command of the Queen, as well as the garden *fêtes* to which they were invited by His Royal Highness the Prince of Wales. During their stay of upwards of two months in London considerable

much precipitation, and their fall is as crushing as ordinarily it is inevitable. The coolie of to-day may be the minister of to-morrow; and a month hence he may be spread-eagled in the court of the palace, with a vertical sun beating down upon him and huge stones piled on his chest and stomach. Or he may be treated even more summarily than this.'—'The Burman,' by Shway Yeo.

attention was also paid to them by the Lord Mayor, and several members of the nobility and gentry. The various civic bodies also received them with hospitality and distinction. The same may be said in reference to their experiences in the principal commercial and manufacturing towns of the United Kingdom.

The real aim of the mission was of a somewhat drastic character, calculated to cause not a little embarrassment to the English Government; but the Envoy abandoned this idea, under advice of the Political Agent. Its avowed object, as embodied in the letter with which the Mengyee was entrusted by his sovereign to the Queen, was merely to 'cause the great friendship that exists between Burma and England to be placed on a secure, lasting, and firm basis,' and to promote 'the confidential intercourse which independent sovereigns should have with each other.'

The sentiments of the Envoy in reference to the responsible duties with which he was charged found expression on several public occasions, and were to the following effect:

'The object of my royal master in sending this mission to England was to pay that respect to your gracious Queen which is due to her virtues and her wisdom, and, by personal intercourse with your leading men and the representatives of the many influential commercial communities of Great Britain, to cement the friendly relations now so happily existing, as well as to further measures best calculated to develop commerce and the mutual prosperity of both countries.'

Arriving in England at the height of the London season, and remaining till its close; visiting the great centres of commercial and manufacturing industry in the different parts of Great Britain and Ireland, under the most favourable auspices; witnessing reviews of troops at Aldershot, Woolwich, and Wimbledon; inspecting arsenals, gun-foundries, dockyards, museums, hospitals, jails, libraries, markets, and other public institutions; attending operas, theatres, races, and other places of general resort; putting in an appearance at balls, *fêtes*, and *réunions*, wherein they met members of the Royal Family, the nobility, and the *élite* of society; joining the social gatherings of England's merchant princes and middle-class; making themselves acquainted, in short, with every source of England's wealth, prosperity, and greatness, as well as every phase of English life of the best sort; everywhere well received and welcomed; everywhere promptly, generously, and efficiently aided in prosecuting their inquiries and their studies, they had ample opportunities of satisfactorily carrying out the programme which the envoy early announced as the basis of his policy.

To attempt to analyse the impressions which an experience of Western civilisation gave to the members of the embassy would be futile. Two of the attachés, it is true, had visited Europe before, but it was under entirely different auspices. They had seen and learned much, but it was in a somewhat desultory fashion, and, though they had the advantage of their companions in this respect, much of what they have seen now, under different circumstances, assumed new proportions or altogether a different aspect. The Envoy and his secretary, on the other hand, learned and well-informed in every way though they were from a Burmese standpoint, and liberal and enlightened in their efforts to acquire and to promote the knowledge of Western arts and sciences, in their hearts clung more or less tenaciously to the old ideas regarding cosmogony and the world's history held by their forefathers, till they were rudely awakened therefrom by actual experience. Suffering then these quaint and time-honoured fancies, which had hitherto been part and parcel of their very faith, to be consigned to that limbo of exploded notions which the isolation of the East leaves behind it when conquered by the civilisation of the West, they were prepared for, and ready to take advantage of, surprises that awaited them in matters which did not so deeply offend their ancient prejudices.

London, with its intricate network of railways, its vast population and interminable traffic, its numerous bridges and splendid embankment, its docks, its shipping, and magnificent public buildings, its enormous wealth, industry, and resources, struck them perhaps more than anything else on their arrival, and kept a lasting hold on their imagination. Marvels of applied steam and electricity, triumphs of mechanical and manufacturing skill, old-established institutions for the legal, fiscal, revenue, and educational administration of the country, our glorious army and navy, splendid war *Matériel* and impregnable forts guarding our great naval arsenals, each and all gave them a justly exalted view of the wealth, stability, power, and prestige of England, which they contrasted favourably with Italy and France, although in minor matters they occasionally gave the preference to the latter. The insecurity, want of stability, and frivolity that marked the then *régime* in France were somewhat naïvely condemned as characteristic of the weakness of their own Government.

Though the dispatch of the embassy was merely an act of vain-glorious assumption on the part of the Lord of the Rising Sun, enthusiasts encouraged the hope that it would result in convincing His Majesty of the error of his ways as regards the administration of his country and his dealings with the outer world; but those who fancied the embassy had the moral courage to effect this wonder had never visited the royal City of Gems, and knew nothing of the complaisant imperturbability of the Lord of the Celestial White Elephant. Nor were they aware of a Court etiquette which rigidly tabooed questions which failed to flatter the King or the country and people His Majesty deigned to govern, and which forbade the Envoy telling His Majesty wholesome but unpalatable truths. Nevertheless, the results of the mission were not entirely negative, for its members, being men of considerable influence, were listened to by the ministers and others in authority with respect, instead of with the incredulity and derision accorded to men of lesser note who had given their impressions of foreign countries. They also by degrees impressed upon their compatriots some of the lessons which they themselves had learned, and in time might perhaps have persuaded them to undertake in earnest the thorough reforms necessary to prevent the entire collapse of their country involved in an adherence to the antiquated policy which was then fast urging it to destruction.

Taught by the light of history, and reckoning on the many disturbing elements for fostering revolution that exist in Burma, all who had given attention to Burmese affairs were profoundly convinced that the death of King Mengdôn would result in complete anarchy, to be ended either according to precedent by the 'survival of the fittest,' after the murder of the weaker aspirants, or by possible interference on the part of the British. Both of these contingencies were temporarily averted by the courage, wisdom, admirable tact, and wonderful facility of resource displayed by the Keng Woon Mengyee, ex-ambassador.

The Burmese, like the French, are a quiet and orderly people, easily governed, but at the same time easily excited, and prone to turbulence and riot when their passions have been roused. Several princes had numerous adherents in the provinces as well as at the capital, and if any of them had taken advantage of the confusion that existed when the throne was about to be vacant by escaping from surveillance and raising their standards at Motshoboh (the historical site of successful revolution) or other prominent place, he would undoubtedly have attracted thousands of the disaffected and others ready for any excitement, and a reign of terror would have ensued till one or other of the contending factions had obtained the upper hand.

Till King Mengdôn was *in extremis*, it was impossible to say which of his forty odd sons would be his successor. In sporting phrase, many prophets were prepared to name the winner, but it seemed 'anybody's race.' The moribund King, when the shadow of death came upon him, named the Nyoung Yan Prince, a young man of education and refinement, as well as a general favourite. Theebaw, it seems, was entirely out of the running, probably due to grave doubts as to his legitimacy—a slur continually cast in his teeth by his half-brothers, who were his fellow-scholars at the S. P. G. school at Mandalay, from which he was transferred to the Royal Monastery College to complete his education. Although his collegiate career was disfigured by 'high jinks' which nearly caused him to be rusticated, he took his degree in the first class of the 'Theological Tripos,' an event which pleased his pious father so much that he for the first time took notice of his promising son, though there was nothing in the royal favour shown the prizeman to make either himself or friends dream that he was the 'coming man.'

The Chief Queen, who, according to Burmese custom, was King Mengdôn's half-sister, though thoroughly loyal to her husband during his reign, was decidedly a strong-minded woman of unbounded ambition. She by no means relished the idea of dwindling into a mere nobody after having for many years enjoyed the position of Queen of the South or Chief Consort. She therefore allowed no sentimental feelings, as to soothing the last moments of her spouse, to interfere with her own prospective interests.

There were three princesses, daughters of Mengdôn, known as Soopayah, destined to remain single during their father's lifetime, but eligible as consorts of his successor. It was an open secret that Theebaw was over head and ears in love with the senior Soopayah, while the Queen's own daughter, Soopayah Lat, or middle Soopayah, had a tender passion for Theebaw, with whom she used to flirt in his college days. With the instinct of true genius, Her Majesty was fully equal to the occasion. She therefore promptly elected to pose as the fairy godmother in the interests of the young people, and, like the wicked steward, 'hedged' on her own account by making sure of the Queen Dowagership when her daughter, as Theebaw's consort, became Queen of the South.

The wily Queen was quite aware that her scheme was perfectly absurd unless she secured the co-operation of the Keng Woon Mengyee, who as premier was then all-powerful. She accordingly sent for that minister, and persuaded him that compliance with her wishes was tantamount to his being King of Burma; as the grateful Theebaw, in consideration of this unlooked-for promotion, would be a mere puppet in his hands. The Mengyee fell into the trap, and by a forged royal order inscribed on a palm-leaf, he hastily summoned the King's sons to hear their father's dying wishes and bid him farewell. All obeyed the summons excepting the Nyoung Yan and another prince, who, suspicious of danger, took refuge in the British Residency, and thus saved their lives. The others, on arrival at the King's private apartments, were incontinently seized and imprisoned. Theebaw, to his joy, was summoned from a loathsome dungeon to a throne, with his sweetheart as Chief Consort, and the girl that loved him as his second, while his brethren, to their intense chagrin, were kept in durance vile.

The cleverness with which the Mengyee secured the persons of all the princes likely to prove dangerous to the peace of the country, the wise precautions he took to check disaffection in the provinces, his careful police administration, and finally his being able to proclaim the death of the old King and the accession of the new, without endangering the public peace, speak volumes as to his capacity in a great crisis. To a people wedded as the Burmese are to precedent, the slightest innovation in the time-honoured custom of absolute monarchy would be repugnant; but, as the youthful King professed to be ignorant of the art of ruling, and delegated his authority to the ministers, and as the latter were ready to accept any alternative rather than brook interference on the part of the English, circumstances combined to favour the new departure.

So entirely successful was the *coup d'ètat*, and so great the calm after the storm, that the Keng Woon Mengyee stifled his natural feeling of resting on a slumbering volcano, and actually indulged in long-cherished ideas of introducing a constitutional form of government in his native country, instead of absolute despotism. Shway Yeo was, we may remark parenthetically, under the impression that the greater part of the scheme was written out for him by the late Dr. Clement Williams, the first political agent in Mandalay, and subsequently an independent trader. This may have been the germ of the idea, but we believe it did not assume concrete form till in 1872, when the embassy visited the Houses of Parliament with the present writer. The Mengyee was greatly struck with our system of government, which was kindly explained by members of the Houses deputed for this purpose. His attachés were charged with making copious notes on the spot and collecting information from every available source, all of which His Excellency recorded in an elaborate minute in the compilation of which the present writer had the pleasure of assisting. The Mengyee endeavoured to carry his idea into practice. His Constitution was published to the world with considerable *éclât*, and ought not to have appealed in vain to the fullest sympathy, if not to the active support of the British Government.

After all, it cannot be said that Theebaw's lines had fallen in pleasant places, for he was deliberately jilted by his lady-love,—who, rather than marry him, shaved her head and took refuge in a nunnery,—was henpecked by the wife provided for him, and bullied by his mother-in-law, both of whom egged him to fury by taunting him with mistaken kindness in proposing to provide suitable accommodation for his imprisoned brethren, and pointing out that he would never be safe till they were out of the way. Theebaw was by no means the drunken monster depicted by rumour, and fain would have avoided bloodshed; but, goaded to madness by his cruel consort and harridan mother-in-law, he uttered the fatal order, resulting in a massacre which caused such a sensation all over the civilised world.

Suffice it to say, in winding up this notable episode,* King Theebaw soon kicked over the traces and acted independently of his premier, who retired into private life.

* Although it is almost impossible to ascertain the exact truth of this affair, the evidence in the natural course of things being somewhat conflicting, the writer believes that his narrative, based on reliable information substantially confirmed by Shway Yeo, is as correct as can be expected under the circumstances.

CHAPTER VI.

THE TALAINGS AND ARAKANESE.

The Môns and Talaings within Recent Times enjoyed a Distinct Nationality—Now Practically the Same as the Burmese—Ancient City of Thahtun—Arrival thereat of Buddhist Missionaries—Marco Polo's reference to Talaings—Mythical Origin of the Arakanese—Nothing Notable in their Annals till the Twelfth Century—Beginning of Close Connection of Arakan with Bengal—Archers of the King's Body-Guard—Likened to the Pretorians—Sufferings of the Arakanese at the Hands of the Portuguese—The Great Mogul Determines to Abate the Scandal.

AFTER disposing of the Burmese, we naturally turn to the Talaings or Môns, whom the former, with all their pride of race, acknowledge to be practically one and the same people. Within, comparatively speaking, recent times, the Talaings enjoyed an individuality as pronounced as the Burmese. The same may be said of their country, comprising the delta of the Irawadi and adjacent regions, long known as the independent Kingdom of Pegu. Absorbed by the Burmese of the upper basin of that river, Pegu became a mere geographical expression, its government as much a thing of the past as the Commonwealth, while the nationality of its people is practically as much ancient history to the present generation as that of the Huns or Goths—emphasised by the fact that the appellation Talaing was simply a nickname, as will be explained presently. Contenting ourselves with this rather crude preamble, it may be as well to refer briefly to the indigenous inhabitants, as well as to the settlers on the seaboard, to enable the reader to understand and fully appreciate what Aryans have succeeded in accomplishing.

According to local tradition, Indian colonists from the coast of Coromandel had, at a remote period, formed settlements in the delta of the Irawadi and adjoining provinces. In Buddhist legends the country they occupied became known as Suverna Bhumi, or Golden Land. The first settlement was effected by two Indian princes, whose chief mission, according to the wildest part of the legend, was to bring up a child, born of a dragon, who was destined to found a city to be called Thahtun. This city, whose ruins are still to be seen, was formerly a great seaport, and possibly may have been visited by the navies of Kings Solomon and Hiram when they came to this region in search of materials for building the temple. Within comparatively recent times it existed in great prosperity, as it is certain that so late as the sixth century A.D. ships visited the port from Ceylon and Coromandel. The whole of the neighbouring country having silted up in a marvellously short space of time, Thahtun, which was utterly destroyed by the King of

Burma in the eleventh century, is now twelve miles from the sea, and, of course, cut off from all maritime intercourse. It was the capital of a territory identical with the ancient kingdom of of the Môns or Talaings, which we rather arbitrarily call Pegu.

In the third century B.C., or when the third Buddhist synod was held at Paliputra, and missions were sent to foreign countries to propagate religion and extirpate heresy, Sono and Uttaro were deputed to Suverna Bhumi, or the region now known as Pegu, to introduce Buddhism. They were at first violently opposed by the natives, but subsequently succeeded in converting them. After the missionaries left the country, or died, Buddhism declined, but its humanizing influences worked for the good of the people; for when other missionaries visited the descendants of the first converts, long afterwards, they received the word with joy. They were not in possession of the 'Pitika' or Buddhist scriptures till early in the fifth century, when Buddaghosa, the great apostle of Farther India, second only in fame to Buddha himself, brought Pali copies of them from Ceylon to Thahtun. He is also credited with giving the people an alphabet, and teaching them to read and write, in order that they might take hold of the scriptures more readily. The cognate tribes of the upper basin of the Irawadi did not secure these inestimable privileges till very long afterwards—apparently not till the eleventh century, when King Anoarahta, famous for his enterprise in the cause of religion, took from Thahtun to Pugân in Burma a number of monks and teachers versed in religion, in order to convert the people.

The Môns are considered by some authorities to be the aborigines of the country. The people themselves side with this view, and are the only nationality in Burma who have no tradition of having come from some other country. All the other races declare they came from the north, or the seat of the solar and lunar races, the scene of chivalrous adventures, and the abode of all those who were celebrated in the legends, the mythology, and the philosophy of Hindus.

According to Môn tradition, the first inhabitants of the country were savages, who rejected all intercourse with civilised beings, and even stoned Goadama Buddha when he visited the country. Sir A. Phayre is of opinion that the original inhabitants of the Irawadi delta belonged to the same family as the Mongoloid peoples in the upper course of the river, but that their ancestors left the great hive on the north of the Himalaya mountains, from which both swarmed, at an earlier period than the progenitors of the former.

'It is interesting,' remarks Sir A. Phayre,* 'to compare the difference of method, and to some extent of result, in the two instances of Mongoloid tribes in the north and south of the basin of the Irawadi who received their civilisation from Indians of different races. In the north (as

* Phayre's 'History of Burma.' London, 1883.

already explained) the tribes were civilised by Aryans, in the south by Dravidians. In the south the original settlers were traders. Eventually they became rulers, but there was an absence of any purpose of consolidation, and the native name of the race they found, or some designation other than their own, has been continued in the language of the people. The term Talaing is not acknowledged in the Mun (Môn) language, and the Dravidian settlers have become entirely absorbed in the indigenous and, except in ancient chronicles, obscured race.'

The capital of the kingdom was transferred from Thahtun to Pegu, which in the classic language was called Hansawadi, or Goose Town, 'from a legend of sacred geese, or, indeed, of the great teacher himself in that birth form, having lived on the spot when it was a sand-bank just appearing above the sea.'*

In the Burmese and Môn histories it is recorded that the peoples of the seaboard were subject to many and strange vicissitudes. After the city of Ava was founded in 1364, we read incidentally of Shan kings being at Pegu; two hundred years afterwards, we find Pegu under a Burmese king; later in the same century, both countries were ruled by a Burmese sovereign, and after a short interval independent of each other, and again united under previous conditions. In the middle of the seventeenth century, the Peguans secured a decided success over their rivals; but early in

* Phayre's History.

the eighteenth century they were finally crushed by the famous Alonugpra, founder of the dynasty of which King Theebaw was the last representative.

Previous to this event, the Môns were a distinct people, possessing a national language and differing in many essentials from their conquerors. But influenced by a gradual assimilation of manners and customs, with a community of social interests and identity of religion and language,* they have become thoroughly amalgamated with the usurpers.

The Burmese proper of the upper Irawadi, separated for centuries from kindred tribes to the south of them, only came tc know the Môns long after they had among them settlements of Telingas from the Coromandel coast; and, with a perversity for altering names only equalled by the British, they dubbed the former Talaing—their equivalent for the temporary residents—a name which has stuck to them ever since. For what the Burmese and Môns know of commerce, they are indebted, in a great measure, to the *bonâ-fide* Talaings or Telingas. It is true that the real commercial instinct has not as yet been given them; but they are great dabblers in small ventures. This, at any rate, is an advance on their former system of barter. The Telingas influenced the people for good in many other ways, and some particulars regarding them ought not to be

* Though endeavours have been made, for academical rather than practical purposes, to conserve the Môn language, it is spoken now by only a few persons in Pegu. It, however, survives among many thousands who fled in the last century into Siam.

out of place. They cannot be introduced more appropriately than by quoting what Marco Polo says of them and their country. Referring to Maabar, which corresponds to the Coromandel coast or the mother-country of the Telingas, he remarks: 'It is styled INDIA THE GREATER; it is the best of all the Indies.' Of the people he gives the following quaint description: 'You must know that in this Province of Maabar there is never a tailor to cut a coat nor to stitch it, seeing that everyone goes naked! For decency only will they wear a scrap of cloth; and so it is with men and women, with rich and poor; ay, and with the king himself, except what I am going to mention.'* There is now no lack of tailors in the country to supply the wants of the people, the majority of whom have adopted decent clothing. The great traveller's account is still applicable to the minority, consisting of catamaran men and masoolah boat-rowers, who are the first people one encounters on the surf-bound coast of Maabar or Coromandel. The Telingas, bold and adventurous mariners in by-gone days, still uphold their prestige. They visit Rangoon and other great ports which have superseded Thahtun, in probably greater numbers than ever; for, thanks to the arrangements made by the British Government, the perils of the sea in the shape of piracy, so rife in days of yore, need no longer be encountered.

Next in order are the Rakaing or Arakanese, a

* Yule's 'Marco Polo.' London, 1871.

cognomen derived from the Pali Raksha, applied to beings who guard the throne of Indra, but in their vernacular equivalent to Bilu, or monster of the ogre kind. They are doubtless descended from Mongoloid tribes closely akin to the progenitors of the Burmese, whose language they speak, but obscured by so many dialectic and phonetic differences as to be frequently unintelligible to the Burmese proper.

The Rakaing claim to be the elder branch of the Burmese family; but, influenced doubtless by traditions in vogue with the aborigines, are content to pin their faith on a far more prosaic origin than the ineffably glorious one aspired to by their more imaginative younger brethren. Their chronicles, as is the case with other peoples not of Aryan or Semitic descents, open with the revolution of the world from a deluge, and also give credence to a legend declaring that the first King of Arakan was the offspring of a wild doe. There is nothing further particularly notable in the native annals till the beginning of the twelfth century, when the country became subordinate to the Pugân monarchy, and remained so till the latter was broken up by the Mongol Emperor, Kublai Khan. The next remarkable episode was in the last quarter of the fourteenth century, when Arakan became involved in a quarrel between Burma and Pegu, and her sovereign was obliged to take refuge in Bengal, an event which was the beginning of a very close connection between the two countries, lasting for more than two centuries. In this interval, the kingdom suffered much from internal disorder, owing to the excessive employment of natives of India as archers of the King's body-guard, who gradually acquired much power, which they exercised without scruple in the promotion of their own interests. For a score of years these guards, like the Pretorians when at the pinnacle of their insolent ascendancy, deposed, robbed, and murdered one puppet king after another, till an Arakanese official of determined character gathered round him a number of devoted men, and dispersed or expelled this band of foreign robbers.

As already shown, the people of the Irawadi delta had many reasons for showering curses on the heads of Portuguese adventurers led by the infamous De Brito; but the sufferings of the Peguans were mild in comparison with the miseries endured by the Rakaing at the hands of compatriots of those 'miscreants.' In the beginning of the sixteenth century, when the Portuguese came 'from the great ocean in big ships,' they were cordially welcomed by the inhabitants and invited to trade. Before long, however, the latter bitterly complained that the visitors repaid this welcome by wantonly plundering their villages on the coast. The historical facts of the Portuguese connection, recorded by Sir A. Phayre and M. Bernier, formulate a terrible indictment against the interlopers. Neither the grave historian nor the picturesque writer, however, even were they to give the rein to fervid imagination, instead of confining themselves to bare fact, could adequately describe the cruelties and indignities suffered by the Arakanese at the hands of their guests.

As the Government was unable to restrain the Portuguese renegades, it is not surprising to find that their only trade was rapine and murder. They scoured the seas in their light galleys, entered the various mouths of the Ganges, ravaged the islands and villages of Lower Bengal, made slaves of their unhappy people, sold them to their countrymen at Hugli, and boasted—'the infamous scoundrels—that they made more Christians in a twelvemonth than all the missionaries of the Indies do in ten years.'* The pirates, becoming bolder by reason of immunity from punishment, proceeded to such extravagant lengths that they utterly cowed the King of Arakan, who was so impressed by the power wielded by the pirate chief Sebastian Gonsales, once a common sailor, that he gave the 'scoundrel' his daughter in marriage. Gonsales, in his arrogance, made a formal offer of Arakan to the Portuguese Viceroy at Goa; but the latter did not see his way to accepting the nefarious offer, which, as Bernier says, 'was quite in keeping with the general conduct of the Portuguese in Japan, Pegu, Ethiopia, and other places.'

The Great Mogul, finding his Bengal subjects were at the mercy of these infamous freebooters, determined to put a stop to a scandalous state of affairs so prejudicial to his administration. He

* Bernier's 'Travels.' Constable's *Oriental Miscellany.* London, 1891.

accordingly entrusted the task to the famous Shaista Khan, viceroy of that province. By a clever, though unscrupulous ruse, this able ruler, working on the cupidity as well as the fears of the Portuguese, acquitted himself entirely to the satisfaction of the Emperor. Whether mindful of the punishment awaiting them for the diabolical murder of a high Arakan official, or moved by Shaista Khan's promises and threats, 'certain it is that these unworthy Portuguese were one day seized with so strange a panic as to embark in forty or fifty *galleasses* and sail over to Bengale, and they adopted this measure with so much of precipitation that they had scarcely time to take their families and valuable effects on board.'* The Viceroy, having got the Portuguese into his power, treated them, as Monsieur Bernier drily remarks, 'not perhaps as he ought, but certainly as they deserved.' When they clamoured for the double pay and the land allotment promised by Shaista Khan, that astute commander coolly told them that 'they were traitors in whom it was folly to confide; wretches who basely betrayed the prince whose salt they had eaten for many years.'

Situated between Bengal and Burma, the strength of Arakan lay mainly in woods and swamps which, aided by artificial contrivances, opposed the passage of an enemy.† Had the

* Bernier's 'Travels.'

† Purchas tells us that the King of Rachim or Arakan 'hath certaine sluices, with the which, when the King of Pegu pretendeth any

Kings of Arakan trusted to these defences, and been content to remain in obscure independence at home, they might long have remained secure from landward foes. But, electing to become unnecessarily aggressive, their country lay at the mercy of foes on both sides. They had extended their territory northward during the rule of the feeble Kings of Bengal. The vigorous Mogul race, however, possessing the imperial throne at Delhi, rigorously governed even the remotest parts of their empire, and lost no time in driving the Arakanese within their ancient boundary. So, as says Sir Arthur Phayre, 'weakened by constant strife among her own children, the ancient kingdom of Arakan eventually became a prey to the successor of Aloungpra, and was destined only to find rest when annexed to the Empire of British India.'

harme towardes him, he may at his pleasure drowne a great part of the country. So that by this meanes he cutteth off the way whereby the King of Pegu should come with his power to hurt him.'—Purchas' 'Pilgrimes.' London, 1625.

A SHAN FAMILY

CHAPTER VII.

THE SHANS.

Shans very Widely Dispersed—Antiquity of their Civilisation—Chequered Career—Origin of Name—Divided into Three Branches—Shan Records found at Manipur—Chinese Emperor's Expedition to India—Frustrated by Shans—Kingdom of Pong long Existed in great Splendour—Broken up by King Anawrahta—The Koh-Shan-Pyi—Their Inhabitants—Shan Politics plain in Mengdôn's Time—Complications under Theebaw's *régime*—British Sphere of Influence Undefined—Prospects of Shan States under a Strong and Friendly Government.

THE Shans or Tai, the most widely dispersed nation in Farther India, invariably Buddhist, comparatively speaking, cultured and everywhere conserving their mother tongue, constituting a fringe to our land-locked frontiers of Burma, excepting where they impinge on Bengal, and still keeping touch with the ancient cradle of their race in Ssu-ch'uan, can, according to Monsieur Terrien de Lacouperie, boast of a civilisation dating back twenty-three centuries before Christ. Their career since they left their ancient *habitat* has not been a little chequered. Declining to acquiesce in the Chinese policy of absorption, whose aim was to efface the external characteristics of their neighbours by superior energy and civilisation, the Shans were forced out of their original places into Yunnan. Maintaining their conservation in that province as well as in Burma and Siam, their national idiosyncrasies, strange to say, were gradually obliterated in their contact with the Hindus of the Brahmaputra valley, which they invaded in the eighth and completely occupied in the beginning of the thirteenth century. They then arrogated to their own dynasty the title of Aham—the unequalled—softened afterwards into Assam. 'With the consolidation of their rule, however, the fate of all Eastern conquerors overtook the Shans. In the sleepy hollow of Assam they lost the qualities which won them power and prestige; while by adopting the language, customs, and religion of their Hindu subjects, they speedily sank into the condition of a mere ruling caste, and ceased to present the characteristics of an alien race.' * According to tradition they were once a great and united people; but the race has split into three principal branches, namely, the Siamese, the Laos, and the people whom we, imitating the Burmese, call Shan, who, however, repudiate the name, and dub themselves Tai, an appellation all three recognise for themselves.

The Shan race, at a period unknown, was evidently a victim to the fate which, in Marco Polo's time, overtook the peoples of Indo-China and the Eastern Islands, when 'a variety of kingdoms

* Mackenzie's 'North-East Frontier of Bengal.' Calcutta, 1884.

and dynasties were expanding and contracting, of which we have at best but dim and shifting glimpses.' At one time famous for its consolidated grandeur, their kingdom of Pong was shorn of its vast proportions by losing Burma, while the remainder, representing the national element, having been broken up for the most part into small principalities, and retaining only a semblance of its ancient dominion in the comparatively effete kingdom of Siam, is now, alas! noted for its decay and disintegration. It is impossible to determine how the various races that inhabited Pong in the zenith of its greatness were distributed. It is, however, probable that Mogoung, the capital of the kingdom, the metropolitan districts, and the mid-Irawadi riparian provinces, were peopled for the most part by Shans, whilst various rude tribes, as is now the case, occupied the country between these last and India. In days of yore, as metropolis of an important empire, Mogoung was probably an attractive place of residence—possibly the Paris of Farther India! It has since, however, dwindled into an insignificant village, visited periodically by Chinese traders in search of jade, and is noted only for an intolerable dulness, which recommended it to the late Burmese *régime* as a suitable place of exile for political prisoners. *Sic transit gloria mundi.* The kingdom of Pong is now as completely forgotten as the kingdom of Armenia, yet the Shans, like the Armenians, temperate, frugal, and with an aptitude for commerce, still exist and even flourish. It has long passed away, and would probably have been consigned to oblivion were it not that, sixty years ago, Captain Pemberton found valuable Shan historical records at Manipur, a translation of which he submitted to the Indian Government with a report, which, though published, was lost sight of apparently till information was required regarding a disputed boundary between Manipur and Burma.

In the days of old, Pong was more intimately connected with India than Burma, formerly its chief province, is now. The peoples on both sides of the borders, whether on peaceful or warlike thoughts intent, seemingly made light of the physical barriers between the two countries, upon which experts now-a-days lay so much stress. The remark also applies to a later period, when written records supplanted tradition. Marco Polo, alluding to events which occurred in the twelfth century, tells of 'the King of Mein, or Burma, and Bangala, a very puissant prince, with much territory and treasure and people.' This reference is very interesting, as it proves that the appellative, King of Bengal, was not merely local, but was recognised in distant countries, possibly at the court of Kublai Khan at Karakorum, where our great traveller was a distinguished guest. It also furnishes ground for assuming that the charge of intolerable presumption hurled at the head of His Majesty of the Golden Foot by the English Government only exposed its complete ignorance of mediæval Asiatic history.*

According to the 'Maharajah Weng,' or Burmese National Chronicle, King Anawrahta, who reigned in the first half of the eleventh century, extended his conquests to the frontier of India, and married an Indian princess. The son of his successor married another, and their son again eventually became King of Burma—facts corroborative of the alleged close relations between the two countries.

The Singpos and others have clashed with the Shans all along what is now the northern frontier of Burma, excepting in isolated places, and driven them into the arms of the Burmese. The latter, while influencing the last and being influenced in turn, owing to community of interest in various ways, have to a certain extent interfered with their pronounced proclivity for colonising the Irawadi Valley, and driven them eastward to the Salwen and Mekhong basins, which have been almost exclusively occupied by Shans for ages. No effort should be spared to encourage this industrious and enterprising people, not only to follow the bent of their own inclinations, but also to resume their ancient *habitat* on the frontier, and thus improve the Burmese, as well as stiffen the small colonies of their own people, which, bend-

* Lord Hastings, in his journal, dated September 16, 1818, records: 'The King of Burma favoured us early this year with the obliging requisition that we should cede to him Moorshedabad and the provinces to the east of it, which he deigned to say were all natural dependencies of his throne.'

ing somewhat towards, but not broken by the flood of Singpo barbarism, still manage to eke out an unsatisfactory existence, surrounded by unsympathetic tribes.

A century before the Christian era, it appears that the Emperor of the Han dynasty fitted out an expedition to find its way through South-Western China to India, which was frustrated by the obstructiveness of the 'barbarians' or Shans, who then occupied Yunnan, resulting in their chastisement and expulsion from the country of the Upper Mekhong and Salwen rivers to the Irawadi Valley. This movement developed to such a degree that the immigrants, after awhile, found themselves strong enough to overthrow the monarchy established by the Aryan settlers and founded a kingdom of their own. As already shown, the Shans completely effaced themselves, but their dominion was gradually extended in the fluviatile region of Indo-China, and eventually expanded into an important empire. Even within comparatively speaking recent times, when Kublai Khan dispatched an expedition against Pugân in the thirteenth century, Shans predominated in the kingdom of Burma, and many of that race acquired great influence therein. Of these the most noted were three brothers, governors of important districts near the capital, who owed their position entirely to royal favour. Unmindful of this obligation, they elected to worship the rising sun, and on the fall of the Pugân monarchy, which inevitably followed the Mongol invasion and the flight of the King, used their power to arrange for the subordination of Burma to China. A son of the absconded monarch, it is true, nominally reigned, but, by a plot contrived by the Shan brethren, was seized and forced to become a monk; in other words, to renounce the world. He having appealed to the Emperor of China as suzerain, a Mongol army was sent to restore him. The Shans, acting on a suggestion in a song sung at a dramatical performance, killed the King, and, showing his head to the Mongol general in proof of the collapse of the dynasty, bribed that official with valuable gifts, and persuaded him to acquiesce in an arrangement allowing them to rule the country as a triumvirate. This story is capped by another ridiculous version of the same event related by Marco Polo. 'You see,' says that distinguished narrator, 'at the court of the Great Khan there was a great number of gleemen and jugglers, and he said to them one day that he wanted them to go and conquer the aforesaid province of Mien, and that he would give them a good captain to lead them and other good aid. And they replied they would be delighted. So the Emperor caused them to be fitted out with all that an army requires, and gave them a captain and a body of men-at-arms to help them; and so they set out and marched until they came to the country of Mien. And they did conquer the whole of it!'*

Both Burma and China essayed to force the

* Yule's 'Marco Polo.'

Northern Shan States—which had hitherto managed somehow to remain independent—to acknowledge their suzerainty; but the Shan confederacy was, for a long time, sufficiently powerful to resist coercion. China took notice of this stubbornness by invading Pong in the fourteenth century, and taking Muang-Marong, its capital, after the horrors of an Asiatic siege which lasted two years; she did not, however, retain possession of it, annexation not being her policy. Burma, involved in many struggles with the Shans, had meanwhile dwindled in territory and power; but she knew how to wait, and, seizing the opportunity of internal dissensions among the chiefs, succeeded in annexing these States. Having existed for many centuries in great splendour, this kingdom, in the beginning of the eleventh century, was broken up by the conquests of King Anawrahta, the darling hero of the Burmese people. His exploits in this region, especially in connection with his love adventures, wherein a Shan princess was the heroine, form the subject of one of the most popular dramas in Burmese literature, of enthralling interest to this day.

The Shans pulled themselves together again; in the middle of the sixteenth century, however, their power again waned, for the Burmese king Bureng Noung seized on the city of Ava, ruled by a Shan sovereign, and following up his successes, conquered the Shan States of the Upper Irawadi, and compelled the powerful chiefs of Mogoung and Mongin to swear fealty to the

'King of Kings,' as he styled himself. About this time the Shans adopted the Burmese style of dressing the hair and clothing, which seems to bear corroborative testimony to the record of their subjection. During the reign of Aloungpra, or in the middle of the eighteenth century, the kingdom of Pong was finally dismembered, and Mogoung ruled by a delegate from Ava.

The Shan States, though easily governed, have, from 'a fatal want of coherence,' been separated into numerous principalities, which for the sake of convenience are called Chinese, Burmese, and Siamese Shan States, according to their proximity to, or as they are influenced by, China, Burma, and Siam respectively. Some of the chiefs of the principalities farthest away from their suzerains, retain the form and paraphernalia of royalty; but these latter 'they possess,' as Colonel Yule says, 'only as the Vicar of Wakefield's daughters possessed their crown-pieces: they were theirs, but must not be made use of.' They nominally paid annual tribute to their respective suzerains, but the payments were rather honoraria than substantive, as they merely consisted of gold and silver flowers, pieces of silk tinsel, and the like.

We learn from Mr. Scott that the Shan country, frequently called Cambawsa, 'was, according to universal modern assertion, divided into Ko Shan Pyi, the Nine Shan States . . . It appears, however, more than probable that the Nine Shan States will prove to be a mere historical expression, and that they no more had a contemporaneous existence than the Saxon Heptarchy . . . The name of Ko Shan Pyi is even sometimes applied solely to the so-called Taiche—Shan Chinese—States north of Senwi, acknowledging the authority of the Chinese Empire.' *

To these we can turn with pleasure and interest, for, cradled in the little nest of valleys in the parallel ranges between the Salwen and the Irawadi, they have preserved their subordinate independence and represent the chief component parts of the ancient kingdom of Pong. Sladen and his companions, on their way from Bhamó to Yunnan, coming upon them after encountering considerable hardship and trouble in their passage through the territory of the turbulent Kakhyens, were delighted to meet with a people who contrasted favourably with those truculent caterans. Bowers † describes both men and women as robust, healthy, and pleasing in appearance, and some of the girls as fair, and good specimens of Eastern beauty. Frugal, temperate, and industrious, the Shans have, he says, the perseverance and aptitude for business, as well as the trading proclivities of the Chinese, and will bear comparison with the occupants of many European valleys, who for centuries have had the advantage of Western civilisation and education. Anderson records ‡ that the great body of the

* *Asiatic Quarterly Review.* July, 1889.

† Bowers' 'Report on Trade Routes.' 1869.

‡ Anderson's 'Mandalay to Momein.' London, 1876.

population is engaged in agriculture; and as cultivators they rank even with the Belgians. They pay particular attention to irrigation, conveying by ingenious aqueducts, from distant places if necessary, the water required for their fields and gardens. The men are superb blacksmiths, while the women are adepts at needlework and embroidery, and are constantly engaged in weaving and dyeing the yarn spun from home-grown cotton. These genial Shans, while expressing regret at the departure of their guests, entertained hopes that before long the revival of a vigorous trade would result in binding closer, in the interests of both countries, the friendly feelings so happily inaugurated. It is now hoped that owing to the improved means of communication, by roads and railways, which will be available, and under a just and firm administration, the country under the recent dominion of King Theebaw will offer a great attraction to these enterprising and industrious Shans, who, even under adverse conditions, have for many generations exhibited a great partiality for settling therein.

It was not till some time after the conquest of Burma Proper that the British had leisure to pay attention to the Shan States; aud not the least embarrassing part of their duty was to solve the problem as to what portion thereof constituted their inheritance. For, while Shan politics were easily understood by persons of the meanest comprehension during the benign suzerainty of

King Mengdôn, they became a sealed book, even to experts, owing to the eccentricities of his successor Theebaw.

'Though Burmese arms did no more than sweep Siam and the Laos, they retained a firm hold of the Shan States. Burmese troops garrisoned Keing Tung and Keing Hong on the upper waters of the Mekong, and when Siam strove thirty-four years ago to extend her colonies north of Keingmai (Zimmè), the Shans united with their Burman rulers to drive back the invaders of Keing Tung. The Burman grip was strong, and the rule not too burdensome, and the Shans were prosperous, contented, and wealthy. With the death of King Mengdôn, and the accession of King Theebaw, all, however, was changed. The lethargy of the sovereign and the extravagance of his queen caused the ruin of the Shan States. Huge sums of money in the way of benevolences were exacted from the hill-chiefs. States and portions of States were sold over the head of the reigning potentate. Any man, Shan or Burmese, who possessed the necessary wealth, had but to go to the Burmese Court, begin bribery with the Secretaries, who established a hereditary claim for him, substantiate this by more money with the Ministers of State, and finally buy the territory outright for a round sum from the monarch himself. The process was expensive, for the purchaser had then to engage the support of the Burman exarchs in the Shan hills to enable him to establish himself, and not unseldom he was jockeyed by a higher bid made by the ruler in possession, or by another speculator. But, whoever eventually prevailed, the population was ground down and robbed of all it possessed. Ruined cultivators took to the fells and joined the following of some recognized freebooter, and the system of dacoity, which had been developed in Burma by the cunning and greed of ministers like the Taingda Mingyi, took, in the Shan States, more of an independent robber type.' *

Things being thus somewhat mixed, a considerable period may possibly elapse before the British will be in a position to determine their sphere of influence. In the interests of the more satisfactory administration of Burma Proper, they have contented themselves with inaugurating the machinery of Government in the Cis Salwen States only, and have thus given a handle to recent writers for jumping to the conclusion that they have adopted this river as their boundary. But, even if they desired to have so well marked a frontier, it would be out of the question, as at least three of the principal States Cis Salwen possess and have for centuries possessed considerable territory on the other side. We may here conveniently quote *The Times* on the subject of the Shan States.

'The conquest of Upper Burma has not only imposed on the Indian Government the task of dealing with a new series of border tribes, accus-

* Mr. Scott, *Asiatic Quarterly Review.*

tomed, under the late native dynasty, to an existence of lawlessness and plunder; it has also brought under the British suzerainty semi-independent States beyond the frontier, which acknowledged the paramount claims of the Burmese kings, but, whenever convenient, defied them. Captain Younghusband, on his interesting ride of eighteen hundred miles through the Indo-Chinese peninsula, was able to study the present attitude of these States, and his account of them disclosed what may be termed the international difficulties of the situation. For example, Kiang Tung, the great semi-independent Shan State on the east of the Salwen river, was subordinate to the King of Burma, and yearly sent a tribute of ivory, ponies, and gold. But, a few years before our annexation of Burma, it had suspended its relations with the Court of Mandalay by murdering the Burmese Resident and his staff. It now lies between British Burma, China, and Siam, and is being rapidly encroached upon by the two latter Powers. The Chinese encroachments, so far as Captain Younghusband could learn, already amounted in 1887 to over one thousand square miles. Are we to enforce our suzerain claims on the State, claims which passed to us with the dominions of the late King of Burma, or are we to leave it to be eaten up piecemeal by China and Siam? "It is scarcely realized by most Englishmen," wrote Captain Younghusband, "that our newly-acquired kingdom of Burma does, through its subsidiary State of Kiang Tung, actually touch Tonquin, and through Tonquin the French." If we assert our claims over Kiang Tung, we advance our frontier several hundred miles beyond the defensible boundary of the Salwen river mountains, and add to our responsibilities a long, straggling, ill-defined strip of country which runs between three nations—the British, the Chinese, and the Siamese—and ends near the borders of a fourth, the French. The soundest policy, Captain Younghusband thought, would be to hand over Kiang Tung to the Chinese, not as a possession, but as a tributary State, and subject to safeguards for British trade. We cite the case of Kiang Tung to indicate the large ulterior questions involved by a delimitation of the Burmese frontier. But in this matter the longer the Government of India shrinks from facing the difficulties inherent to the situation, the more aggravated will those difficulties become. The six years which have passed since the annexation of Upper Burma should have sufficed to collect the needful *data* for the delimitation of its eastern frontier.'

With Burma advancing in giant strides, achieving results more satisfactory than the most enthusiastic believers in its capabilities ever dreamt of; with its rude tribes made more amenable to the usages of civilisation; with the hitherto disunited congeries of Shan States amalgamated under the auspices of a strong, progressive, and friendly Government; and with Siam giving evident signs of progress, there is every reason to believe that, before very long, what constituted the ancient Shan kingdom of Pong, will attain to far more than its pristine splendour.

A KAREN MARKET BOAT.

CHAPTER VIII.

THE KARENS.*

Karens Divided into Three Principal Tribes and Numerous Clans—Information as to Origin, Based on Tradition, Nevertheless Reliable—Migrated to Burma with the Chinese—Ancient Kingdom—Their Habits and Customs denote Central Asian Origin—Language Reduced to Writing—Bghai Dress and Ornaments—Karen Talent for Melody—Belief in a Supreme Being—Spiritualism—Fetish Stones—Augury by Fowls' Bones—Sorcery Compared with what used to Prevail in England—Notions Regarding the Future Life—Origin of Christian Mission.

KAREN is a name we have adopted from the Burmese, conveniently designating a people divided into three great tribes—the Sgau, the Pwo, and the Bghai, comprising numerous inferior clans known to outsiders by nicknames derived from various peculiarities in dress or occupation, each tribe calling itself by its equivalent for man, but having no common appellation for themselves and congeners in the family of nations. We are dependent on oral tradition alone for information as to

* Portions of this chapter have been 'boiled down' from the author's work 'Karens of the Golden Chersonese.' London, 1876.

their origin; but this testimony, which points to Central Asia as their ancient home, and indicates the route by which they came therefrom, has perhaps more ethnological value than the pretentious records of the more advanced races that surround them. Obscure as the retrospect may be, in imagination they see in the dim horizon 'the river of running sand' which their ancestors crossed when coming southwards—a fearful tractless region, where the sands rolled before the wind like the waves of the sea—apparently referring to the dread terrors of the Gobi desert, graphically described by Marco Polo and the celebrated Chinese pilgrim Fahian. In it, says the latter, 'there are a great many evil demons; there are also sirocco winds which kill all who encounter them. There are no birds or beasts to be seen; but so far as the eye can reach the route is marked out by the bleached bones of men who have perished in their attempt to cross the desert.'*

Their ancients have handed down to them that they accompanied the Chinese force which invaded Burma; and their legends also take more tangible shape by indicating a connection with the Chinese in places whereof the narrators know nothing but the bare names. Thus Bhamó, through which the invading Chinese army came on its way to Mien or Pugân, frequently occurs in their old rhymes as the name of a Burmese town near which their ancestors dwelt. Again, 'Mien with its gold and silver towers,' as Pugân was called

* Beal's 'Travels of Buddhist Pilgrims.'

in Chinese history, is apparently the same as the 'Gold and Silver City' near which they were located with the Celestials. The latter, after overrunning Burma, returned to China, while of the Karens who remained behind, some were dispersed among the Burmese and Mons of the plains, while others eventually secured territories in hilly regions, which, from natural advantages, afforded them desirable and secure resting-places, where they have been able to remain more or less independent for centuries.

Karen tradition refers to a period when they were an undivided nation with a king of their own, and some of their aspirations point to a monarchial government under which they anticipate great temporal prosperity. These hopes take shape in the form of a prayer to the Almighty in the following strain: 'O Lord! we have had affliction for several generations, and now should have our share of the good that the gods provide. The Burmese, Talaings, and Siamese, as well as European foreigners, have obtained their desires in this respect, while the Karens have been left out in the cold.' The Millennium which they expect when their prayer has been granted is indicated in the following stanzas, which have a sufficiently close resemblance to the prophecy in the eleventh chapter of Isaiah to suggest the notion that it may be one of their biblical traditions:

'When the Karen King arrives,
There will be only one monarch.
When the Karen King comes,
There will be neither rich nor poor.

'When the Karen King arrives,
The beasts will be happy.
When the Karens have a King,
Lions and leopards will lose their savageness.'

In spite of these aspirations, there is no evidence to show that the Karens ever tried to bring them to any practical conclusion. In fact, they seem reconciled to the state of dependence which has been their lot for ages.

Although the historical traditions of rude and unlettered tribes seldom have much ethnological value, those of the Karens, in reference to their origin and older movements, have the support of evidence not accorded to their neighbours. And when we compare these with their physical and mental characteristics, the state of social relations, system of government, religious observances and customs, as well as their monosyllabic language, with its numerous intonations involving as many changes of signification, we are involuntarily reminded of that well-marked civilisation characterised by distinctive social, domestic, and religious institutions, whose original seat is commonly assigned to mid-Asia.

The Karens believe that spiritual power over health and life, extending even to the realms of the dead, is obtainable by the living, and wizards and necromancers are both respected and dreaded. The practice of sorcery, divination, and ordeal is universally practised by them, and deeply influences their life by holding it in an atmosphere of distrust, dread, and revenge. They also opine that all objects, natural and artificial, have their presiding deities, which must be appeased or kept in good humour, and their habit of propitiating the ghosts of the dead by the consecration of miniature houses to their use, is among the Sythic and other branches of the archaic Asiatic faith. Their belief is precisely the same as the Naturalism and Shamanism of the Tartars, in that besides the recognition of spirits and spiritual influence over the affairs of this world, the idea of a supreme God has been attained—' the Maker of all things visible and invisible, and the Distributor of good and evil in this world; but they worship him not with prayer or praises, or any kind of service.'*

The custom of placing in and upon the graves of the dead articles for the use and consumption of the living, concealing the burial-places of their chiefs, as practised by the Red Karens, the binding of slaves and ponies near places of sepulture in lieu of the obsolete custom of human sacrifice at the funerals of influential persons, all point to identity of origin. Their social system, under which each village or group of villages is a little republic under a hereditary chief or patriarch, without ever attaining to conditions favourable to the growth of monarchy, obtains also among Himalaic peoples. As with the Tibetan tribes, so with the wilder clans of the Karens, humanity has made little progress. Selfishness reigns supreme, producing indifference to bloodshed. Bitter feuds, lasting for generations, with their usual con-

* Yule's 'Marco Polo.'

comitants of rapine and murder, are the normal condition of their society. Finally, Karen personal adornment follows the ordinary Himalaic fashion in which heavy tiers of rings on the arms and legs, with enormously distended ear perforations, are conspicuous. All these indications mark the Karens as the descendants of the ancient Tartar hordes who, leaving their inhospitable steppes, swept across central Asia into that portion of China which history teaches us was the site occupied by the nucleus of numerous States which subsequently developed into the Chinese Empire. Incidentally we may remark that their Celestial fellow-travellers were not the first occupiers of the Flowery Land. Indeed, they admit the fact, inasmuch as their traditions tell us that on their first arrival they became acquainted with 'tattooing' populations, probably the Shans, who, on being driven out of their ancient *habitat*, travelled southwards, and settled in Farther India.

The habitations and villages of Karens of the plains are essentially the same as those of the Burmese. Among some of the hill clans the equivalent thereto consists of one or two oblong houses built on piles, and divided into sixty or seventy compartments, each occupied by a separate family, so that the size of a hamlet is estimated by the number of hearths it contains. Viewed from a distance, these structures, especially those near pine forests, are apt to remind one of Swiss châlets; but the enchantment that distance lends them is unfortunately broken on a nearer view, which gives one the impression of Brobdignagian rabbit-hutches on scarlet-runner sticks, occupied by human bipeds, instead of specimens of the rodent genus. At first sight it was a puzzling matter to decide how the men, women, and children, busy in various ways in the verandahs or roof, arrived at their coins of vantage; but we soon were aware that they easily accomplished this feat by means of ladders made from giant bamboos, cut in notches a foot or so apart, convenient enough for people with bare feet, but difficult to those wearing boots. Similar steps communicated with the roof from the landing on which the people spread their cotton, chillies, &c., to dry in the sun.

The Karen language is rather a family of dialects than a single one. Like all Indo-Chinese speech, it is monosyllabic, and each syllable changes its signification by a change of intonation. This peculiarity is more pronounced in Karen than in Burmese, as each Karen syllable has five varieties of pronunciation with as many changes of meaning, while Burmese can only boast of three. In Annamite, said to be a cognate tongue, the syllable *ba*, for example, with its five intonations properly rung, may mean 'three ladies gave a box in the ear to the favourite of the prince.' Léon de Rosny, in reference to Cochin Chinese, declares 'the same syllable signifies twenty-three different things, according to the difference of accent, so that people never speak without singing.' Quoting this, Professor Max Müller remarks, 'This description, though somewhat exaggerated, is correct in the main, there being six or eight musical accents or modulations in this as in other monosyllabic tongues, by which the meanings of one and the same monosyllabic root are kept distinct. These accents form an element of language which we have lost, but which was most important during the primitive stages of human speech.' *

The Sgau and Pwo clans comprise the bulk of the agricultural population of the delta of the Irawadi, and are also found in the lower basins of the Sittoung and Salwen rivers and their adjacent mountain ranges. As the earlier missionaries wrote, 'They are a meek, peaceful race, simple and credulous, with many of the softer virtues and few flagrant vices.' They afford a marked contrast to the warlike and independent Bghais of the hilly regions, who differ as widely in their moral characteristics from their congeners of the plains as in their physical peculiarities. They also boast with truth of having ever successfully defied all efforts of the Burmese to exercise control over them. For the most part, however, preferring to live far from the bustle of cities and towns, from choice ensconcing himself in dense forests, perching on the eyrie-like heights of mountain ranges, or hiding in the tall elephant grass on the margin of rivers and streams, the lowland Karen is occasionally found

* Max Müller's 'Science of Language.'

hovering round the outskirts of modern civilisation, ministering to its necessities but not caring to join in its pleasures or in its pursuits. Differing as the various tribes do in many ways, they have many points in common which allow us to speak of them as homogeneous. All, however, are the very antipodes of the Burmese. Our description of the contrast between the Burmo-Mongoloid and the Burman equally applies to the Karen in the same comparison, and in no trait is this so conspicuous as in their relative sense of humour,—the typical Karen being as impervious to a joke as Dean Swift's Scotchman; the Burman, on the other hand, having a very keen sense of the ludicrous.

The strong personality of the Burmese, even where the Karen element predominates, is so pronounced that casual observers are naturally attracted thereby, and tempted to depreciate the less obtrusive characteristics of the Karens. Officials and others brought in constant contact with the former, more or less succumb to the glamour of their genial disposition and winning manners, which contrast favourably with the stolid and matter-of-fact bearing of the Karens, with whom flattery is so foreign to their thoughts that they have no word for it in their language. They are also apt to look at all that concerns the latter through Burmese spectacles, which unfortunately are obscured by a prejudice that relegates them to a position little higher than mere animals. It is surprising that one of the most interesting peoples in our Indian Empire should thus be ignored, and such scant justice should be accorded to their exemplary attitude, of such paramount political importance in the late revolution in Burma. A silver lining to the dark cloud, which long hung over the country, then showed itself in the conspicuous loyalty and admirable behaviour of the Karens, victims though they were of unsympathetic treatment, eminently conducive to disloyalty and disorganization. The very tribes who, under the Burmese *régime*, were truculent and apparently untamable caterans, justified the conciliatory policy of the British Government by becoming its staunchest supporters in the duty of restoring order in districts which had become partially disorganised. For they not only, as a law-abiding people, afforded a praiseworthy example to their disaffected neighbours, but by placing themselves at the disposal of the officers of Government or their missionaries, upheld British authority at a critical period—an attitude the more commendable, as some of them were smarting under a sense of grievous wrong in having been taxed for the cost of extra police in districts which would have lapsed into anarchy had it not been for their timely intervention.

Though, as will be explained presently, Karen tradition has it that the Karens anciently possessed written records, the bulk of the people were sceptical as to the possibility of their language being represented by signs till Dr. Wade, who was the first missionary to labour among them, reduced it to writing,—an event that caused not a little excitement. As a tentative measure, both the Roman and the Burmese alphabets were used for this purpose. But instead of adopting either, which apparently would have been the most reasonable course, those responsible for the new departure chose to go out of their way to invent a new one.

Although the Karens originate nothing, they are apt imitators, and evince such a capability for instruction, that the children of those who a generation ago were dubbed 'wild men,' can now survey land and plot their work, use the sextant, measure heights and distances, take the sun's meridian, and calculate for latitude. Others exhibit a decided talent for printing, carpentry, and other forms of handiwork, proving what can be done by well-considered and persistent efforts for promoting education.

The lowland Karens have ever been submissive to authority, whether ground under the heel of Burmese tyranny or enjoying the security and comfort of the *pax Britannica.* The same may be said regarding the Highlanders, who have been influenced by the latter, while the less tractable are like the Scottish clans in the days of Rob Roy. Each tribe has its chief, but as a rule his influence is merely nominal. Under exceptional circumstances, as was the case in Ancient Caledonia, he enjoys a certain amount of power in his different relations of landlord, leader, and judge of his clan; but his authority is far from absolute, as he has to consult his elders in matters of importance. The Karens imagine that their law came down to them in a state of perfection from the Ancients, and consequently, like that of the Medes and Persians, it cannot be altered. Of this unwritten or common law, as we might term it, the elders are the recognised interpreters, just as the Secretaries of State of European powers are the interpreters of royal warrants. These worthies are expected to teach the people to do good and eschew evil, but owing to the frailty of human nature they, feeling they do not always pose as bright exemplars, content themselves with merely expounding the law, and so satisfy their consciences, like the Scotch divine, who, aware of his own backslidings, said to his congregation, 'Dinna do as I do, but do as I bid ye.' It must be confessed that the elders have somewhat an invidious task assigned them, for many of those whom they strive to teach, having no restraint on their passions save superstition and the fear of retaliation, acknowledge no right of control, and, taking the law into their own hands, apply it as suits their savage inclinations. According to Karen polity, it is considered convenient to encourage the people to avenge their wrongs, and, provided they conform to traditional custom, they are absolved from all responsibility so far as the State is concerned. This anomalous state of affairs, though fairly representing the normal conditions of society among the ruder clans, is subject to modification where the people have been directly or indirectly influenced by peoples in a higher stage of civilisation, or where their chiefs, either by a combination of fortuitous circumstances or by sheer force of character, acquire and exercise an influence denied to weaker men. As Dr. Mason says, 'Each village, with its scant domain, is an independent state, and every chief a prince, but now and then a little Napoleon arises who subdues a kingdom to himself. The dynasty, however, lasts only with the controlling mind.' Excepting under such conditions, chiefs are unable to extend to their nominal subjects the protection which an organised form of government affords, or even to insist on payment of taxes, a legitimate demand for this privilege. Defective as the Burmese Government was in the case of the wilder tribes of Karens, Dr. Mason was of opinion that the clans subjected thereto contrasted favourably with those who maintained their independence, proving that a bad government is better for a people than anarchy.

In cosmogany the Karens are more advanced than the Burmese, in that they hold to the Ptolomaic theory, while the latter imagine that the sun, moon, and stars revolve round a great mountain in the north, in lines parallel to the earth. With a somewhat similar conceit regarding the seven daughters of Atlas and Pleione, who, according to Greek mythology, changed after death into stars, they say that the Pleiades consisted originally of seven persons, one of whom has been lost. A meteor is held to be a youth-star visiting a maiden-star, a more pleasing belief than the Arab notion, which assumes it to be Azrael's death-summons. As is the case with more enlightened people, the Karens regard the appearance of comets as indicating wars, famine, pestilence, or other calamity. Milton speaks of a comet

> 'That fires the length of Orphiuchus huge
> In the Arctic sky, and from his horrid hair
> Shakes pestilence and war.'

Shakespeare also tells us that

> 'Meteors fright the fixed stars of heaven;
> The pale-faced moon looks bloody on the earth,
> And lean-looked prophets whisper fearful change:
> These signs forerun the death or fall of kings.'

The Bghai family of Karens has its chief *habitat* on the left bank of the Salwen river, near Toungoo. Beyond the Bghais again, extending far into China, are numerous tribes allied to them, but exceeding them in lawlessness and ferocity, prone to kidnapping and slave-dealing. Some of its clansmen wear short drawers with radiating red lines, while others patronise white, sack-like, garments with perpendicular red bands. The American missionaries have accordingly distinguished them as Pant-Bghai and Tunic-Bghai. Tsawkoo males never vary their scant apparel, which consists of dun-coloured drawers with red stripes, supplemented by a profusion of beads of many colours. The women ordinarily wear the white and red short tunic adopted by their neighbours, with a short blue petticoat with red stripes. Their favourite necklace consists of three or four leaden coils of the thickness of an ordinary finger; and, not satisfied with bracelets of brass coils extending from elbows to wrists, they case their lower limbs in brass greaves, weighing each sometimes seven pounds, while, as a matter of course, beads are worn as well. On rare occasions, they put the finishing touch to their toilet by surmounting all with a remarkable head-dress consisting of a brimless hat of cane-work about eight inches high, embroidered in fanciful patterns with beads. The hat is without crown, but this defect is concealed by plumes manufactured from the brilliant feathers of birds, stuck in front and arranged so as to fall over it, giving it, at a short distance, somewhat the appearance of a Highlander's plumed bonnet decked out with beads and green beetle-wings. They were induced to appear in full dress on the occasion of the present writer's visit to one of their villages when a Tsawkoo opera was performed for his edification, which, if the interpreter was to be believed, was the local version of 'Don Giovanni.' It must be admitted that the confessions of their Leporello—emphasised by a band accompaniment of harmonicons, flutes, flageolets, and drums, hastily improvised from bamboos cut in the adjacent jungle—were as much appreciated by the audience as those of his prototype in Mozart's famous opera, interpreted by a powerful orchestra, are by Westerns.

Most of the Karen tribes have a decided talent for melody, which the American missionaries have taken much pains to develop; so that, in the very wildest localities, one occasionally finds congregational singing in their chapels rendered by the naturally sweet voices of the women and the hearty, if less harmonious, tones of the men, in a fashion that would gladden the heart of many an English vicar.

The Karens are distinguished from the peoples that surround them by their belief in the existence of a supreme being, God eternal, the Creator of heaven and earth, who at one time favoured them with His special protection, but withdrew His countenance from them in punishment for their sins. In one of their traditions we have it,

> 'God is truly unchangeable and eternal.
> He existed in ancient Time, at the beginning of the world.
> The life of God is endless;
> A succession of worlds does not measure his existence.
> God is perfect in every meritorious attribute,
> And dies not in succession on succession of worlds.'

Their indigenous faith would seem to bear traces of the Mid-Asian mythologies, which were characterised by the broad simplicity of Man in various parts of the world. Every object of nature, say the Karens, has its presiding genius or Nat; thus all celestial and terrestrial bodies, all animate as well as inanimate things which can be brought into the practical use of mankind, have their guardian spirits. The air they breathe is also thickly peopled with the ghosts of the unburied dead, and the spirits of their departed ancestors crowd around them. The mighty ocean and trackless desert which inspire awe, the rice-field, the vegetable-garden and hill-clearing which minister to their bodily wants, have each and all their tutelar deities or Nats, which, as subordinate beings to some greater power, must be propitiated. These Nats, which some call demons, are only so in the Greek signification, for they are not naturally aggressive; unluckily, however, mortals are apt to trespass inadvertently on their domains, and are punished for these breaches of etiquette by sickness and death. Hence, to avert these calamities, they must be appeased with offerings of food and libations of intoxicating drinks. The Karens, according to tradition, seem, like the Chinese, Hindus, and Egyptians, to have practised the Noahic religion, in which, according to Carlyle, 'fable and fancy could find no place, and all was genuine, unsophisticated truth.' Their indigenous faith, however, does not rise to the level of idolatry, which Sir John Lubbock tells us 'characterises a somewhat higher stage of human development.'* Simple as is their creed, it is burdened by a somewhat complicated psychological conceit with reference to the attributes of all animated nature, which they call La or Kela. The idea, say some, seems allied to the Psyche of the Greeks, others attribute it to the Genius of the Latins, while the present writer would class it with the Ka of the Egyptians, as interpreted by Miss Edwards.† It has also other inherent

* Lubbock's 'Origin of Civilisation.' London, 1870.

† 'Fellahs, Pharoahs, and Explorers.' London, 1891.

qualities peculiar to itself, reminding us of the good and bad angels, which, in our own classic literature, are said to attend on every human being. This La, they say, 'existed before Man was born, comes into the world with him, remains with him until death, and, for aught that appears to the contrary, is immortal. Yet no moral qualities are predicated of it. It is neither good nor bad, but it is merely that which gives life to mortality.' * The Karen, as can well be imagined, endeavours to keep on good terms with all the *genii loci* of his surroundings, but finds it particularly incumbent on himself to make things especially pleasant for his La, lest through pique or inadvertence it should cease to protect him from his bad demons, viz., madness, epilepsy, lust, wrath, bad dreams, disease, and languor.

Under certain circumstances, they imagine that some favoured individuals have power over the spirit world so far as to compel the La of a recently deceased person to return to its corpse and revive it;—reminding one of ancient Danish mythology, wherein a ghost or La, which has re-taken itself to the land of Shades, can be made amenable to similar pressure. Ethert Brand's La, we learn from Sir Walter Scott, was thus released by the intrepidity of his sister.

> 'She crossed him thrice that lady bold;
> He rose beneath her hand.
> The fairest Knight of Scottish mould,
> Her brother, Ethert Brand.' †

* Dr. Mason, *Journal Asiatic Society of Bengal.*

† 'Lady of the Lake.'

Spirit-rapping and other phases of spiritualism have a great hold on all Karens; and the missionaries confess with sorrow that it is one of the most impracticable of the illusions with which they have to grapple in the case of their converts. In some of the Sgau funerals they use an apparatus by which they firmly imagine that the La can be induced to respond to the summons of its most beloved one, either by rapping or other visible sign—a great comfort to all concerned, who thereupon adjure it to depart in peace. An unsympathetic missionary, however, tells the tale that when he kept the crowd of simple folk away from the machinery, 'there was no more answer to the calls than there was to the cries of the priests of Baal before Elijah.'

Though the Karens, as a rule, are not idolaters, some of the Bghai tribes have fetish stones, supposed to be the *habitat* of malignant as well as benevolent Nats, possessing miraculous powers, like those in the temples of the Todas of the Nilghiri hills, but not in themselves actual objects of worship.

Indifferent as they are in matters connected with the world to come, they are keenly anxious to anticipate the future in this life, and never enter into the very commonest undertakings that involve uncertainty, much less the more important, without consulting and obtaining a favourable response from the augury of fowls' bones—a process which Gaule, in his 'Magastromancers Posed and Puzzled,' terms *Spatulancy*. According to their traditions, God gave the Chinese a paper book, the Burmese another of palm leaves, and the Karens a third made of parchment. The Chinese and Burmese, prizing the divine gifts, took every care of them, while the Karens, with reprehensible carelessness, allowed a hog to tear up their copy, the fragments of which were eaten by fowls. The Karens, though much concerned at this misfortune, took comfort in the thought that as the fowls had digested their book, and become as it were depositaries of the lost law, they must possess all the wisdom it contained, and therefore could be consulted through their bones. This superstition is doubtless of great antiquity, having originated probably in Central Asia; for we know that the common barn-door fowl, like the Karens themselves, came from that region. After leaving its ancient home, it passed into Persia, over which country, according to Aristophanes, it reigned supreme, prior to Darius and Magabasus. From Persia it found its way to Greece, and thence through Italy to France and Britain. It also became domiciled in India and China. In all these countries it was utilised for purposes of divination; a cock, for instance, assured Themistocles of his victory over Xerxes, influenced the decision of Romulus in choosing the site of Rome, and inspired Numa Pompilius, who was the first to make augury a profession. The Santals in Bengal, the Buddhists in Ceylon, and some of the low castes of Southern India, used to sacrifice red cocks in honour of their

Lares rurales; there is also an instauce on record in the fourteenth century of an Irishwoman having been arraigned before the Ecclesiastical Court, presided over by Richard Ledered, Bishop of Ossory, and charged with having sacrificed nine red cocks to her familiar spirit.* So the Karens are not singular in the matter of having venerated the bird which is now universally used as an article of food.

To what date we may refer the cessation of the prejudice against eating poultry is unknown, but they certainly were favourite food in the seventh century. In the course of a few centuries, their merits lived down the ill-fame that accompanied them to England, and achieved the popularity they have since maintained. The cock then, in archaic times, was evidently an honoured guest, though subsequent ages have so far modified the veneration paid him as to utilise him as food, just as the South Sea Islanders utilised their missionaries after their first feelings of reverence wore off.†

Their system of augury appears by the accounts of some travellers to be essentially the same as that practised by Miau-tsze‡ tribes of China, with

* 'Kilkenniensis Annales Hibernia,' published for the Irish Archæological Society, 1842.

† 'South Sea Bubbles,' by the Earl and the Doctor.

‡ The Miau-tsze are found in Kweichau, Yunnan, Ssu-ch'-uan, Hunan, and Kwang-si. The sign Miau (a compound of the words flower aud meadow) signifies 'germinating seeds,' 'blades of grass springing from the seed vessels.' The sign Tsze, ou the other hand, is that usually employed to express son or descendant. In accordance with this explanation, the Chinese seem to consider the Miau-tsze

whom probably the Karens have some affinity. To describe it: the services of an elder supposed to have achieved the distinction of Passed Master in the science having been called into requisition, he causes a fowl to be killed, and, after extracting the leg and wing bones, holds them so that the minute air-holes therein shall be at the top. Into each of these he inserts a tiny straw to indicate its direction, accurately noting at the same time the number thereof and their relative positions, many nice distinctions having to be observed in connection with these particulars, to enable even an expert to read the oracle correctly. Thus by the mere turn of a straw it is decided whether war shall or shall not be declared; whether an important expedition shall be undertaken or abandoned; whether the marriage of a maiden, who has already plighted her troth, shall be consummated or not; whether a wizard shall die or be suffered to live; whether an accused person be guilty or innocent, and, as if to exemplify the very small margin that often exists between the sublime and the ridiculous, an orthodox Karen would never tempt Providence so far as to take an emetic or purgative without resorting to this oracle. We may smile at the infatuation of divining by chickens' bones; that we are not altogether free from the taint of this superstition is, however, proved by the common practice of children plucking the merry-thought.

as children of the soil or indigenous inhabitants.—'Voyage of the Novara'

If we refer to our own early history, it will be noted that sorcery was one of the oldest and most deep-rooted articles of the superstitious belief of the Anglo-Saxons. It was rightly considered by them as a relic of paganism, and as such proscribed by all the earliest ecclesiastical laws. It was only made a punishable offence by secular law when it was resorted to for the purpose of inflicting personal injury. Subsequently, the ecclesiastical courts seem to have lost jurisdiction. But the existence of sorcery was not doubted, and it was looked upon with the more horror as representing the supposed results of some kind of intercourse with the spirits of evil, the demons who were supposed to have been the main supporters of idolatry. These demons, it was imagined, were rather compelled to perform certain things by spells which bound them, or were incited to act in favour of persons who performed certain superstitious rites. The Karens held somewhat the same belief as our forefathers, and the analogy between the two systems is further borne out by the fact that in neither do we find any traces of those compacts with the evil one which became so famous in after times. In Karen mythology there is therefore nothing to correspond with the ordinary definition of witch, an individual who is supposed to derive her power from an understanding with Satan. They have, however, necromancers who profess to have eyes to see spirits unseen by others, to tell what they are doing, and even to go to Hades and converse with the spirits of the dead who have their *habitat* therein. These professors of the diabolic art are ordinary persons who, under certain circumstances, are supposed to be subject to demoniacal influence, and who, if rumour does not bely them, are quite as malignant as the veritable witches of Western lore.

The Karens have very peculiar conceits in reference to persons possessed with a familiar spirit which some tribes call Na, others Ne or Kephoo, who incontinently develop into beings, compared with whom the terrible ogres of our nursery days are mild, harmless, and benevolent creatures. According to one myth, it is said to be a horrid vampire which sallies forth at night, in the repulsive form of a human head and entrails, seeking whom it may devour. A person possessed of a Na, to say the least of him, is a decidedly objectionable member of society, inasmuch as he devours mankind when under the strange hallucination that they are rats, dogs, pigs, or other animals; a dread superstition, somewhat relieved of its gruesomeness, when the person possessed utilises himself as an article of food, and thus rids the world of a veritable monster.

Dr. Mason tells a story of one of these highly eccentric individuals who thus expiated his sin of cannibalism:—

Once upon a time there was a worthy couple who had two little daughters. It happened, one fine morning, that the younger followed her father when he went to work in the forest, and when they arrived at the foot of a certain tree the bewitching power of an evil spirit came upon the man, and he devoured the child. He then returned home, and, persuading his wife that the younger child fretted for her playmate, took her away and, when they arrived at the same tree, devoured her also. With unappeased appetite he essayed the same tactics with his wife, which would have ended in the same way had it not been for a friendly lizard, who forewarned her and dragged her to the tree-top by his tail, just as her husband appeared armed with an impaling stick, calling out 'Old rat, where are you?' Possessed of a Na, the man's wife appeared to him as a rat, and he accordingly purposed to impale her on his stick and roast her as he would this species of rodent, which Karen epicures consider a dainty dish. After fruitlessly searching for his wife, the man, after slicing himself up with a dah, devoured his own head and limbs, leaving nothing but the trunk. On this the lizard, remarking that her husband was no longer dangerous, let the woman down to the ground by his tail. When the man, or rather his spirit,* saw her, he cried out and entreated her to restore him to life, but she was too wise to listen to his proposal, and ran off to her friends. A puerile narrative, some may say, but excusable, perhaps, as it indicates the profound belief in the marvellous entertained by some of the 'enlightened' among the Karens.

* This was, doubtless, the La of the deceased, not the man himself, for, as remarked elsewhere, in Karen representations of the future state, he was absorbed in his La, which, after his death, entered on a new phase of existence.

According to another myth, a person under the influence of a Na has the power to destroy the La or vital principle, and by means of sorcery cause others to be attacked by disease, resulting in death. He is therefore held to be accursed, and it is considered quite as meritorious to get rid of him as to kill dangerous animals or poisonous snakes. Their Criminal procedure, in fact, conforms to the Hebraic law, in which it was commanded that 'a man also, or woman that hath a familiar spirit, or that is a wizard, shall surely be put to death.' *

While, therefore, we may deplore these superstitious practises on the part of the Karens, it must not be forgotten that, even now-a-days, simple persons are to be found in some parts of England every whit as credulous as these poor people. We should also bear in mind, at the same time, that little more than two centuries ago thousands of people, including persons of the highest rank, were put to death on charges of witchcraft, approved and confirmed by King James I., who gave his countenance to these proceedings by publishing a work entitled, 'Dialogues of Dæmonology.'

Karen ideas regarding a future life, though crude, are analogous to those held by the ancient Greeks and Romans, so far as regards the classification of the dead. According to Dr. Cross, they distinguish departed spirits under four heads. The first are the Plupho, whose repre-

* Leviticus xx. 27.

sentatives shuffled off the mortal coil naturally, and were decently buried. These go to a beautiful country and renew their life on earth. As the North American Indian, with his dog and bow, betakes himself to the happy hunting-grounds, so the Karen, with his axe and cleaver, builds himself a new domicile, grows his rice, cotton, and vegetables as before, free from the worries of his former existence. The second are the Sekha, ghosts of infants and persons who by accident were not buried, which wander about the earth, and occasionally show themselves to mankind in a benevolent kind of way, but, being considered harmless, are not propitiated. The third are the shades of those who have met with violent deaths, known as Theret, who are supposed to seize the Las of mortals, causing death. Hence they must be appeased by offerings to induce them to free the Las they have captured. The fourth, known as Ta-mu, are the spectres of tyrants, unjust rulers, and other wicked people, who are condemned to wander about the earth, and, in sheer spite, torment the Las of mankind in the shape of apparitions of various animals or birds. Varied offerings, according to circumstances, are made to this last class of disembodied spirits, and in serious cases of illness, according to Dr. Mason's experience, the patient is sprinkled with pounded charcoal, and prayers are made to the Ta-mu beseeching it to desist from its wicked purpose.

Victims as the Karens are of a superstition

which trusts to the efficiency of propitiatory offerings to demons in order to save them from all the ills to which flesh is heir, and which discourages disbelief in a future state, they appear—humanly speaking—to be impracticable to the teachings of a purer faith. They, however, prove that rude tribes, with exceedingly crude ideas on the subject of religion, occasionally present a virgin soil, in which novel ideas of morality take root and fructify. Thus with few prejudices, and no deeply rooted convictions to get rid of, the heathen Karen is more susceptible to the teachings of Christianity than the Burman Buddhist trammelled with the dogma of metempsychosis.

The Karens, says Dr. Mason, are like the Samaritans who at the first hearing 'with one accord gave heed to the things that Philip spake,' but the Burmese are like the Bereans who 'searched the Scriptures daily whether those things were so.' Christianity has certainly wrought a vast change in the habits, the feelings, and the hearts of the Karens. Instead of the strict system of taboo which obtained when heathenish rites were in the ascendent, a glad welcome is now offered in their chapels to all who wish to join in prayer and praise to the living God. It has also achieved such marvellous success in these regions as to cause the Karen mission to be recognised as one of the most promising in the world. These results were primarily due to the influence of their traditions, which taught them to look to the west for white strangers, who, coming by sea, would bring with them the book, once theirs, and make them acquainted with the true God. The portentous advent of the English in right of conquest, and the appearance of American missionaries with the Holy Bible, were accordingly accepted in simple faith as a literal fulfilment of the promises foreshadowed in this legend. That a nation, oppressed as were the Karens, should have traditions promising deliverance is natural enough. The coincidence with similar stories regarding white foreigners in China, Mexico, and Siam is, however, remarkable. A great impetus was simultaneously given to the cause of Christianity which claims our widest sympathy, because the triumph of the sacred cause, and the consequent breaking down of the strongholds of ignorance, superstition, and savagery, have been mainly achieved by the aid of the people themselves, who voluntarily and freely gave of their substance in earnest of the sincerity of their religion.

The mission of Augustine to England is said to have owed its origin to the presence of English slave-children in Rome, whose lovely faces, 'non angli sed angeli,' so fired Gregory with religious zeal that he deputed him to convert their countrymen. The mission to the Karens orginated in a Karen slave, named Koh Tha Byu, who, as the 'Karen Apostle,' proved a second Augustine to his countrymen.

As our Lord chose his first disciples from among the poor fishermen of Galilee, so the American missionaries, in selecting their first assistant, were fain to be content with the services of a man belonging to an equally low stratum of society, who in early life had been guilty of robbery and murder. In spite of his villainous antecedents, Koh Tha Byu, acquiring extraordinary influence over his countrymen, was the instrument of converting many to Christianity. He was the first to encourage his timid compatriots to break through their habits of reserve and leave their secluded jungles in order to visit the Christian teacher, Mr. Boardman, and ask his opinion regarding a little book of whose contents they were ignorant, but held by them in great veneration in hopes it was the promised volume. Mr. Boardman found the tattered volume they placed reverently in his hands to be the 'Book of Common Prayer' used in the Established Church of England. 'This is a good book,' said the missionary; 'it teaches that there is a God in heaven whom alone we should worship. You have been ignorantly worshipping this book; that is not good; I will teach you to worship the God whom the book reveals,'—paraphrasing, perhaps involuntarily, the words of St. Paul to the Athenians, when he stood in the midst of Mars Hill and declared unto them the unknown God whom they ignorantly worshipped.

In any notice of the Karens, however crude and brief, some reference to the religious traditions which have earned for them sympathetic interest throughout Christendom is essential. The people are fully impressed with the idea that in ancient times they possessed the Word of God, written on books of skin, the description of which, in a poetical fragment quoted by Dr. Mason, especially that part of it in which allusion is made to 'one-sided letters,' points to an identity with the parchment records used by the Jews before paper was known to them.

> 'The palm-leaf book that is written in circles,
> The elders drew out the lines in coils;
> They became great winding paths:
> The letters of the palm-leaf books teach ancient wonders;
> God sent us the book of skin;
> It is at the foot of the King of Hades;
> God sent us the book which has neither father nor mother;
> Enabling everyone to instruct himself.
> The book of one-sided letters, the letters ten,
> Is at the feet of the King of Hades;
> The book of one-sided letters, of letters many,
> All men could not read.'

None of these writings, unfortunately, have been preserved, in consequence, say they, of the accident thereto detailed in the puerile myth already quoted. Their ancients have, however, handed down to them oral traditions, the resemblance of which to various incidents in the Mosaic record seem to prove that, if derived from a written source, they owe their origin to the Old Testament, and not to the New, as there is no reference therein to Christianity. Though, as some declare, these legends may have been too highly coloured by the American missionaries, owing to preconceived notions regarding the origin thereof, yet as a matter of fact they substantially agree with the traditions possessed more or less intact by all the tribes before they had any intercourse with either Americans or Europeans. Indeed, it was owing to the verification of these very traditions that the apathetic indifference of the Karens to ordinary events was changed to an attitude of absorbing interest. A single example of their religious traditions referring to the fall of man will suffice:

'Anciently God commanded, but Satan appeared bringing destruction. Formerly God commanded, but Satan appeared deceiving unto death.

'The woman Eu and the man Thanai pleased not the eye of the dragon. The dragon looked on them, and beguiled the woman and Thanai.

'How is this said to have happened? The great dragon succeeded in deceiving unto death.

'How do they say it was done? A yellow fruit took the great dragon, and gave it to the children of God. A white fruit took the great dragon, and gave it to the daughter and son of God.

'They transgressed the commands of God, and God turned away from them. They kept not all the words of God—were deceived unto sickness.

'They kept not all the law of God—were deceived unto death.'

Christianity has made rapid strides wherever it has been firmly established, and has, moreover, paved the way to a rapidly increasing confidence between our Government and a people now eminently loyal and law-abiding, but who, under the Burmese rule, were distinguished either for their turbulent and undisciplined character, or for sullen submissiveness to a Government cordially detested.

When old and evil customs have been suppressed by the teachings of a purer faith, even the most sceptical must admit that the missionaries have done good. But putting religious polemics aside, and looking at missionary work merely in the interests of political economy, the Christian propaganda in this region deserves our deep sympathy, if we bear in mind that, when the common weal was in danger, the Christian Karens were, to a man, most loyal to the Government. The attraction which primarily induces the ministers of various denominations who labour among the Karens, is doubtless the hope of promulgating their own views of Christian faith and hope; but, fortunately for the general welfare of the people, they have also learnt the lesson that, though it is impossible to instil abstruse Christian dogmas into the mind of the untutored Karen, he can profitably be taught Christianity when reduced to its simple essence of his duty towards God and his duty towards his neighbour. While, therefore, not neglecting these essentials, they confine themselves chiefly to furthering the education and civilisation of their converts, eschewing abstract doctrines as much as possible. This praiseworthy interpretation of duty has been attended with marvellous results, not the least of which was the transformation of grossly intemperate and good-for-nothing reprobates, into sober, industrious, and estimable people. The policy of the Government of India, though paved with the best intentions, is cursed with a want of sympathy provocative rather of profound respect than of ardent affection, which prevents it keeping touch with the people. The missionaries, however, often furnish a link between the Government and the people of great political importance. Lady Dilke, fully impressed thereby from personal experience in the North-west Provinces, opines 'that a day may come when the influence of their patient and self-sacrificing devotion will have created a bond of union between ruled and rulers which shall offer a stronger resistance to the advance of foreign foes than the weight of our sceptre or the sharpness of our sword.'* Her conclusions are by no means fanciful; for the admirable conduct of the Christian Karens, when we had to deal with foes in our own houshold, was mainly due to the influence brought to bear upon them by their missionaries. It will be to our lasting reproach if our present or future policy mar the glorious achievements connected with one of the most loyal peoples in Farther India.

* *Fortnightly Review.* May, 1889.

CHAPTER IX.

CHINO-BURMESE BORDER TRIBES.

Lord Dalhousie ignores the Teaching of an Aphorism—Result of Lord Dufferin's annexation—The *status* of the Border Tribes—Hilly regions between Burma and India successfully Negotiated by Burmese and Shans—Singpos badly treated by the English—Rule relating to Succession—Caterans with redeeming Characteristics—Tea (Cammellia Thea) found in this Region—Zardandan or Gold Teeth—Sorcery among Them—Dagroian Cannibalism—The Kaya or Red Karen—Kaya as Manufacturers—Conspicuous loyalty of Hill Karens—Marriages—Funerals of a Chief and Common Folk compared.

For reasons of high policy which swayed our Government in 1853, but which, for our present purpose, it is needless to discuss, Lord Dalhousie, setting at nought the teachings of a well-known aphorism, refrained from swallowing the whole of Burma when at his disposal, and merely contented himself with the better half, comprising the seaboard province of Pegu. So impracticable, however, was Mengdôn, the King of the country, in coming to an understanding about boundaries, owing to his sentimental objection to having his name handed down to posterity as the sovereign who surrendered Rangoon, that the great proconsul, declaring it was useless to treat with a man of that stamp, cut the Gordian knot by adopting as frontier an imaginary line, representing a parallel of latitude. On the 1st January, 1886, Lord Dufferin indulged in the remaining half, commonly known as Upper Burma.

His lordship's annexation has brought us face to face with responsibilities connected with congeners of the Burman race, as well as other typical specimens of various rude societies having their *habitat* on all sides of our new frontiers, whose proper management must needs be a potent factor in successfully dealing with the development of commerce, especially in connection with the furthering of telegraph and trade routes, which, now all important, were necessarily under abeyance during the late *régime*. A notable fact has thus freshly been brought home to us that 'in every extensive jungle tract, through the vast continent of India, there exist hundreds of thousands of human beings in a state not materially different from that of the Germans described by Tacitus,* generally characterised as uncivilised.' It cannot be said that this description gives a clear, definite or precise idea of tribes whose civilisation is a variable quantity—one of degree as well as a matter of opinion. The civilisation of the East differs materially from the civilisation of the West. But even taking the term in its most limited sense—that is to say, where both may be said to meet on a common platform—the attainments of these

* Hodgson's 'Coech Dhimal and Bode tribes.' Calcutta, 1847.

peoples hardly warrant our using it in its ordinary signification, which suggests the idea of communities advancing cautiously and methodically, in promoting the best possible organisation of society in view to the improvement of its social relations and the furthering of its material progress.

As on the borders of India proper and India beyond the Ganges, excepting where they are washed by the Indian Ocean and the Bay of Bengal, so on those of our recent inheritance, a vast number of peoples are found of every degree of civilisation except the highest, who, having somewhat vague notions as to the necessity of good government, practically set at nought what we in our philosophy define it to be. As a matter of course, these border tribes are continually at issue with our frontier officers, many of whom are prone to adopt coercive measures in order to bring them to their proper bearings. The Burmese Government favoured this policy in dealing with rude peoples; but its efforts to compel them to submit to authority were entirely abortive. On our occupation of the province of Pegu in 1853 and Upper Burma in 1886, we consequently found ourselves hampered with peoples declared to be so wild and so untamable that the authorities we supplanted were only able to exact nominal tribute at irregular intervals, and never ventured into the country occupied by them excepting in armed force. Secure in the almost unassailable positions they selected on the mountain ranges between the Sittang and the Salwen rivers, or in obscure gorges whose normal stillness is only broken by the rushing of perennial streams, cool, refreshing, and pure as crystal, which adds such a charm to this region, the self-reliant and indomitable Karens, aided by their reputation for turbulent and undisciplined behaviour, hurled defiance at their would-be oppressors, and achieved for themselves an unique and independent position. With few sympathies in common, with disdain and oppressive bearing on the one side, and with fear, hatred, and a desire for vengeance on the other, the Burmese and the Karens of the plains, though living together for centuries, have ever pursued parallel courses, making no attempt to bridge the gulf between them by efforts towards a better social intercourse, or the more humanising influence of the marriage tie. Neither have they learnt the lesson that concession must precede union, and that two races are not easily welded into a single nationality unless they consent to make some advances towards being one socially.

Though the so-called wild tribes have doubtless been influenced by long contact with peoples in higher grades of civilisation, they have not been affected to an appreciable extent. Conservatism in its integrity is their *rôle*. The situation is the more complicated owing to the unsympathetic attitude of Shans and Burmese, who disdainfully decline to make any attempts towards a better social intercourse, or the promotion of more intimate relationship. They dispose of them even in their histories simply by the term barbarian, and thus furnish no aid to inquirers seeking information concerning the despised races. We know that, in common with other Tibeto-Burman tribes, the practice of sorcery, divination, and ordeals deeply influences their lives. We are also aware that their religion, which is allied to the Scythic and other branches of the ancient Asiatic faith, comes under the head of the 'Heathenism' denounced by King Ethelred: 'That is, that they worship the sun or moon, fire or rivers, water, wells, stones, or forest trees of any kind; or love witchcraft, or promote *morth* work of anywise; or by blot or *fyrht* perform anything pertaining to these illusions.' But we have got much to learn concerning their physical and moral attributes, their customs and the affinities of their different dialects —a critical examination of which will probably aid us in arriving at reasonable conclusions regarding their archaic history. So far as we can now judge, however, they seem to refute the notion that different races cannot live long together without resulting in a process of assimilation affecting their physical and mental attributes.

One's knowledge of geography and ethnology is often enhanced by fortuitous circumstances, such as direct personal interests or events attracting general attention; there is an exception to this rule, however, in the ignorance displayed regarding the theatres of our 'little wars' in Burma and the people exploited—a subject of more than passing interest to the relatives and friends of those condemned to inglorious warfare in a region unhealthy and inhospitable. Even after a five years' occupancy of Upper Burma, our authorities knew very little more of the border tribes than was the case some six decades ago, when Wilson, Hannay, Pemberton, and Bayfield furnished interesting accounts of their experiences—the great value of which has been gratefully acknowledged by Colonel Woodthorpe and several others, who have lately done much in the matter of geography to atone for previous shortcomings.

To bring the Chins, Lushais, Kakhyens, Singpos, *et hoc genus omne* to their proper bearings, the British Government abandoned the conciliatory policy which was found so effective in converting equally impracticable hill Karens into loyal subjects of the Queen Empress. It seemingly took a leaf out of the Burmese book of diplomacy, and even to have out-heroded Herod in their efforts to coerce them. Yet diplomacy, it is said, has been extended to its utmost limit in order to avoid harsh proceedings and teach these rude peoples that it is preferable for them to enjoy the fruits of honest labour than to incur the risks and troubles incidental to their former methods of obtaining a livelihood.

Pemberton pointed out that Yunnan had become of peculiar interest to us, owing to its vicinity to the north-eastern borders of our Indian Empire. He was also of opinion that, if judicious efforts were made, there was every prospect of a hopeful trade between the industrious tribes of the Irawadi basin and the people of Assam. During this interval, however, little has been done in furtherance of this idea. Excuse there may have been when an impracticable people like the Burmese had to be consulted; but none exists now, and it will be to our lasting reproach if we do not prove equal to the occasion, by carrying out some definite policy—hitherto absolutely wanting —for the management of the Singpos and other tribes, as well as the encouragement of trade in this region.

As already noticed, early in the eighth century the Shans successfully overcame the traditionally formidable physical difficulties of the hilly region between the Brahmaputra and Irawadi valleys, with forces strong enough to conquer the country now known as Assam. In the beginning of the present century again, Burmese armies, sufficiently powerful to render material aid to successful revolution, to dictate terms as to the administration of the country, and even to threaten English territory, repeated the same feat. That the Indian colony came by this route to the Upper Irawadi, and did not ascend from its delta, is also proved by the history of Pegu. These cases in point are evidence of the absence of engineering difficulties. It was known generally that, contiguous to the passes, truculent Nagas, Singpos, and other caterans levied black-mail, and harried travellers as well as their weaker or more peaceful neighbours. Spasmodic efforts, it is true, were made to obtain more information; but the petty chiefs on the Indian borders, and the Burmese in Arakan, excelling our political officers in diplomacy, baffled all their efforts in this direction, and caused thereby a deplorable loss of life and treasure.

These Singpos seem to be identical with the Kakhyens, who, after the break-up of the Shan kingdom of Pong, began a career of aggression and conquest of the country lying between Assam and Bhamó. Crossing into Assam by the Patkoi pass, they were at first welcomed by the peasantry as deliverers, for they restored order in the territory devastated by their oppressors; but when they took to pillage and man-stealing, causing the country to be well-nigh depopulated, the too trustful husbandmen had not a little cause to modify their opinions.

The Singpos are a fine athletic race, above the ordinary standard in height, and capable of enduring great fatigue. With merely a stone for anvil, and a rude hammer, they manufacture excellent 'dahs.' The women are equally ingenious and as industrious as those of other tribes, especially when they are burdened with family cares. Proud of her position, a married woman marks her status indelibly by tattooing both legs in parallel lines, and weaves the family clothing, colouring the threads with local dyes.

During the progress of the Burmese war of 1825–26, we were either politically dishonest, or guilty of a lamentable want of foresight, when we induced the Singpos to release their captured slaves, on the strength of a promise of giving them a lion's share of the profit of a projected commerce between India and Burma. Arrangements were also made whereby the tribes, bearing this consideration in mind, were to guard the Patkoi pass, and prevent Burmese incursions into Assam. With inexcusable want of foresight, however, the British authorities failed to provide these rude people with the means of repelling invasion; and when the Burmese arrived, as anticipated, the Singpos—very naturally considering discretion the better part of valour—surrendered their stockades and fraternised with the invaders. Wise in their generation, they also sent a request to the English to come and rid them of their unwelcome visitors. Whether the English delayed in responding to the appeal, or the Singpos, on further acquaintance, were convinced of the superiority of the Burmese, does not appear; but, when the English came, they had to reckon with both. The British troops, by a series of gallant assaults, expelled the Burmese. The Singpos shared in the discomfiture of the latter, their villages being destroyed, and their slaves, representing their only tangible property, set free. In the subsequent process of settling the country, pressure was also brought to bear on the people of neighbouring tribes who had remained passive during these disturbances, in order to make them also give up their slaves, in furtherance of our policy of cheap philanthropy. The Singpo or Chingpaw—man *par excellence* of that day, be it known—never condescended to manual labour, but, esteeming himself a gentleman at large, made others work for him. He consented to part with his slaves, who were as much his property as cattle with other tribes, with the distinct understanding that he was to obtain due compensation for his loss.

The English shamefully neglected to fulfil their promises, and provoked a rebellion which was only crushed after much bloodshed. Owing to a subsequent more sympathetic policy, the Singpos give no trouble, and aid us in keeping other Patkoi tribes in order. An opportunity now offers for making amends to the successors of these ill-used people, when we perform our duty to this neglected region by developing it in the interests of trade and agriculture.

Interlaced with the Shans, in the direct route from Bhamó to Yunnan, is a people belonging to the same family as the Singpos, whom we, imitating the Burmese, conveniently call Kakhyen, or Kachin. They have their *habitat* in the hilly regions north of Bhamó, and as far south as the old city of Tagoung, while they extend to the Chinese frontiers on the east. They comprise several clans, each with its own chief, but recognise no common authority; and owing to blood feuds, which often last for generations, this disintegration results in a rigid exclusiveness between members of the different tribes. It is noticeable that, in their patriarchal system, the chieftainship devolves on the youngest

KACHIN WOMEN.

son, or, failing sons, on the youngest brother of the chief.* Their marriage ceremony is also peculiar, as 'it combines the idea of purchase from the parents with that of abduction, so frequently found to underlie the nuptial rites of widely separated races.'† Like their congeners, whom we have been discussing, the men hardly ever work, while the women are condemned to lives of drudgery. With an evil reputation as cattle-lifters and man-stealers, they are regarded as outlaws by the Burmese. Hence hostilities and reprisals are rife; and, whether by the injustice of Chinese traders or high-handed Burmese extortion, they are thievish, lazy, and untrustworthy.

They rank, nevertheless, fairly high in the matter of civilisation, as the women spin and dye cotton, of which they weave a strong, thick cloth in fanciful coloured patterns. They are also adepts at embroidery in silk and cotton; while the men show a certain æsthetic taste in wood-carving. Referring to the Kakhyens, Dr. Anderson goes so far as to say that it was impossible to help being reminded of Scottish Highland clans of the olden time, so many were the points of resemblance that occurred in the customs and indeed character of these mountaineers. They are further alleged to be impracticable in the matter of opening out the trade routes, but will

* According to Mr. Baber, the same custom obtains among the Lolos of China.

† Anderson's 'Mandalay to Momein.' London, 1876.

doubtless be perfectly amenable under firm and judicious treatment, when they are thoroughly made to comprehend that they will be fairly and generously dealt with, but at the same time taught that any attempt to put obstacles in our way will be sternly repressed. They are quite alive to the fact that their profits depend on the amount of traffic that passes through their country, and they will be only too glad to offer all facilities for trade if it be made worth their while. In short, they will learn the essential difference between certain and regular receipts in acknowledgment of services rendered, and the fitful and very irregular assets depending on 'black-mail.'

Kakhyens have managed to wedge themselves in between Bhamó and Ko Shan Pyi or the Nine Shan States on the Yunnan frontier, and so prevent the connecting link between the Anglo-Chinese telegraph systems intended to put London and Pekin in communication *viâ* Calcutta. For acting loyally in the spirit of Lord Rosebery's Convention of 1886, the Chinese lost no time in extending their western line to Yang Chang (the Vochan of Marco Polo) within easy distance of the Yunnan-Burmese frontier, and are prepared to push it thereto when the English do their part. Two-thirds of the remaining gap for which we are responsible is occupied by those delightful Shans who gave Sladen such cordial welcome, and the other third by the hitherto impracticable Kakhyens, who, little to the credit of British management, are still permitted to dominate the trade routes between the ancient *entrepôt* of Bhamó and Yunnan.

From information compiled by General Walker* we learn that the Kachins (Kakhyens) are very numerous north of Bhamó, and show signs of vitality sufficiently pronounced to reject the notion of their being absorbed in contact with civilisation. Impelled by those behind them, they are fast pushing their way into districts undeniably British, and thus demand serious attention from the fact that they look upon the country they occupy as their own, and scout the very notion of any possible intervention in their affairs. Their brethren living in the hills athwart the trade routes were, like them, a fine race, so long as they were obliged to struggle with the Burmese Shans for their very existence; but, since they have dislodged the latter, they have lost the incentive to martial ardour and so have degenerated.

There are many Chinese as well as Shan-Chinese Settlements among the Northern Kakhyens—examples of the long-standing tendency of these peoples to take up their abodes in the Irawadi Valley. This emigration from the Flowery Land is alleged to be due to excessive tyranny and extortion on the part of Chinese officials. If this be true, the immigrants' former lot must indeed have been hard, to induce them to exchange it for the tender mercies of the

* Proceedings of the Royal Geographical Society, March, 1892.

Kakhyens, in order to realise what at best must be a precarious existence. It is now customary for both Chinese and Shans to place themselves under the protection of the chief of the place wherein they intend to settle. The Kakhyens welcome them and treat them on the whole fairly, as they find them useful members of society to whom they can dispose of their rubber in exchange for salt and other necessaries. They do not demand any other equivalent for this protection, which consists in warding off, if possible, attacks of would-be marauders intent on kidnapping and cattle theft, or endeavouring to obtain restitution by ransom or otherwise if they are not strong enough to cope with the filibusters. 'The system,' as General Walker says, 'is a very objectionable one, but cannot be avoided unless the country is placed under British protection: no Shan or Shan-Chinese village can afford to be without its protecting Kachins, as otherwise life and property in the village would not be worth a moment's purchase.'

Among other natural productions in Kakhyen-land, according to Dr. Anderson, is the tea-plant (*Cammellia Thea*) which grows freely in its eastern slopes, 'suggesting dreams of future tea-plantations cultivated by improved Kakhyens or imported Shans or Palongs.' In the *Eurya*, which flourishes in many parts of the Karen Hills near Toungoo, it was hoped we had a certain proof that the true tea of commerce could be cultivated there with advantage. Unfortunately, however, the bare fact of its existence does not help us, as it does not belong to the tea-plant at all. It is quite a different tribe, though of the same family.

The practice of sorcery, described by Marco Polo as pertaining to what were formerly the northern districts of Pong, is identical with what obtains among the Kakhyens, Singpos, and cognate tribes, as we learn from Anderson, Sladen, and others. His quaintest and most telling descriptions thereof are in connection with the inhabitants of the Zardandan province—who, according to Sir Henry Yule, are Kakhyens—and the Dagroians, who, for all that we know to the contrary, may have been Lushais, as the 'wicked custom' of cannibalism, for which the former were notorious, has been told, nearly as Marco tells us, of tribes belonging to the same family in Arakan, or west of ancient Pong. 'Let me tell you,' remarks the great traveller in reference to Zardandan, 'there is never a leech; but when anyone is ill they send for their magicians; that is to say, the devil-conjurers, who,' after a rough diagnosis of their patient's malady, 'incontinently begin playing on their instrumeuts, and singing and dancing; and the conjurers dance to such a pitch that at last one of them shall fall to the ground lifeless, like a dead man. And then the devil entereth into his body. And when his comrades see him in this plight, they begin to put questions to him about the sick man's ailment. The magician's reply, it appears, was in accordance with his notion as to the probable issue of the complaint. If the case seemed to him hopeless, he would declare that 'such and such a spirit has been meddling with the man, for that he hath angered the spirit and done it some despite, so that the spirit will not pardon him on any account. . . . But, if he is to get better, the answer will be that they are to bring two sheep, or maybe three; and to brew ten or twelve jars of drink, very costly and abundantly spiced . . . And then those things are to be offered in sacrifice to such and such a spirit, whose name is given. And they are to bring so many conjurers and so many ladies, and the business is to be done with great singing of lauds, and with many lights and store of perfumes. And when all that the spirit commanded has been done, with great ceremony, then it shall be announced that the man is pardoned and shall be speedily cured. And when at length they receive such a reply, they announce that it is all made up with the spirit, and that he is propitiated, and they fall to eating with great joy and mirth, and he who had been lying lifeless on the ground gets up and takes his share. So, when they have all eaten and drunken, every man departs home, and presently the sick man gets sound and well.' *

The responsibilities of the Zardandan sorcerers were mild in comparison with those of their Dagroian *confrères*. For, when the latter decided that the patient's case was hopeless, they caused

* Yule's 'Marco Polo.'

'certain judges of theirs' to do the sick person to death by suffocation. 'And, when he is dead, they have him cooked, and gather together all the dead man's kin and eat him. And I assure you that they suck the very bones till not a particle of marrow is left in them; for they say that if any nourishment remained in the bones this would breed worms, and then the worms would die for want of food, and the death of those worms would be laid to the charge of the deceased man's soul. And so they eat him up stump and rump . . . It is a very evil custom and a parlous.' *

Mr. Scott, referring to a savage race found in the Salwen basin, remarks: 'The assertion that they eat their own parents to relieve them of the miseries of old age, and to ensure them a respectable grave, one that cannot readily be dishonoured, is too singular and too much like the known customs of the more enlightened cannibal races to be altogether a fiction.' † Other travellers record equally gruesome reports; a tribe known as Wa being particularly noted for a very pronounced propensity for devouring their guests, a lugubrious eccentricity which makes careful people somewhat chary of accepting their hospitality.

All the world over, notably among the Greeks and Romans, a certain discipline was considered inspensable to give the power of interpreting the signs of the gods its full development. The rude

* Yule's 'Marco Polo.'

† *Asiatic Quarterly Review*, July, 1889.

tribes in all parts of Farther India are to this day no exceptions to this rule. Major Sladen tells us, in his official narrative of the expedition to Western China, that anyone among the Kakhyens who aspired to the dignity of medium or necromancer, must climb a ladder with rungs formed of naked swords, edges upwards, and sit on a platform thick set with spikes, without personal inconvenience, before he passes his examination and acquires credit—verily, a practical test for convincing the most sceptical.

The province of Zardandan, meaning gold teeth, was so called from the highly eccentric custom which distinguished its inhabitants of casing their teeth with the most precious of metals. Whether the practice fell into disuse from its manifest inconvenience, or the people, having since been absorbed into the Chinese population, have voted it out of fashion, does not appear; the fact is that it no longer exists. That Marco did not invent a fable, nor was a victim to a hoax, is proved by Chinese annals, as well as by Klaproth and other writers. Admitting all this, Mr. Baber suggests that the practice of chewing areca-nut with lime, which colours the teeth red and causes profuse expectoration, confined as regards China to this region, may go some way to account for its ancient name, 'Chin-ch'ih' or 'Golden Teeth.' 'We first met with this practice,' he says, 'near Talifu. In fact, we had been for some days importuning our geologist to account for certain red streaks on the roadside rocks. His explanation was plausible enough, (some people can explain anything,) but he was soon found out.' *

The men of Zardandan, says our traveller, 'are all gentlemen in their fashion, and do nothing but go to the wars, or go hunting and hawking. The ladies do all the business, aided by the slaves who have been taken in war.' † Marco's pungent description is true of their alleged congeners, who are as much 'gentlemen' as their ancestors were, preferring , like many members of more advanced societies, to remain idle when they can get slaves and 'ladies' to work for them. They, as is the case with other border tribes, treat females with scant courtesy.

To this rule there is a remarkable exception in the case of the Pani Cocch tribe beyond the Bengal border, in which women 'rule the roost,' though, like all those of similar clans, they do most of the work. For the men, in consideration of being 'gentlemen' at large, make over to the women the whole of their property unconditionally ; so much so, that, on the death of a wife, her property does not necessarily revert to her husband, but can be claimed by her daughters, if she be blessed with female progeny. A female, even during her nonage, in this delightful society, has the privilege of selecting her husband, restricted only by etiquette, which insists on allowing her mother to make the actual proposal of marriage. When she is of age, however, she is at full liberty

* 'Royal Geographical Society's Supplementary Papers,' vol. I.

† Yule's 'Marco Polo,' 2nd edition. London, 1875.

to take the initiative herself. If she happens to become a widow with property, she has the whole world of eligible males at her feet, and can pick and choose at discretion. A man's prospects being strictly limited to what his wife is willing to allow him, money-lenders are obliged to bear this in mind when making advances, and, if the unhappy male incurs fine, he has to become a slave to his creditors, unless his wife can and will redeem him. With these drawbacks to matrimony, it says much for the women that any bachelor becomes a Benedict, especially when it involves not only living with his mother-in-law, but also subjecting himself to her rule!

It is curious to note that, when military expeditions accompanied by English officials passed through the villages of newly-exploited Kakhyens, the people hardly exhibited any curiosity or alarm at this entirely novel proceeding. Most of the so-called 'wild' tribes have an intense curiosity to see white people for the first time, though they are not demonstrative in yielding to this weakness. To this rule the Kayas, according to O'Riley, are an exception; for he says that under these circumstances he has never met them without exciting their intense laughter, accompanied by an intense fearfulness of his presence, and was therefore at a loss to decide whether it indicated abject barbarism or advance towards civilisation.

Abutting the Shan States are the Kaya whom we, imitating the Burmese, call Karenni or Red Karen. The attitude of this people has a distinct bearing on the question of trade between Burma and China, as the prospect of realising satisfactory commercial results, based on the well-known trading proclivities of the Shans, depends much on whether they are amenable or otherwise. After passing through several tribes of hill Karens for some forty miles as the crow flies from the ancient city of Toungoo, in the days of yore the seat of a powerful Burmese dynasty, one arrives at the notable peak of Nattoung on the borders of Karenni, famous in mythological story as the Ararat of Karen tradition. Standing on its summit, at an elevation of nearly seven thousand feet above sea-level, with one's feet resting on grassy undulations like English downs, and the flora giving evidence of a temperate climate, one obtains a bird's-eye view of the country of the Kaya, consisting of a fine table-land, contrasting not a little with the jungle-clothed territory within our old frontier, inasmuch as not a vestige of primeval forest remains therein, and great attention is paid by the people to the land, the farms being divided by walls or hedges. It also enjoys a better climate, as proved by the interesting fact that hoar-frost is seen in December, that the dandelion, the violet, and the forget-me-not, as well as other flowers pertaining to temperate zones, are found on the highlands, that neither fogs nor miasmatic vapours prevail, and no dense jungle exists to tarnish the air with its noxious exhalations.

Karenni consists of a number of petty States,

each having its particular chief; for all practical purposes, however, it may be divided into Eastern and Western Karenni, which are ruled by chiefs more or less independent. The former, it is true, by the annual tender of a silver flower, acknowledged the King of Burma as his suzerain, but did just as he pleased, for he could well hold his own against any Burmese troops that tried to coerce him, and kept in awe the most powerful of the Shan chiefs. No wonder, then, that he defied the British when they called him to account for his alleged misdoings. Though the term 'government' is a misnomer when applied to the polity that obtains among the Red Karens, and though they have no tradition of a Licurgus, they are burdened with an oral law for the regulation of society almost as cumbrous as the written law of more advanced peoples. Each village, with its scant domain, constitutes an independent State, of which the chief is the ruling prince, and only 'now and then,' as Dr. Mason says, 'a little Napoleon arises who subdues a kingdom to himself, and builds up an empire; the dynasty, however, only lasts with the controlling mind.'

Karenni affords an exception to the ordinary rules of political economy, which takes it for granted that the uses and necessity of Government are such that a country cannot exist without some sort of civil administration; for it possesses neither law nor dominant authority, the only semblance thereof being the almost nominal power exercised by its chiefs. The Wehrgeld of the ancient jurisprudence of the Germans, as well as the Mosaic law which says, 'an eye for an eye and a tooth for a tooth,' is fully appreciated in this system. The forays of the Kayas may be accepted as its special development. Though to persons accustomed to European procedure they are tantamount to unqualified robbery and murder, they look upon them as Europeans regard the execution of magistrates' judgments by sheriffs' officers. Anomalous as it may appear, the duty of living at peace is nevertheless very strictly enjoined. 'The lover of peace,' it is said, 'will be blessed with numerous sons and daughters who will demean themselves with propriety; he will have no enemies to assail him,'—a rough paraphrase of the words of David, 'Happy is the man that hath his quiver full of them, they shall not be ashamed, but they shall speak with the enemies in the gate.' The Kaya are distinguished for their savage and intractable nature, as well as turbulent and undisciplined bearing. They are also notorious for their cruelty, ferocity, and disregard of human life. With manners and customs shaped by gross superstition, fear being their only governing principle, without any sense of natural religion, violating all law, defying all authority, habitually indulging in intoxication, licentiousness, and murder, the Kayas, according to Mr. O'Riley, afford an instance of a society whose social relations, excepting in the matter of cannibalism, are not a whit more civilised than that of the most barbarous tribes in Africa.

Dr. Mason, distinguished by reason of his success in evangelising kindred tribes in British territory, on the other hand, declared that 'they have no police, no prisons, no penitentiaries, no schools for the reformation of young thieves; and yet they have no locks on their doors, no watch-dogs in their yards, no man-traps or spring-guns in their gardens, and still thefts are very uncommon.' He also remarked with pleasure that they were anxious to have missionaries sent to them in order to teach them religion. Both of these gentlemen had afterwards reason to modify their opinions—Mr. O'Riley acknowledging that there was every room for hope that civilising influences would have a most beneficial effect on the people, while Dr. Mason, alas! was forced to admit that the pleasant arcadia depicted by him existed only in his imagination. There was abundant excuse for this divergence of opinion between experts, for the characteristic differences of the various tribes of the Bghai family, to which the Red Karens are affiliated, are often very marked.

The Red Karens preserve a distinctive difference in mould of form and feature compared with the Karens proper, the Burmese, and Shans, whose physical characteristics are more decidedly Mongolian. The appellative Red Karen probably originated from the prevailing colour of their turbans and garments, and not from that of their skin, which approaches a medium copper tint. The men are, as a rule, taller and better set up than those of neighbouring tribes; while the women, who are mere drudges, exceed them in height and bulk, especially in the abnormal development of their lower limbs, caused by the pressure of heavy strings of beads below the knees, and their habit of carrying heavy burdens on their backs. Like all the tribes in this region, they also wear heavy brass greaves and armlets as well as leaden coils on their necks, arms, and legs—facts that confirm their mid-Asian origin. Though ignorant of many useful arts, the Kaya make their own knives, axes, swords, spears, hoes, bracelets, silver ornaments, earthenware, bridles, bits, saddles, stirrups, etc. They also manufacture gunpowder, an art they very probably acquired from the Chinese, when in ancient times they had more intimate relations with Celestials than is the case at present.

Tempted by the abundance of available land in Burma, the hill Karen can there indulge in his natural nomadic tendencies, and migrate in the forest from site to site, burning down at each remove new areas on which to carry on his wasteful husbandry. For he 'cares as little to be the proprietor of the land on which he erects his booth, as the bird to own the tree on which it builds its nest or perches to pick the fruit.'* In Karenni, however, where the population is comparatively great in proportion to the cultivatable area, the Kaya is forced to pay more attention to agriculture, and there is every reason to hope that they, like cognate tribes in the Toungoo district, will be

* Dr. Mason.

able to cultivate chincona, tea, coffee, and potatoes successfully when a demand for these products shall arise.

During the late revolution in Burma, the Karens, as already remarked, were conspicuous for their loyalty under circumstances eminently conducive to disaffection; affording at a critical period a praiseworthy example to their disaffected neighbours by unreservedly placing themselves at the disposal of Government for service against the disturbers of law and order. As the Burmese police were found to be utterly untrustworthy in dealing with turbulence and disorder, this duty had, in a great measure, to be relegated to Goorkhas and Sikhs, imported from India at considerable expense. By a happy inspiration, an excellent alternative was found in the enlistment of Christian Karens, who, when pagans, were renowned for their fighting propensities. They proved fully equal to the occasion, and acquitted themselves so admirably, especially in jungles which at certain seasons of the year are practically inaccessible to Burmans or to the fighting men drawn from India, that additional companies were raised who also did most excellent service. These very gratifying results justify the idea of trying a similar experiment with the Red Karens, who, we learn from excellent authority, are 'a fine plucky race, which would make a good levy for us in future years.' Long before Havelock invented 'Mounted Infantry' for our military tactics, the Kayas anticipated the notion; for, as Dr. Mason says, every man owns a pony, so that in time of war they are a mounted militia, when all turn out to service.

When first encountered, there was not a little difficulty in effecting commercial arrangements with the Kayas and other hill tribes, as they were wedded to a cumbrous system of exchange which found an equivalent for money in rough silver ingots containing about one-third of alloy, and in kyeezees or drums, similar to those possessed by the Miautzis in China, consisting of copper or spelter cylinders rudely ornamented with figures of animals, birds, or fish, and varying in value from five to fifty pounds, according to size and volume of sound. Very soon, however, the Red Karens appreciated the value of the more convenient rupee as much as the Tibetans* did a like equivalent for tea bricks, or the Red Indians the potency of the 'almighty dollar' in exchange for beaver skins. The kyeezee, nevertheless, is still one of their most cherished possessions. Its music, say they, inspires them with martial ardour when ready for the fray, and soothes the savage breast when in a sentimental mood.

Besides the big feast, with excessive license, the normal characteristic of all social events pertaining to cognate tribes, the Kaya marriage ceremony possesses some distinctive features. For instance, the bride, in presence of the assembled

* In Tibet, according to Mr. Baber, 'Those which bear a crowned presentment of Her Majesty are named *Lama tob-du* or vagabond Lama, the crown having been mistaken for the headgear of a religious mendicant.

guests, pledges the bridegroom in a cup of spirits; the bridegroom like young Lochinvar reciprocating in like fashion.

> 'The bride kissed the goblet, the knight took it up;
> He quaffed off the wine, and he threw down the cup.'

In the middle of the carouse, the bridegroom takes a hoe and proceeds to the garden followed by the bride. He digs the earth with his hoe for a little, and she follows suit, and thus pledges herself to work equally with her husband, and be subject to his orders. After this the bride, attended by the company, takes a bamboo bucket to the spring, draws some water therefrom in her bucket, which, after being filled by the bridegroom, she carries to the house, walking behind the latter,—an act of like significance which completes the ceremony.

The Bghais are distinguished from the Sgaus and Pwos proper by burying their dead. Much ado is generally made on the occasion of funerals, especially those of their chiefs. To this rule, however, there is a notable exception in the case of the Kaya chiefs, who are secretly buried at night in a grave fifteen to twenty feet deep, care being taken that the place of sepulture shall not easily be discovered, as they have an ancient tradition to the effect that if the Burmese or Shans succeed in obtaining a Kaya chief's head, they would be able to conquer Karenni and reduce its people to slavery. The fact is interesting as we find from Hwiu Seng and Sung Yun, who visited Central Asia in 518 A.D., that although it was customary in Khoten (Cotan) to honour the ashes of the common dead by building towers over them, 'when a king dies they do not burn his body, but enclose it in a coffin and carry it far off, and bury it in the desert.'* It is curious also to note that the Goths had similar prejudices in regard to keeping secret the burial-places of their chiefs. For we learn from Roman history that on the death of Alaric, his followers 'turned the stream of the Bisenzio, caused their slaves to dig a grave in the bed of the river, and, after burying him there with all his treasures, they turned back the waters into their course, and slew all the slaves that had been employed in the work.'†

If the upshot of our little war with Eastern Karenni be its annexation, and the establishment therein of the *pax Britannica*, a brilliant future may be anticipated for this distracted country. But if, on the contrary, the people are left to seeth in the anarchy which has long been their normal portion, this prospect seems as hopeless as ever. Carrying fire and sword into Karenni, without furthering its moral and material welfare, may temporarily check the turbulence of the Kayas, but whether it will promote their civilisation, and develop among them the arts of love and peace is, to say the least, highly problematical.

* Beal's 'Travels of Bhuddhist Pilgrims.'

† 'Landmarks of Ancient History.'

CHAPTER X.

CHINO-BURMESE BORDER TRIBES (*Continued*).

Yindiline—Low Social Condition—Taru—Acute Sense of Shame—Turbulence of Gaykho and Tsaw-Koo Tribes—Treaties—Ordeals—Gunpowder—Marriage — *Crim. Con.* — Sporting Proclivities—Khyen or Chin—Girl's Faces Tattooed—Marriage—A Game of Forfeits—Omniverous, barring Cannabalism—Oaths Pertaining to Border Tribes—A Karen Curse—Rice-Beer—A Barrel always on Tap—Bamboo Buckets—Great Capacity—Karen and Santal Legend—Redemption of Captives—A Karen Robin Hood.

We may now conveniently refer to various tribes with whom the Kayas are more or less affiliated. To begin with the Yindilines, their hewers of wood and drawers of water. The social condition of the latter as described by O'Riley is decidedly revolting to our sense of the fitness of things; for parents send their children adrift so soon as they can shift for themselves, just as birds turn their young out of their nests when they can fly. Society is consequently so mixed, that in some cases the people cannot determine whether those with whom they have social intercourse are blood relations or otherwise. Unlike the inhabitants of the Northern Island of Burmese cosmography, they have no test by which they can avoid the awful possibility of a man marrying his grandmother! In this delightful region the women abandon their babes immediately after birth, and leave them to Nature. Like Topsy they 'grow,' but as all are of exactly the same size, build, and colour, inconvenient mistakes would undoubtedly occur were it not that when a couple, 'moved by reciprocal affection, wish to unite in wedlock,' they are obliged to go under a certain tree which gives them permission by lowering its branches; if, however, it makes no such sign, its immobility is tantamount to forbidding the banns.* The Tarus, again, though equally primitive in their habits, preserve much more decorum in their social arrangements; while their sense of shame is so acute, that accused persons commit suicide rather than pose as objects at which the finger of scorn can point—thus indicating, perhaps, a connection with China as regards the curious alternative known as the 'happy despatch.'

With a character for ferocity only equalled by the Kayas, and living for generations in a state of chronic warfare with their neighbours, the Gaykhos long had an unenviable notoriety for their lawlessness and independence of control of any kind. The Tsaw-koos, residing in what used to be a debatable land between the Sittang and Salwen Valleys, might well go in double harness with the Gaykhos, who are so unfavourably known

* Father Sangermano's 'Burman Empire.' Rome, 1833.

for want of hospitality towards strangers that none valuing their lives ever cared to visit, much less to exploit a country where each man's hand was against his fellow, and casual visitors were looked upon as lawful prey. Their passion for the possession of kyeezees is so pronounced that it is said instances are by no means rare of their bartering their children and other near relations for them, in subservience to a superstition that the deep-sounding note of these monotoned instruments propitiates the Nats and averts evil from themselves. In the settlement of serious quarrels, or in the redemption of captives, the indemnity with them always takes the shape of a kyeezee, with buffaloes and pigs as a makeweight, just as in Western countries a concession of territory or perhaps some men-of-war is insisted on. In their social disputes also it forms an important feature, for according to Dr. Mason a girl who has been jilted can claim from her false lover a kyeezee for her body, another for her head, and a gong to cover her face for shame. They and all their congeners have established forms for making covenants of friendship and reciprocity treaties, which savour of the archaic civilisation to which so many of their customs belong, rather than to a more recent development which insists on documents duly signed and sealed. The blood of bulls and of goats, of swine and dogs, of fowls and men, mixed with rice-beer or spirits, is with them far more efficacious than the more matter-of-fact pens, ink, sealing-wax and paper of such importance in other countries. In the ratification of treaties of peace between various tribes, as well as of marriage compacts and civil agreements, the parties concerned cut notches in the stem of a big and durable tree. Beyond this peculiar notch, says Dr. Mason, no monuments of peace or war are known to exist. With little faith in the infallibility of their judges, they prefer to have recourse to certain ordeals for deciding suits for determining the guilt or innocence of accused persons. In the water ordeal they have a test of lung power rather than simple hydromancy, for the accuser and accused are simultaneously 'ducked,' and he or she who remains longest under water is pronounced the winner. In the candle ordeal, whoever keeps his taper alight the longest wins the case.

Among septs of less importance are the Pray. Ishmael among other clans, their hand, till lately, was against everyone, and everyone's hand against them. Their neighbours, the Hashu or Hashwie, possess like unenviable characteristics, but console themselves for their exclusion from society by drumming on their kyeezees and self-adornment—the women carrying out the absurd fashion of leaden and brass coils round their necks and limbs in more pronounced fashion than those of other tribes. From decomposed animal matter as well as the nitrates of lime, magnesia, and soda, found in their limestone caves, they by an ingenious process obtain nitrate of potash and saltpetre. Mixing this with charcoal of their own make, sulphur purchased elsewhere, lime juice, spirits, and 'Perry Davis' Pain Killer,' which is supposed to give it pungency, they mauufacture a coarse kind of gunpowder.

The social ceremonies, connected with domestic occurrences among the tribes of Kaya affinities, call for no special remark, excepting on the occasion of marriage in some of the more advanced communities, when the candidates are married by proxy, though they themselves must also put in an appearance at the function. Two elders represent them, one being the bridegroom's 'best man,' the other officiating for the bride's maid. Each sponsor holds a loving-cup of spirits, and, acknowledging the obligations incurred by the person he represents, offers his cup to his fellow and adjures him to be faithful to his covenant. The parties most concerned do not interchange vows, but by silence give consent to the promises made by the elders in their behalf. Their ritual insists on a formula somewhat similar to that in the English Church Service which runs, 'to have and to hold from this day forward, for better for worse, for richer for poorer,' etc. But, instead of the bride and bridegroom saying this, the congregation take up the refrain and say, 'Amen! they are man and wife and may live together; have plenty to eat, or starve; may clothe themselves as they please, or go naked; may exist in peace, or fight and quarrel; it is nobody's business but their own; no one has any right to interfere.'

At a Kuki wedding the officiating elder considers

it unnecessary to tender advice to the bridegroom, but duly impresses on the bride the duties of matrimony so far as she is concerned. Instead of the marriage homily addressed to all whom it may concern, as noted in the Church of England prayer-book, the Kuki peroration is as follows: 'This man has taken you to be his wife; be you faithful, and have not evil communication with other men; cheer him with liquor and meat, and make him happy all the days of his life; may you be blessed with numerous progeny; if you act otherwise, you will be a worthless creature and will be fined heavily.'*

The practice of the hill Karens in cases of *Crim. Con.* are by no means so drastic as that pertaining to some of the tribes on the Bengal border. They are taught by their traditions, however, that not only the parties guilty of this phase of incontinence are punished by the God of Heaven and Earth, but a general calamity is inevitable, unless averted by sacrifice and prayer. The transgressors therefore have to purchase a hog, slay it, allow its blood to flow into a furrow in the ground which they have to scrape with their own hands, and repeat the following prayer: 'God of Heaven and

* Among the Lolos, according to Mr. Baber, this ceremony is opened by the bridesmaids with a melancholy song, bemoaning the bride's unhappy fate. To which the bride responds acknowledging in song, broken with bitter weeping, that she is a hapless victim. A scene of tearfulness ensues, when the male relations of the bridegroom burst upon the scene, seize the maid, place her pick-a-back on the shoulders of the best man, and carry her off on horseback to her own home.

Earth, Lord of the mountains and hills, I have destroyed the productiveness of the country. Do not be angry with me, do not hate me, but have mercy and compassionate me. Now I repair the mountains, now I repair the streams. May there be no more failure of crops, no more unsuccessful labours, no more unfortunate efforts in my country. May the paddy be fruitful, the rice abundant, the vegetables flourish.' After submitting to this ordeal and paying damages to the plaintiff, a decree *Nisi*, with costs, is pronounced by the village elders who act as judges of the Divorce Court.

Many of the hill Karens are noted for their sporting proclivities. They have a peculiar breed of small dogs with little pretensions to good looks, but keen in the pursuit of game, and, unlike the common village curs, always accompany their masters in their rambles. A notable instance of the Tsaw-koo Karen passion for the chase was some years ago afforded at a great open-air gathering of their clan presided over by the present writer, and arraigned for the purpose of discussing the important question of opening up trade routes with the Shan States. When in full conclave, it happened that one of their hounds gave tongue in the jungle, and by so doing broke up the meeting. For their canine companions, who, with their masters, were assisting at the function, incontinently rose from their slumbers, and, in full cry, joined the hunt which they, like Towzer in Pindar's sonnet, were enjoying in their dreams.

'Eager he seemed to hunt indeed,
The rabbits to their holes;
Thus dogs can dream like gentlemen,
Altho' they've got no souls.'

Interesting as the future trade in cotton twist and grey shirtings might be, the present chance of sport could not be foregone by people so devoted to the chase, so all with one accord followed their dogs in pursuit of game. The escapade resulted in the capture of a wild boar, but, as the consequent excitement precluded any chance of rational discussion that day, the meeting was put off *nem. con.* till the next.

The Chins or Khyens, who have given us so much trouble in Upper Burma, contrast unfavourably with their congeners in Lower Burma, who are among the most easily governed of our fellow-subjects. Like the Shans, they are scattered all over Farther India. No special description need be given of these veritable caterans, as, *pari passu*, what has been said of the Kayas applies equally to them. Sir A. Phayre is inclined to accept their own version as regards their origin, which, in effect, is that they are offshoots from Burma-Mongoloid races which have pressed southwards from the Great Central Plateau. Dr. Mason again would class them with Karens. Reasonable arguments can be adduced in favour of both theories. Though much has been written about the equally non-obtrusive Karens, little was known of the Chins, till they recently asserted themselves by turbulent behaviour, except that they were merely a mild industrious people whose women were noted for the extraordinary custom of tattooing their faces. So little interest, in fact, did they inspire, that Padre Sangermano's explanation of this eccentricity has been generally accepted without protest. The worthy Padre stood godfather to its being a heroic remedy devised by the people as a counterblast to the amorous propensities of Burmese Kings of Pugân for possessing Chin girls in their harems—a solution quite as preposterous as the reason he assigns for Burmese males tattooing their legs. If the custom does not date back to the period when the Chinese entered the Flowery Land and encountered 'tattooing peoples,' it is probably of earlier date than the Pugân monarchy broken up by Kublai Khan in the thirteenth century. The tattooing question in various parts of the world offers a wide if not particularly interesting subject for inquiry. Suffice for our present purpose to cite the Naga male, whose tattooed face is his equivalent for the Victoria Cross—the reward of valour; the Burman or Shan who cannot achieve 'beautiful legs' unless his nether limbs are clothed in knee breeches or trousers manufactured by the tattooer's stylus; the Kaya who indelibly stipples his coat-of-arms on his back, and the Singpo woman who tattoos her legs in parallel lines, indicating that she is subject to the bonds of matrimony. The compiler of the 'Burma Gazetteer' accords space to the popular fallacy and also admits two alternatives—one that the Chins disfigured their girls to prevent outsiders, captivated by their

CHIN GROUP

charms, eloping with them; the other that the process furnishes an indelible mark for identification, in the event of the girls being kidnapped. Another peculiar custom pertaining to the Chins is that a girl's parents are not, by law, considered her guardians. A girl at birth is assigned to one of her brothers, and failing him to a male cousin, who is *in loco parentis* in all matters relating to her marriage. The marriage ceremony is performed at the bride's residence, the bridegroom providing the necessary khoung, or rice-beer, his friends furnishing pork, and her friends fowls. It then resolves into a game of forfeits, the groom and his representatives sitting on one side, and the bride and hers on the other side of a peeled bamboo with a cross piece stuck into the beer-jug. The only rule in the game being that trespass by anyone belonging to one party to the domain of the other entails a forfeit of a pot of beer, it is hardly needless to say that it is one meant to be broken, and the guests act accordingly; so the fun becomes fast and furious, developing into a Bacchanalian orgy.

The Chins have the character of being omniverous. They do not absolutely deny the soft impeachment, but wish it to be clearly understood that they scrupulously draw the line at cannibalism. 'We eat,' say they, 'everything that cannot speak.' It was not always so, according to a tradition quoted by Captain Lewin,* from which we learn that beasts and birds at one time had the

* Lewin's 'Wild Races of South-Eastern India.' London, 1870.

gift of speech, and spoke the same language as mankind. From our Bible we know that 'when men began to multiply on the face of the earth and daughters were born unto them, that the sons of God saw the daughters of men that they were fair; and they took them wives of all which they chose.'* According to the Chin version, the Creator's daughter 'stooped to conquer' the affections of a great chief, the patriarch of their race. She took the keenest interest in her adopted people, and noticed with concern that they degenerated because they abstained from animal food. The legend has it that the beasts and the birds begged for dear life 'with pitiful words, making the hearts of men soft, so that they could not slay them.' The chieftainess accordingly represented the matter to her Father, who took away from them the power of speech, so that men's hearts, moved by their sad entreaties, should no longer melt within them like wax, and thus deprive their bodies of proper sustenance.

Among some of the Chin clans, there are men supposed to be media of intercourse between Khozing, the patron deity of the nation, and themselves. The individual, so distinguished, becomes, they imagine, 'filled with and possessed by the divine afflatus.' In his intervals of inspiration, he is also believed to be endowed with the gift of tongues and to be invulnerable. He can then caress tigers, as a matter of course; for, as the Chins say, 'the tiger is Khozing's house dog, and

* Genesis vi, 1, 2.

he will not hurt us, because we are the children of his master.'

None of the tribes will venture to embark on any undertaking out of the ordinary tenor of their lives without propitiating the Nats by animal sacrifice. So very particular are they in this respect, that, when on raiding thoughts intent, they often take animals with them in case they may be required for this purpose when they are far from home. Dogs are naturally preferred, under these circumstances, as they follow their masters and thus save the trouble other animals would give. Incongruous as it may appear, the Chins, as a matter of fact, pose as veritable arbiters of destiny. They can circumvent the unseen spirits, or, as a budding diplomatist puts it, 'Nats are sometimes humbugged by the wily Chins.' They have implicit faith in the old nursery adage, 'If at first you don't succeed,' etc.; thus, if the Nats are obdurate on the first asking, they are bound sooner or later to be hoaxed into acquiescence, if the inquirer be sufficiently persistent, and can afford to satisfy the Nats' requirements. A single dog may be enough for a complaisant demon, while it may take a pack of hounds to reconcile a more obdurate one.

Our diplomatist, talking of a sub clan, also informs us that it is not partial to much clothing, the male Chimbon being reckoned by fashionable people to be decidedly over-dressed if he happens to wear anything so large as the historic fig-leaf. Though, according to Chin notions, the body when unadorned is adorned the most, Fashion permits of the excessive ornamentation of the head. The hair of a Chin dandy is worn in a large top-knot decorated with coils of beads of various colours. Brass pins are stuck into this coiffure, to which are attached gaudy red tassels of goat's hair and the teeth of the hog-deer, sometimes supplemented by green parrots' feathers, or a huge cock's tail stretched on a bamboo frame, which to the European eye has a somewhat ludicrous effect. Women also wear brass pins in their hair, though a *chic* damsel eschews feathers.

The same informant tells us that in the Chin country there are no engineering works of much consequence, yet in the same breath he records the very interesting fact that the people construct wonderful bridges of bamboos on the cantilever principle—a system which has lately become familiar to the British public from having been adopted by the great engineer who built the Forth Bridge. He also notes that they cross their streams by swing bridges, and have ingenious aqueducts of considerable length for household as well as irrigation purposes, and also have more substantial and better-built houses than the Burmese. All of which, though they may not be reckoned as triumphs of engineering skill in our sense of the word, may be called so in comparison with the achievements of most of the neighbouring peoples. Some of the Chin tribes eke out a precarious existence either by raiding weaker clans of the same race, or others who have not the same claim to their forbearance. They pay little or no attention to cultivation. These raids are organised chiefly for the sake of plunder and obtaining human captives, but never solely for heads. All prisoners not ransomed are either kept in bondage or change masters so often in distant villages that their friends, when they obtain the means for their redemption, are unable to trace and recover them. Wherever this terrorism prevails, there is no hope for Chin improvement; for those who, if left alone, would be industrious people, have no incentive to industry when liable to lose all they possess at any moment.

Though the borderer is characterised by freedom from any moral sense of his duty towards his neighbour, nevertheless, influenced by dread of the malignant Nats, he attaches a decided importance to an oath on his weapons of offence or defence, as well as on things necessary for existence. Thus the Naga holds his gun, spear, or sword in his teeth when making a solemn affirmative, which signifies that he is prepared to fall thereby if he fails to fulfil his obligations; while the Kuki swears by cotton, water, rice, and dah, meaning, under similar circumstances, that he is prepared to forfeit all that makes life worth having. With the hill Karen the equivalent of the Christian maxim, 'Swear not at all,' is 'Swear not without cause.' In his superstition, he thoroughly believes in the efficacy of a deliberate curse; in fact, he is taught that it is a legitimate way of obtaining satisfaction for injuries which the ordinary law does not recognise. His curse is not the oath of the bargee or coal-heaver, vigorously delivered, probably, but without any wish that the fearful imprecations he enunciates shall be really fulfilled. It is a deliberate affair. He knows that if he curses without reason his anathemas recoil on himself. So, when he has made up his mind to curse some one, 'he goes on to the verandah of his house and curses him three evenings in succession. On the third evening he takes an expiring faggot, an addled egg, and the last dropping of the dishes, which are usually given to the pigs, and says, "May his life expire like this expiring faggot; may he be destitute of posterity like this addled egg; and may his end be like the refuse of the dishes."'*

Marco Polo, referring to the national beverage of the Tartars, says, 'Their drink is mare's milk prepared in such a way that you would take it for white wine, and a right good drink it is, called by them kemiz.'† One who knew the nomads well describes it as 'the drink of all from the suckling upwards; it is the solace of age and illness, and the greatest of treats to all.' Though we can understand from his description that the intoxicating power 'varies according to the brew,' it is also interesting to learn that its effect is light and transient, producing in its climax a tendency

* Dr. Mason, *Asiatic Society's Journal.*

† Yule's 'Marco Polo.'

merely to refreshing sleep. All the border tribes use copiously a fermented liquor brewed from rice or millet, equivalent to the classic *Zythos* *Ζῦθος*—beer without hops, which as Æschylus, nearly five hundred years before Christ, tells us was made with barley by the Greeks, and used by them in their daily life as well as at festive gatherings. It is called khoung by the Karens and sheroo by the Kakhyens. Not a little trouble is taken by both in its preparation, and with the latter, according to Dr. Anderson, it is even 'regarded as a serious and almost sacred task, the women while engaged in it having to live in almost vestal seclusion.'* They not only have to be very careful to follow the instructions contained in their traditional recipes, but also not to forget to mix, with the initial ingredients, chillies, ginger, and certain sun-dried herbs, in order to avert trouble from malignant Nats. The doctor, more courageous than the present writer, tasted this beer, and passed a favourable verdict thereon, while another authority declares the Chin beer to be very palatable, much resembling cider in taste, but more like perry in appearance.

The Kakhyens, as well as some of the Karen hill tribes, have always a barrel of khoung on tap in their reception-halls, in which are inserted several reeds, intended to be used sherry-cobbler fashion by the guests, when, like Mrs. Gamp, they feel so 'dispoged,' provided they observe

* Anderson's 'Mandalay to Momein.'

strict etiquette in eschewing the inner reeds reserved for family use. The Kayas believe khoung to be a veritable panacea for all the ills to which flesh is heir. Moderation in its use, according to Mr. O'Riley, used to be so exceptional, that Dean Swift's fifth reason for drinking was accepted as a valid excuse for intoxication whenever opportunity offered. This beer, while possessing all the pleasurable sensations attributed to kemiz, produces less satisfactory results. In fact, it develops the seven recognised phases of drunkenness: (1) ape-drunk, when it finds vent in vehement dancing and other tom-foolery; (2) lion-drunk, when it resolves itself into a pugnacity that leads to 'battle, murder, and sudden death;' (3) swine-drunk, sufficiently suggestive; (4) sleep-drunk, when it keeps the more phlegmatic in a 'chronic state of mild and sweet inebriety' and somnolence, tending to obesity when made of such consistency as to be an article of food and drink combined; (5) martin-drunk, when they are apt to be supercilious and overbearing; (6) goat-drunk, when it lets off steam in inconveniently amorous proclivities; (7) fox-drunk, when they become crafty in their cups. Nevertheless, as Mr. Hodgson truly says, 'where honest John Barleycorn is free from the dangerous alliance of spirits, opium, and hemp, even if assisted by the "narcotic weed," he need not be set down as a necessary corrupter of morals.' Mr. Hodgson's conclusions are amply borne out by the fact that, whereas habitual drunkenness from spirituous liquors is a well-nigh incurable disease even in the case of Westerns possessed of high moral courage, confirmed drunkards among the Karens, without any pretence to this estimable attribute, have, after they have embraced Christianity, relinquished the 'accursed thing,' and become estimable members of society.

The Venerable Purchas, writing in the sixteenth century, speaks of a wine then produced in the Tenasserim division, the secret of whose manufacture is now unknown. He describes it as having been made from 'the floure of a tree called Nyper' . . . 'an excellent drinke, cleare as chrystall, good to the mouth and better to the stomacke, and it hath an excellent gentle vertue, that if one sorely afflicted with the French disease, drinking goode store of this, hee shall be whole againe, and I have seene it proved . . . as a friend of mine whose nose began to drop away with that disease . . . was counselled of the Doctors of Phisick . . . that hee should go to Tanasary, or Tenasserim, at the time of the new wines, and that hee should drink of the Nyper wine night and day . . . This man went thither and did so, and I have seen him after with a good colour and sound.' *

The multifarious uses to which the bamboo is put, have been so often and so well enumerated by travellers in the tropics, that the present writer will not attempt to exercise the patience of his readers by specifying them. One useful

* Purchas' 'Pilgrimes.' London, 1625.

variety, however, of the grass genus, known as *bambusa gigantea*, which attains to a height of one hundred feet, with stems a foot or so in thickness, and met with in greater perfection on the borders of Burma than in many other regions, may be referred to without incurring this reproach. Captain Gill, in his travels in Burma and China, having never seen a bamboo bigger than six inches in diameter, was rather inclined to doubt the fact; but had he visited the Karen hills he might have seen water-buckets made of single joints of the genus we refer to, at least twenty inches in length and thirty inches in circumference,—a sufficiently modest margin when Dr. Mason is our competent authority for thirty-six inches. A woman sometimes carries as many as five of these buckets on her back, slung on a cord, which is kept in position by being brought round her forehead. This bamboo-bucket is curiously mixed up with the Karen tradition of the dispersion of the human race. The legend runs that a chief, after dividing a bucket into seven pieces, gave one to each of his seven sons, bidding them depart and found separate nations, which would be estranged for a season, but eventually reconciled, while their rulers would return with the several portions and restore the bucket to its pristine shape,—a result symbolical of the Karens becoming hereafter a great and undivided nation. Mr. Hunter remarks that 'as the Santal legend immediately divides the human species into seven families, so the Sanskrit tradition assigns the propagation of our race after the flood to seven Rishis.' *

In both the criminal and civil procedure of all the Bghai tribes, a system of forays for purposes of vengeance, plunder, and the recovery of debts was duly recognised. But those who have come under the British sphere of influence have gradually been taught, not without much searching of hearts, that they can no longer take the law into their own hands with impunity. Debt forays were comparatively mild affairs, unless the debtor and his friends resisted the *posse comitatus* formed of the creditor and his neighbours, while the others were often characterised by fearful atrocities; individuals having a marketable value being carried away captive, while infants and decrepit folk, of no account in the slave-market, were often ruthlessly murdered by the marauders.

The negotiations for the redemption of these captives were always entrusted to an elder of a neutral village. If the commissioner was accepted as an 'ambassador of peace,' a hog was killed in his honour, his lower limbs were smeared with its blood, and, after being hospitably entertained, he was sent back to his clan with the head and legs of the slaughtered animal; exhibits invariably accepted as 'sealed documents that his mission had been successful.' After these preliminaries, the principals of the feud met, and, having sacrificed a hog or a dog, mixed the blood thereof with various

* 'Annals of Rural Bengal.' 151.

ingredients (already enumerated as utilised in other covenants), divided the animal's head in twain, each taking a moiety and slinging it round his neck, solemnly interchanged promises of good-will, and invoked terrible curses on themselves in the event of breach of agreement.

When in the Bghai country, the present writer was introduced to an old chief who, in his salad days—by reason of his truculent forays—was the Robin Hood of that region. With his unkempt locks bound by a turban of tattered muslin, mud-coloured from long usage; his only raiment consisting of breeches originally striped in the fashion affected by his clan, of the same sad hue; carrying the indispensable bag which all the Karen tribes sling from the shoulder, filled with odds and ends, consisting, among other provender, of a fat snake, (for all is fish that comes into a Karen's net,) tall and weird-looking, he was indeed a conspicuous figure. The old gentleman had repented of the error of his ways, and in token of his desire to lead a peaceful life, as well as appreciation of the efforts of missionaries for promoting the welfare of his people, he gave up his sword, with which he had killed thirty men—his most cherished possession—to be sold for missionary purposes.

The writer gladly availed himself of the privilege of purchasing this weapon, and subsequently gave it to a prominent official of a missionary society, who says that he always 'brings down the house' at his lectures when he produces it and tells its story.

CHAPTER XI.

INDO-BURMESE BORDER TRIBES.

General Summary—People considered Impracticable even by the Imperial Dalhousie—Success of Sir Cecil Bendon's Departure—Language of this Region of a Broken and Infirm Type—All the Tribes understand a Common Language—Proverbial Philosophy—Bachelors' and Spinsters' Clubs—Courtship and Marriage—Women Valued in Ratio to Physical Capacity—High Prices demanded for Marriageable Girls—'Girls of the Period'—Clothing, from Fig-leaves to Elaborate Toilettes—Naga Delicacy—Toungya or Jum Cultivation—Manipur—Game of Polo—Origin of Name.

INTERPOSED between Bengal and Burma is a great mountain system, of which, only two decades ago, we knew little more than that it was peopled by numerous savage tribes of warlike habits and predatory instincts—a legacy left us by the Assam dynasty, which we supplanted. Our ignorance of these races, their numerous dialects, their customs and modes of living, was equalled by their complete ignorance of us and our power. Hemmed in and stationary themselves, they could not understand that we had other resources than those in evidence, and therefore were entirely unable to comprehend the inevitable results of their obstinacy.

Of history they have nothing worthy the name, and the oral traditions they possess lack the corroborative evidence that makes those of the Karens so valuable. The Manipuris, who are in touch with Hindu civilisation, in spite of their history being disfigured by a record of barbarism in the shape of internal wars of a revolting type, would fain live up to the ideal standard allotted them in the Indian epics, wherein their country and ancestors are described in glowing terms. Those not so influenced, however, have no such romantic inspiration, and are not to be distinguished from their hill cousins prone to wild paganism, with manners and customs unsophisticated and repulsive. Again, 'the Nagas of the romance are fascinating creatures of the serpent-race, gorgeously apparelled and abounding in wealth, while the Nagas of our day are very undeniable and unsavoury savages.' *

The eccentric notions of duty entertained by these delightful peoples for many years, not a little embarrassed our frontier officers in their attempts to bring them to our sense of the fitness of things; as may be imagined, when every individual was brought up with the genial idea that rapine and bloodshed are meritorious acts.

> 'For why? Because the good old rule
> Sufficeth them; the simple plan,
> That they should take who have the power,
> And they should keep who can.'

* Dalton's 'Ethnology.'

Leniency, mercy, conciliation, and respect for the rights of property as interpreted in the jurisprudence of other races, who in their arrogance claim to belong to a higher civilisation, are all looked upon as signs of weakness, and are treated with contempt.

A policy of direct management by chosen officers, supported by a show of strength, was accordingly brought to bear upon them, in view of suggesting for their favourable consideration the propriety of somewhat modifying these opinions. The experiment at first was attended with the happiest results, but after a while the old Adam reasserted itself in many cases, especially after the English succeeded to their recent inheritance, when the joys and excitements of the old life were brought to their recollection by turbulent congeners on the Burmese side of the border, who, as subjects of the Lord of Many White Elephants, were permitted to remain in unmitigated savagery, and observed the code of morality which they had discarded under British advice.

It would of course be extremely wearisome to enter into a purely ethnological treatise regarding even a tithe of the various tribes in this region, whose name is legion, but incidental references to some of the more prominent of those who come within the scope of our subject may not be out of place.

Up to 1860 the general policy of Government, as we learn from Mr. (now Sir Alexander) Mackenzie, was to have no direct dealings with these border tribes.* The history of our intercourse with them is a tale of often-repeated outrage on the one side and long suffering forbearance on the other. Baffled by the inveterate savagery of the people and the difficulties of their hills, even the Imperial Dalhousie was nonplussed and content to 'relegate them to a kind of political Coventry.' In 1866, however, Sir Cecil Beadon, Lieutenant-Governor of Bengal, persuaded that this policy of 'masterly inactivity' was but a sorry excuse for neglect of duty, inaugurated a new departure, which, after all, 'was merely the reiteration of the old, but still inexplicable fact, that one British officer of tact and firmness, living in the midst of an inferior race, ready to redress their grievances, to sympathize with their wants, and punish their crimes, can turn the heart of that people to himself, and lead them forward to civilisation and peace.'

While insisting on direct control, personal influence, and conciliatory intercourse on the part of his agent, the Lieutenant-Governor supported him by adequate strength in the shape of an armed guard, wisely deciding that it is a mistake to suppose that granting the power to inflict condign punishment for exceptionally gross outrages is any departure from a general policy of reconciliation.

Lieutenant Williamson, the officer selected to initiate this line of conduct, was eminently qualified for the task. Though his advent was viewed with suspicion, he fortunately possessed physical

* 'North-East Frontier of Bengal.'

accomplishments which awoke their wonder and paved the way towards their profound respect. 'Unerring skill with the rifle and a soundness of mind and limb that enabled him to beat the village leaders in a race uphill, were a better introduction for him than even his armed police.' His *savoir-faire*, admirable sympathy, and strict sense of justice accomplished the rest. Chiefs, who hitherto had gloried in their independence, joyfully acknowledged his authority; intertribal warfare ceased; solemn compacts of friendship were entered into and kept; dogs were substituted for human victims in their sacrifices, and holocausts were made of skulls and other ghastly trophies of past murders—all these victories in the cause of civilisation having been accomplished without bloodshed.

'In many a jungle solitude,' remarked an Indian paper twenty years ago, 'where fever lurks in every brake, and uncouth savage races dispute with wild beasts possession of the clearings, we can point to devoted men, little heard of by the public, little noticed by their Government, who are spending and being spent for the sake of the people they control, and bringing by degrees whole tribes to learn the rudiments of civilisation and progress.

The same truth still holds good. Government, from time to time, and by the mere force of events, has been compelled to take up questions which it would have gladly ignored. Its policy may therefore be described as a variable quantity, oscillating between stern repression and flabby conciliation; sometimes carrying fire and sword into the quiet hamlet of a chief whose only offence is the kidnapping of a few individuals in satisfaction of a debt and whom he treats as members of his own family, and anon giving rum, rupees, and green pyjamas to a truculent scoundrel who adorns his premises with the gory heads of his hapless victims.

Sometimes agreeing with those who declare that the only way to impress savage tribes with a notion of our power is to attack those who claim independence in defiance of our opinion on this subject, burn their villages, destroy their crops, and hunt them down as outlaws. At other times admitting that 'the details of border warfare in which disciplined troops mow down half-armed peasants are unpleasant in themselves and afford neither glory to the conquerors, nor lessons in the military art,'* they approve the gentle policy of Augustus Cleveland, on whose tomb the following words are engraved: 'Without bloodshed or the terrors of authority, employing only the means of conciliation, confidence, and benevolence, he attempted and accomplished the entire subjection of the lawless and savage inhabitants of the Jungle Terry (forest frontier) of Rajmahal, who had long infested the neighbouring lands by their predatory incursions, inspired them with a taste of the arts of civilised life, and attached them to the British Government by a conquest over

* Hunter's 'Rural Bengal.'

their minds—the most permanent and the most rational mode of dominion.'*

The speech of the tribes to whom we refer, like that of the aborigines of Bengal when invaded by Aryan peoples, is of a broken and infirm type, with numerous words for what can be seen and handled, but incapable of expressing abstract conceptions of the intellect. The Aryan warrior from whose lips 'flowed a language instinct with tenderness and power, a language equipped with the richest inflections and a whole phalanx of grammatical forms; one which clearly uttered whatever it was in man's lot to suffer and whatever it was in his mind to conceive, and which from the beginning of recorded time stands forth in one form or other as the vehicle of his highest efforts . . . used to pray for victory over the men of inarticulate utterance and of the uncouth talk.'†

The student accustomed to the rich and appetising fare particularised in the Sanscrit philological *menu*, turns with loathing from the meagre and insipid pabulum comprising the lingual bill of fare provided by races in a low degree of civilisation. When he buries himself in a jungle tract to study the language of its people at the fountain-head, and finds that within the radius of a morning's walk from his tent a dozen tribes are to be met, each with its special dialect, to whom his acquisition is an unknown tongue, he can fully sympathise with the Aryan prayer. Among the

* Hunter's 'Annals of Rural Bengal.' London, 1868.

† Ibid.

Nagas alone he would have to encounter about thirty different languages, 'affording a striking proof of the tendency of unwritten speech to split up into different dialects. An intervening hill, a ravine, or a river, is enough to divide the language of a district.'*

Our officers, very properly, are encouraged to learn the various tribal tongues, in order that they may be able to communicate directly, instead of through interpreters, with peoples who have to be judiciously managed. Whatever may be urged in the interests of philology, for practical purposes absolutely no valid reason can be assigned for conserving dialects of a languid type which merely fossilise the disintegration that now exists. Every effort, therefore, should be made to induce the border races to learn Burmese or Shan, subject to the geographical and philological considerations incidental to their influence. By so doing, homogeneous peoples now divided into innumerable clans from diversities of speech may be induced to follow in the footsteps of their ancestors, and become united by the bonds of a common language.

Whatever may be the result of our efforts in this direction, we can never hope to achieve the marvellous success of the Chinese potentate mentioned by Mr. Colborne Baber. 'How comes it,' he asks, 'that the language of the remotest province of China is almost identical with that spoken at the capital, while in the intervening provinces

* Hunter's 'Rural Bengal.'

so many uncouth and distorted jargons are encountered? The patois of Ssu-ch'-uan, at any rate, in the mouths of its country-folk, was more than half-unintelligible to our northern followers. Hunan was, in addition, ridiculous; but in Western Yunnan we were accosted in a familiar and luminous speech, which made us feel as if we were nearing home. Philologers would fail to discover the reason, independently of history, but it is of infinite simplicity. The natives of Yunnan were forced to learn the language of the north on pain of death. Wu San-kuei, the Chinese general who sided with the Tartars at the rise of the present dynasty, and subsequently reduced Yunnan, became its king, and imposed a despotic and grammatical rule upon his subjects. Selecting those of his veterans who spoke the purest Chinese, he set them to instruct the vanquished. Tradition does not state how many dunces were decapitated, but in any case his educational policy has produced admirable results. "At times kings are not more imperative than rhymes." But here was a king more imperative than a whole language.' *

Completely isolated as the tribes of this ethnical and political frontier are from each other, they nevertheless possess a common language, according to Captain Lewin,† sufficiently copious and pungent under certain circumstances, which finds

* 'Notes on route of Mr. Grosvenor's mission through Western Yunnan.'

† Lewin's 'Wild Races of South-Eastern India.' London, 1870.

no place in the curriculum of the philologist. The chief's special messenger, carrying his carved and ornamented spear as an emblem of authority,—potent as a magistrate's seal in other countries,—dumb though he be in the presence of people to whom his dialect is a foreign tongue, metaphorically speaks in accents that cannot be mistaken when he flings down the gauntlet in the shape of the war-dah with strip of crimson cloth in token of defiance, or produces the cross or dagger-shaped *pluroi* or wand, made of strips of bamboo, which, simple as it may appear to the uninitiated, under some conditions furnishes materials for a lengthy despatch, if reduced to a written medium. If the tips of its cross pieces be broken, for instance, it signifies a money demand for each fracture. If one cross piece be charred, it means an urgent summons, directing people to come by torchlight if it arrives at night. A capsicum fixed on the pluroi signifies that disobedience to the order will 'make it hot' for the recipient. If the *pluroi* be made of cane instead of bamboo, it betokens this punishment will take the form of a flogging.* The smooth round stone which was all that Lieutenant Wilcox received from the Abors, in reply

* The *pluroi* reminds one of the 'Fiery Cross' of the Highlanders in the days of Rob Roy, sometimes called the 'Cross of Shame,' because disobedience to what the symbol implied inferred infamy. The extremities were charred and dipped in blood, signifying a rendezvous summons. He who failed to appear suffered the extremities of fire and sword, which were emblematically denounced to the disobedient by the bloody and burnt marks on this warlike symbol.—Sir Walter Scott. Note to 'Lady of the Lake.'

to interminable verbal negotiations suggesting the advisability of their submission to British authority, was utterly meaningless to that very intelligent officer, till interpreted by a rude native of the jungle who happened to be present when the missive arrived. The translation ran thus: 'Until this stone crumbles in the dust, shall our friendship last, and firm as is its texture, so firm is our present resolution.'

Regarding people fond of flowers and tokens, it can readily be imagined that the language of flowers affords a rich vocabulary, effectually utilised by the young of both sexes. The astringent areca nut and succulent leaf of the betel palm, with their concomitant soporific ingredients in the shape of lime and tobacco and various condiments with which they 'chew the cud of sweet and bitter fancy,' are equally suggestive. Even a lump of charcoal or a pinch of turmeric, articles eminently necessary for warmth and culinary purposes, but innocent, one would imagine, of the romantic element, come not amiss occasionally to emphasise a sentiment or give it a different colouring, 'to point a moral or adorn a tale.' The coy maiden, who dares not outrage custom by a verbal proposal to her lover, can send him the birnee rice and flower equivalent thereto, and thus put herself on the same platform as her Western sister, to whom the privilege is accorded only in leap year.

Captain Lewin's policeman, when required to explain why he, in some outlandish locality, desired a week's leave, said, 'A young maiden has sent me flowers and birnee rice twice as a token, and if I wait any longer they will say I am no man.' Thus it will be seen that 'common objects' afford a variety of combinations to the imaginative, making them more or less independent of articulate utterance.

Most of the tribes possess legends of various kinds, but few that deserve quotation. They also are fond of 'Proverbial Philosophy.' Captain Lewin quotes several of their sayings, some of which have English synonyms. For example: 'The elephant is caught by the elephant' finds an equivalent in 'Set a thief to catch a thief.' The Khyoungtha exquisite, though his general toilette may be scanty, pays elaborate attention to his coiffeur, and resents any interference with his hair, which he rolls into a complicated ball on the crown of his head. This weakness resolves itself into a well-known proverb—'If I must die, I must die; but don't touch my top-knot, as the peacock said.' This Lewin neatly caps with Leech's picture of the swell and the robber, and its accompanying legend—'Take all, take money, take life; but spare, oh! spare my collars!'

In the code of morality pertaining to all the border tribes, compassionate indulgence is vouchsafed to the frailties of human nature in tolerating, if not actually encouraging, the freest intercourse between the sexes before marriage. Draconian severity, however, is the rule afterwards, and transgressors against marital rights are punished with the utmost rigour of the law, death even being the penalty in cases of *crim. con.* among the wilder clans, the injured husband posing as judge, jury, and executive. Under their quasi-patriarchal village government—which, as Mr. Hunter says of similar peoples in Bengal, 'rests its system on the simpler political limit of a nomadic society, the family,'—each village has its chief, and, in some clans, under him again are two deputies, one for the boys and the other for the girls, who assist him in duly maintaining social order. When the young people are kept at home, the duties incumbent on the deputies are more or less perfunctory; not so in other communities provided with bachelor clubs and spinster halls, to which boys and girls, at a very early age, are drafted and placed under the aforesaid deputies, who, according to all accounts, rule the clubs in a very despotic fashion, and exact from their subordinates, with unsparing hand, services of all kinds. Both sexes, it appears, have the privilege of being honorary members of both clubs, an advance in civilisation to which Westerns have, as yet, not attained. These privileges, however, cease when they accept the responsibilities of married life. And as the youth is often a Benedict at seventeen, and the maiden provided for at even an earlier age, the former has not much time allowed him for 'sowing his wild oats,' or the latter for pronounced flirtation, and both, therefore, make the most of their opportunities, aided and abetted by the club managers, who, being invariably young, naturally sympathise with their frolics, when they do not interfere with discipline. *Paterfamilias*, also, metaphorically allows his boy to have the latch-key, and *materfamilias* lends her girls the 'key of the fields,' or, in other words, lets them amuse themselves to their heart's content, mindful of their own youthful experience. This extreme laxity in the case of juveniles, followed by inexorable stringency when they attain to years of discretion, far from being attended with demoralising results, acts altogether beneficially, inasmuch as the social evil, with its attendant horrors, —a veritable scourge among peoples who are supposed to be in a higher stage of civilisation,—is absolutely unknown to these primitive Children of the Forest.

Some of the tribes, partially influenced by the Hindu or Buddhist religions, patronise, in somewhat emasculate fashion, certain proceedings which by a stretch of the imagination may be termed marriage ceremonies. The Khyoung-thas of Arakan may be accepted as an instance in point, probably owing to the picturesque description of a wedding function pertaining to these Children of the River, given by Captain Lewin. The indigenous system, however, favoured by the more unsophisticated clans who simply propitiate the *genii loci* of their hills, streams, and forests, may be said to resolve itself simply into a process of natural selection, approved by the beasts of the field and the fowls of the air. The same remark applies, so far as absence of ceremonial is concerned, to the other two great events in their career, namely, birth and death. Their sense of propriety, as Mr. Hodgson somewhat sententiously observes, 'takes less cognizance than it might advantageously do of those great sacraments of humanity, baptism, marriage, and sepulture, withholding all sanction from the first, and lending to the other two, especially marriage, a less decided sanction than the interests of society demand.'*

In the good old times, when chivalry demanded that the wishes of the weaker sex should be taken into account, the enamoured swain had to act in accordance with its behests. It might be his happy lot to woo the gentle maiden, whose appreciation of the beautiful was captivated by the tender grace of a lovely orchid or other rare flower of the forest, or whose material senses were enthralled by some sylvan delicacy in the shape of tender field mice or a plump squirrel. It might, however, so happen that the Fates decreed he should be enamoured of a damsel of sterner type—not so easily pleased. He would have found, for instance, that the Naga girl who respected herself never condescended to listen to the addresses of a lover, unless he either presented her with the skull of a murdered victim—accepted by custom as a chivalrous offering of a true knight to his lady—or appeared before her with a tattooed face—a tangible patent proving that he had already secured a similar trophy, and thus, by the laws of

* Hodgson's 'Kocch Bodo and Dhimal peoples.' Calcutta, 1847.

his clan, was a recognised candidate for the estate of matrimony. Hideous as he might appear to others, to her he was a *persona grata*. In the present unromantic age, no such deference is paid to the claims of woman. It is sad to record, in fact, that in the communities where the male, eschewing work, relegates it to the female, the latter is valued in direct ratio to her physical capacity. Woman, no doubt, is a ministering angel, but altogether in a material and not a poetical sense. Sooth to say she is rated more at her commercial value in the matrimonial market or as a useful drudge than as a comforter and helpmate to man. Consequently, in this degenerate civilisation, she has become more or less a question of money or its equivalent. Like the Babylonians fourteen centuries before Christ, who periodically sold their unattached women in the open market, some parents among these simple peoples, blessed with attractive daughters, occasionally dispose of them to the highest bidder. As polygamy does not conflict with the unwritten canons of their codes, the rich man can purchase as many wives as he pleases, while the impecunious youth must serve for his bride as Jacob did for Rachel. Though the *vinculum matrimonii* generally binds all classes when they arrive at maturity, an exception to this rule occurs in some clans owing to the abnormal prices demanded for marriageble girls. Talking of the Ho spinsters, Colonel Dalton assures us that 'it is not from any yearning for celibacy they continue single. The 'girls of the period,' according to his account, 'tell you frankly that they do all they can to please the young men, and . . . make themselves as attractive as they can, flirt in the most demonstrative manner, and are not too coy to receive, in public, attentions from those they admire . . . But with all this the men will not propose,' as their grasping papas will not abate the price set upon their charms.

Mr. William Black, describing one of his heroines, says there was a great deal of what might be called 'natural religion in that young lady,' a peculiarity which he defines as 'a belief in occult influences ruling the earth, unnameable, undefinable, but ever present and ever active,' the real cry of 'her soul unknown to herself went out to all the vague and imaginative powers of magic and witchcraft—to the mysterious influences of the stars and the strange controllers of chance.' Such is the faith of the various rude peoples of this region who have not been affected by Buddhism or Hinduism.

Sir W. Hunter, contrasting the Aryan usurpers with the Bengal aborigines, remarks, 'The Aryan requiem looked forward to reunion above, that of the aboriginal tribes shrinks from the dead as from an undefined horror, and, so far from speaking of a meeting hereafter, begs that it may be spared the terrors of a visit . . . The great object of the aborigines is to get their dead out of their sight. The North-Eastern hill-men hide the

* Hunter's 'Annals of Rural Bengal.'

corpse in a hole as soon as the breath has left it. No stately rights are observed . . . Among the tribes that have developed funeral ceremonies, a burial is only an occasion for gluttony and drunkenness.'

The same remarks apply to many of the border tribes. To this rule, however, there are exceptions. The Kukis, for instance, dessicate the corpses of influential persons, by means of air, fire, or the sun's rays, and thus manage to keep them for weeks, and even months, in order to allow all friends to assemble, say farewell to the departed, and partake of the funeral feast. Captain Lewin * tells us that among the Dhun and Khoo clans the body is placed in a hollow made of a tree-trunk, with holes in the bottom. This is placed on a lofty platform, and left to dry in the sun. The dried body is afterwards rammed into an earthern vase and buried; the head is cut off and preserved. Another clan sheathe their dead in pith (sola); the corpse is then placed on a platform, under which a slow fire is kept up until the body is dried. After this, it is kept for six months for the convenience of relations and friends, who may be far away on business or pleasure, and subsequently buried. The Howolong clan hang a man's corpse on the house beams for seven days, during which time his widow, should he have left one, has to sit underneath spinning. Custom forbids her stirring from the spot, and, if no one feeds her, she must

* 'Wild Races of South-East India.'

either act in defiance thereto or starve. Thus the Kukis, at any rate, have none of the loathing of the dead which distinguishes the Bengal aborigines. It appears, indeed, that they endeavour to make it as pleasant as possible for the corpse as well as themselves during the interval between burial or dessication. For the deceased is seated in an honourable position in the centre of the house, arrayed in his finest clothes, with his gun or other weapon beside him. The friends assemble and make high carnival, paying much respect to the deceased; filling his pipe with tobacco, they place it between his lips, and, putting choice morsels before him, adjure him to eat, as he is about to start on a long journey. Colonel Dalton * confirms what Captain Lewin says about the Kukis, and notes that the Singpos and Nagas dessicate their dead in similar fashion and with the same object, while the Garos sometimes keep theirs for ten days or so without resorting to dessication. The Abors, he also tells us, while burying defunct relatives before they become offensive to the living, pay every honour to the corpse, consigning it to its last resting-place fully clothed and equipped with arms, food, cooking-utensils, &c., as if for a long journey, a custom probably Himalaic in its origin.

Like all rude peoples, the clans in this region practise augury. They divine by fowls' tongues and the yolks of eggs; there is nothing, however, analogous to the Karen ordeal by chickens' bones,

* Dalton's 'Ethnology of Bengal.'

though the Singpo process of predicting future events by the minute hair-like fibres exposed by bursting nul grass joints by fire, offers *data* somewhat similar to those afforded by the tiny straws stuck in the bones on which the Karens work their oracles. Dropping oil into a vessel containing water, similar to ceromancy or wax-dropping prevalent in other countries, examining the entrails of birds, as the Romans did in ancient times, and testing a pig's liver, are some of their favourite ordeals. Colonel Dalton gives an instance where the Abors pin their faith on this last. Finding that some members of this tribe desired to ascertain the reason of his visiting them by this test, he suggested a simpler plan would be to judge by his words and looks, to which they retorted that 'the words and faces of men were fallacious, but pig's liver never deceived them!'

With our first parents, necessity was the mother of invention as regards clothing. After eating the forbidden fruit, their eyes were opened, and they knew they were naked. In this dilemma they sewed fig-leaves together and made themselves aprons. When the same truth was brought home to the unsophisticated comprehension of the Joangs, a primitive tribe of this region, they were unable to arrive at even this stage of inventive development. Hardly twenty years ago their female toilet consisted merely in the young shoots of any tree with long, soft leaves stuck before and behind in a girdle of beads worn round the waist.* However advantageous as regards cheapness and convenience of a dress provided gratis by Dame Nature for the women during their walks abroad, it had very decided drawbacks in situations where it could not be renewed. For in hot, dry weather indoors, the leaves had a tendency to shrivel up, with consequences more easily imagined than described. Whatever may be said in an artistic sense regarding 'the well-developed and finely-formed' girls seen by Colonel Dalton who, 'as the light, leafy costume left the outlines of the figure entirely nude . . . would have made good studies for a sculptor,' nothing, it was admitted, could be urged in the case of individuals in the 'sear and yellow leaf,' who, if rumour does not err, are apt to develop into veritable hags. A general consensus of opinion was therefore arrived at by the Joangs and other similar tribes, that clothing of a more durable consistency than mere jungle produce was imperative.

Encouraged by the gift of cloth to some of their women, the Joangs accepted this material as a substitute for leaves. But the alternative failed to satisfy other tribes, whose inventive genius positively ran riot in their efforts to devise indestructible clothing. It will suffice to give the Abor group as an example, as they set the fashion in this region. All females belonging to this clan with pretensions to youth wear suspended in front from a string round the loins a row of

* Dalton's 'Ethnology of Bengal.' Calcutta, 1872.

three to a dozen shell-shaped embossed plates of bell-metal from about six to three inches in diameter, the largest in the middle, the others gradually diminishing in size till they reach the hips, which rattle and chink as they move like prisoner's chains. The women of the Miri sub-clan, in lieu of the brass plates of the Abor lasses, wear a small petticoat of cane woven together about a foot in breadth, and fastened so tightly round the loins that it restrains the free use of the thighs, and causes the women to move with a short, mincing motion. The female costume of the Miri hill tribe is also very elaborate and peculiar. It is described as a short petticoat 'reaching from the loins to the knees, secured to a broad belt of leather, which is ornamented with brass bosses. Outside this they wear the singular crinoline of cane-work . . . often the sole garment of the neighbouring clan.'

The costumes of both men and women of many of the other tribes is often very fantastic and picturesque. But it is no part of our design to enter into a detailed description of the various eccentricities of Fashion which must be obeyed by her simple votaries in these out-of-the-way regions, as implicitly as by her more sophisticated slaves in Europe, whether her decree takes the form of a panoply causing a savage to be so hideous as to strike his enemy with terror, or resolves itself into the triumphs of a Worth, making a Western belle 'beautiful for ever.'

A considerable difference of opinion exists

among the various clans as to what constitutes comfort and convenience in domestic architecture. Some, it must be confessed, are extremely moderate in their requirements, others somewhat fastidious. The former, content to be cribbed, cabined, and confined, pack themselves sardine fashion when they retire for the night, and, if rumour be true, sometimes sandwich themselves with their pigs and goats; while not a few indulge in large and commodious dwellings, relegating their cattle and poultry elsewhere. The huts of the Joangs, says Colonel Dalton, are amongst the smallest that human beings ever deliberately constructed as dwellings. They measure about six feet by eight, and are very low, with doors so small as to preclude the idea of a corpulent householder. Scanty as are the above dimensions for a family dwelling, the interior is divided into two compartments, one of which is the store-room, the other used for all domestic arrangements. The 'paterfamilias' and all his belongings of the female sex huddle together in this one stall, not much larger than a dog-kennel, the boys and other unmarried males of the family finding quarters in the bachelors' hall, which exists in all their villages. The houses of some other tribes are comparatively palatial, especially those of the chiefs. Notably those of the Mishmis and Nagas, —who affect the long Himalaic pattern, the largest varying from thirty to one hundred and sixty feet in length, by eleven to forty feet in breadth,— containing numerous compartments. The æsthetic sense of the proprietors of these abodes, as is the case with the Lawas in the Shan States region, finds expression in the adornment of the walls with trophies of the chase as well as ghastly memorials of ferocity and vengeance * in the shape of human skulls, some obtained in fair fight, and others by the most diabolical treachery. These exhibits are records of the proprietor's achievements only, for etiquette forbids retaining in his gallery skulls acquired by his predecessors. We are thus brought face to face with a custom of great antiquity, and the direct cause of tribal isolation and continual warfare. As long as the social position of a man was determined by having his face tattooed, a distinction which could only be attained by producing a human head to his chief, who conferred the 'ak' or patent for such decoration—as much valued as knighthood with us—so long did these atrocities continue. The worst of this practice was that women and children were as often killed as men by individuals who desired the 'ak.' It was quite incomprehensible to them how such dastardly acts could be unmanly.

The border tribes, without exception, are, to all intents and purposes, omniverous. The bounteous forest with its various denizens, the fine rivers and limpid streams that trend therein and their inhabitants, are their unfailing friends, and supply

* All around the walls to grace,
Hung trophies of the fight or chase.
Lady of the Lake.

all their modest wants. Much of the vegetable and animal kingdom which we, in our philosophy, eschew, these Children of the Forest thankfully utilise as gifts from the gods. 'They have,' says Colonel Dalton, 'as keen a knowledge of what is edible among the spontaneous products of the jungles as have the monkeys, and have often to use this knowledge for self-preservation, as they are frequently subjected to failure of crops, and, even in favourable seasons, do not always raise sufficient for the year's consumption.' Besides the animal, ornithological, piscatorial, and vegetarian items of Western fare, the flesh of tigers, bears, elephants, monkeys, dogs, alligators, lizards, squirrels, rats, field-mice, and such small deer, are not only included in their *menu* but are considered very palatable, especially if cooked so as to develop their gastronomical excellencies. Thus 'the Nagas have a partiality for a dog who has just been full fed with rice and milk. He is hastily killed and cooked whole—*chien farci au naturel.*' *

Owing partly to sparseness of population, and partly to climatic causes, a most wasteful system of husbandry, known as Toungya in Burma and Jum in Assam, is tolerated by the Government, though anathematised by its forest officers. It consists in clearing a patch of forest land, setting fire to the fallen jungle, and sowing in the ashes a miscellaneous crop of rice, pumpkins, and other vegetables. 'In ages transcending memory and

* J. L. Kipling's 'Beast and Man in India.' London, 1891.

tradition,' the ancestors of the Toungya workers (says Mr. Hodgson) 'passed beyond the savage and hunter state, and the nomadic and herdman's state, and have advanced to the third, or agricultural grade of social progress, but so as to indicate a not entirely broken connection with the precedent condition of things; for, though cultivators, all and exclusively, they are nomadic cultivators—so little connected with any one spot that there is no equivalent for village in their language.' Increase of population, to the joy of the Forest Department, has, as a matter of course, forced the Government to abandon their policy of non-interference. According to the Pegu Conservator of Forests, the 'Karens themselves say that they were once like the jungle fowl, hiding where they liked, scratching the earth here and there; putting in a grain of rice, and eating what came of it if the Nats permitted; but, now that the Forest Department has put them into boundaries here and boundaries there, they feel like pigs in a pen.'

In the meantime, however, the manifest propriety of utilising malaria-proof people in opening out malarious districts deadly to others, is eminently worthy of serious consideration. This idea was probably in Sir George White's mind when, after his military operations in Burma, he reported that 'a cooly corps composed of suitable hill-men, such as the Kassias, is indispensable.' On the Assam frontier, indigenous, in lieu of unimported labour, has been profitably utilised in making roads. The Nagas who, at one time, had been among the most obstructive in matters connected with this region, now show a good example by offering voluntarily to do work of this kind. This fact is suggestive of equally desirable results elsewhere.

Nestled in the centre of a chain of valleys connecting India with Upper Burma is the small State of Manipur, an *imperium in imperio* about the size of Wales, of very melancholy interest to Englishmen, by reason of the terrible disaster which occurred there in the spring of 1891. A peculiar feature in its administration is that, in lieu of payment in cash or its equivalent, every man gives ten days' labour out of every forty to the Rajah. In lieu thereof the latter allots him a plot of land, and, with commendable public spirit, generally utilises his labour concession in road-making, so that the internal communications of the country are very creditable compared with what obtains among the surrounding tribes.

Manipur has three outlets for its commerce—two by routes which, according to tradition, were selected by the wave of Aryan immigration which settled in the upper basin of the Irawadi. But, owing to difficulties in connection chiefly with want of cheap carriage, it is practically cut off from the outer world, as we found to our cost when troops had to be sent there to restore order. The geographical position of the little State naturally attracts attention, but, surrounded as it is by hills of considerable elevation, the question as to whether it can be included within the projected system of trade intercommunication between Burma and India appears highly problematical.

'Manipur,' says Sir James Johnstone, formerly its Political Agent, 'contains scenery of surpassing beauty, every variety of climate from an almost tropical one to one almost colder than that of England; it is the home of an intelligent race of people quite distinct from any other Indian one, and with a history and civilisation of its own well worth a little study.'*

The Manipuris, traditionally of Indo-Chinese origin, claim, it seems, like the Burmese, to have Aryan blood in their veins. Even by their own showing, however, they are of very mixed race, for till very recent times they admit they have had the most intimate intercourse with the surrounding tribes, and to this day conform to Naga usage in some of their most important rites. They are described as far more industrious and energetic than their neighbours.

Sir J. Johnstone tells us that the Government of Manipur is a 'pure despotism tempered by assassination and revolution,'—a downright system which we, in our possibly less robust philosophy have discarded, but of which the people are proud. 'It reflects credit, in their eyes,' he goes on to say, 'on all their race; and associated with it in their minds are their pageants, their processions, their boat-races, their festivals, their golden bazaar, their miniature military triumphs, and

* *Nineteenth Century*. June, 1891.

their royal progresses; all these are dear to the people, and are the outcome and natural growth of their own native system.'*

Like the ancient Roman general who, after returning from a successful campaign, esteemed the crown of laurel as the highest possible reward for his services, so, under similar circumstances, the Manipur commander covets the benediction of his Rajah beyond any material recompense. 'Happy were it for us, perhaps,' remarks the former Political Agent, 'if our tastes were so simple, and if we aspired no higher than to do our duty and earn the approval of our fellow-creatures!'

In the beginning of the century, Manipur was noted for its excellent ponies and cattle, but these seem to have altogether disappeared after the Burmese invasion in 1819, when the inhabitants were nearly exterminated. The English have endeavoured to aid the people in restoring these famous breeds, but unhappily with only partial success.

Everyone now knows that the popular game of polo, or hockey on horseback, was introduced from Manipur, where it forms a great national pastime for everyone who can get a mount, while those not so privileged are content to play it on foot. It is ingeniously suggested that the English name for the game is derived from pulu, the Tibetan for ball.

* *Nineteenth Century.* June, 1891.

CHAPTER XII.

A FIELD FOR COMMERCIAL ENTERPRISE.

Ancient Fascination of Far Cathay—Vasco da Gama and his Successors—Mineral Wealth of Yunnan Proverbial—Ssn-ch'-uan Population Congested—Eastern Yunnan Trade Dominated by French—Persistence of Commercial Chambers for Construction of Railways to China—Railways in Burma Successful—Chinese Emigration should be Encouraged—Purchas and other Mediæval Travellers—Power of King of Pegu—Commissariat in Burmese Armies—M'Leod's Journey in 1839—Burmese Rubies in the Sixteenth Century—Statistics of Burmese Trade—The Great Drawback to Commerce—Want of Roads—Burmese and Chinese Customers—A well-known Fable Quoted.

From the very earliest times, the Indies and Far Cathay exercised a special fascination on Western peoples. Though 'the ancient policy and habits of Rome were opposed to commercial development, and her landholders in the heyday of her insolent adolescence denounced both commerce and the arts as business of slaves and freed men,' * she subsequently changed this line of conduct, and nowhere did the pulse of mercantile life beat more energetically than in the great city which afterwards became the nucleus of the commercial

* Merivale's 'History of the Romans.' London, 1875.

activity of the world. The impetus was given by Augustus, yet, as Gibbon says, it was reserved for the Antonines to open out new communications with India and China by sea, a policy which owed its origin to the public losses caused by the abnormal prices demanded for silk, carried overland at great cost and risk from the land of Seres or China, which had become indispensable to the luxurious Romans. Besides encouraging improvements in navigation, there is also reason to believe that they brought diplomacy to bear on the Celestials in the interests of commerce. According to Chinese annals of that period, it appears there was considerable foreign traffic with Kiau-chi or Hanoi, the capital of Tong-King when actually incorporated with the Chinese Empire. Particular mention is made therein of a famous embassy from Antun, King of Tat-sin —*i.e.*, Marcus Aurelius Antoninus in A.D. 166. Though no record of this event is to be found in Latin authors, who never condescended to allude to anything so vulgar as trade, it is worthy of note that silk and other commodities, which heretofore had been so expensive that only the rich could indulge therein, became so cheap in the reign of that famous Emperor as to be within the reach of all.

To Westerns, the Red Sea then, as now, was the legitimate highway to the East; hence the isthmus that prevented water communication therewith was wont to be denounced as an invidious freak of nature. After various abortive attempts had been made to counteract this anomaly, commencing with Pharoah-Neco's in B.C. 610, success was only lately achieved by a rare combination of diplomatic ability, perseverance, energy, skill, and tact on the part of Monsieur de Lesseps, which resulted in the meeting of the waters of the Orient and the Occident, bringing Far Cathay as it were to their very doors. In vain hope of reaching India by any such short cut, Vasco da Gama was glad to arrive at the goal of his aspirations by a very round-about way. The Portuguese, Dutch, French, and English, successively taking advantage of the great discoverer's initiative, formed settlements in that country, which at various periods were to all a source of glory and of wealth. It was long before the English committed themselves to this policy. Only, in fact, after the accession of Henry VII. did they feel the impulse of maritime discovery and commercial enterprise, the germs of which were sown when their merchants attended the markets of Bruges, where the produce of the unexplored North was exchanged for the treasures of the East. The English, in spite of getting a bad start in the race for this great prize, passed the winning-post first, distancing all competitors and effectually discouraging them from any further competition.

Immediately after the opening of the Suez Canal, however, the long dormant tendency of the European continent to exploit the East awoke to new life, impelled by an almost insatiable 'earth hunger,' which in 1885 or 1886, Italy's *anno dell ardimento*, or year of enterprise, Signor Mancini, the Premier, somewhat euphemistically termed 'the modern pacific crusade in behalf of Civilisation.' But with an enormous Indian trade which is ever expanding; with her actual and prospective profits in Cathay and Farther India; and commanding at the same time more than three-fourths of the Canal traffic, England can well afford to allow other nations to share with her the gifts provided by the gods, and can make allowance, with perfect equanimity, for the eccentricities of the new departure.

Before the Chifu convention was arrived at, British trade was confined strictly to a few seaports, but now has reached many important regions in the interior, and in course of time will probably influence the South-Western provinces which various mercantile communities in Burma have marked as peculiarly their own. British expectations in the latter region were directly aided and abetted by their commercial brethren at home and in India, who were not a little excited at the prospect of an overland trade with China, starting from the seaports of Rangoon and Moulmein, the chief of whose attractions was the possibility of exchanging their manufactures for the produce of the rich provinces of Yunnan and S'su-ch'-uan by a short cut, instead of carrying them by the long and rather dangerous sea route *viâ* the Straits of Malacca and the Indian Archipelago.

Some twenty years ago, the indefatigable Captain Sprye put this project before the public in tangible shape when he urged upon the British Government as well as upon several Chambers of Commerce in England, the great importance of a railway between Rangoon and Esmok (Ssmau) on the border of Yunnan. In reference to this scheme, Sir Arthur Phayre officially recorded that 'direct British trade with the Shans and Western Chinese, overland from Rangoon, is of vast importance. To British Burma it is all in all. Increase in trade and increase in population, and this increase from the finest population in Asia, the Chinese.' Lord Salisbury, when Secretary of State for India, emphasised the interest he felt in the scheme, by sanctioning surveys and exploring parties. His successor, however, reversed his policy, and the Under-Secretary for India, from his place in Parliament, stigmatised Captain Sprye as a visionary and a semi-lunatic. No wonder the gallant officer died of a broken heart. The whirligig of Time, nevertheless, has brought with it revenge to his memory in a general concurrence of opinion in favour of his views, which have been practically adopted by experts. British merchants, meanwhile, supported by influential Chambers of Commerce, put such pressure on the Home Government, that the Viceroy of India was instructed to take the matter into serious consideration. The latter, after due enquiry, came to the conclusion that Captain Sprye's plan, whether chimerical or otherwise, could not compete with the immediate possibility of opening out the ancient trade routes between Cathay and Farther India, which were sufficiently practicable in days of yore for the passage of the Chinese armies which overran and conquered Burma, as well as for large trading caravans. As considerable commerce between Bhamó and Yunnan had existed within recent times, the mercantile world, as well as Government officials, had also long been anxious that inquiry should be made as to the causes of its decline, and the probabilities or otherwise of its resuscitation.

From the reports received from the leaders of various missions, as well as independent travellers from China and Burma, we learn that the trade collapse was undoubtedly due to the Panthay revolution in Yunnan, and consequent anarchy so pronounced that its complete recovery can only be anticipated in the distant future. All agreed that the physical difficulties to be encountered in running a railway from the Irawadi valley to Yunnan-fu and Talifu would involve enormous expense, while the line would have to pass through a region depopulated by grievous famine and pestilence, consequent on a war which lasted two decades. Mr. Colborn Baber describes the line it would have to take, as the worst possible route with the least conceivable trade, and drily adds, 'I do not mean that it is absolutely impossible to construct a railway . . . By piercing half-a-dozen Mont Cenis tunnels and erecting a few Menai bridges, the road from Burma to Yunnan-fu would doubtless be much improved.' Alternative lines, intended to tap the richer districts of Southern Yunnan, advocated by Messrs. Colquhoun and Hallett, are heavily handicapped by political as well as physical difficulties.

'Fortunately, however,' says Mr. Scott, 'there is another way of approaching Yunnan which does not imply either Menai bridges or corkscrew tunnels. It has the further merit of passing entirely through British territory, and of opening up the Shan instead of the Lao States. Such a line would traverse a country which produces everything from indigo to tea and opium, from potatoes and cabbages to forests of teak, and is, moreover, rich in ores of various kinds, so rich that an Indian mineralogist grows eloquent over a spot so singularly wealthy in metal that he calls it a solid mountain of iron, and records the absolute paralysis of his compass. Lead and iron have long been found in abundance, and the paltry holes dug by our new Shan subjects yield an amount which promises to skilled labour a return which will probably eclipse in interest the much-vaunted ruby mines. Hot springs and mineral waters await the arrival of the speculator in table drinks, and the mines of sulphur may probably be as valuable as the seams of coal which have yet to be scientifically examined.' *

The ancient trade route, starting from Bhamó, acquired so great a prestige from the fact of the Chinese having utilised it for centuries in

* *Asiatic Quarterly Review.* July, 1889.

the interests of commerce and occasionally for the passage of aggressive armies, that enthusiasts hoped against hope that they might be able to exploit it by railway, and thus tap the rich South-Western provinces of China, to which Yunnan is a great mountain barrier. Although, in these days of successful enterprise, this difficult feat does not actually amount to an engineering impossibility, still the drawbacks are so very pronounced that they are by no means prepared to adopt the heroic remedy suggested by Mr. Colborne Baber. They know that a certain amount of trade can be reckoned on by the time-honoured system of carrying goods on the backs of porters or mules; but the degree of development attainable by this crude alternative, under the most favourable circumstances, is, they admit, by no means such as to provoke exuberant feelings of hilarity on the part of merchants looking out for new markets for their manufactures.

It would be idle to ignore the fact that by strenuous and persistent efforts of the British mercantile community on the Chinese sea-board, the head waters of the Yangtse river have been so very successfully negotiated by English steamers that, even allowing for the crass obstructiveness of Chinese officialdom, it cannot be long before the trade of Ssu-ch'-uan and Kweichaw takes advantage of this natural outlet to the sea. Ssu-ch'-uan is known to be thickly populated; Kweichaw fairly so. Both possess great natural resources, which, comparatively speaking, are lying idle from want of means of export, but capable of immense development, now that there are immediate prospects of obtaining a favourable market for products far in excess of their requirements.* Yunnan, on the other hand, whatever it may have been in ancient times, now presents the reverse side of the medal. Owing to war, famine, and other untoward causes, its population has practically disappeared, and the comparatively few people left are quite unable to utilise the latent capabilities which, in former times, were a source of wealth and comfort to its numerous inhabitants. That gold, silver, copper, coal, and other valuable minerals exist both in Yunnan and Burma, according to the legends in our maps, which are undoubtedly based on facts more substantial than the imagination of cartographers, still most of this treasure remains hidden in the bowels of the earth. The following extract from the *Quarterly Review* of July, 1890, bearing on the question, may advantageously be quoted here:

'All the travellers whose names we have placed in the margin† of this article are unanimous on two points: one, the richness of the resources and the natural wealth of Western China; the other,

* Mr. Baber, describing Ssu-ch'-uan says, 'Cultivation is everywhere dense; indeed, with the exception of graves and the immediate neighbourhood of houses, and Government works .... and the few slopes which are too steep for agriculture, every spot of ground is tilled, and most of it terraced.'

† Mr. Davenport, Mr. E. Colborne Baber, Emile Rocher, Captain William Gill, R.E., Mr. Holt S. Hallet, Mr. Archibald John Little, A. H. Exner, Leipzig, Mr. Alexander Hosie.

the rudimentary condition of its material development, and the (shall we say consequent?) deep poverty of the great number of its inhabitants. Taking Western or rather South-Western China as consisting of the three provinces of Szechuen, Kweichaw, and Yunnan, we find it comprises an area of three-hundred-and-forty thousand square miles, or about twenty thousand square miles more than the combined area of Great Britain, Ireland, and France. Its aggregate population is estimated at about eighty millions, or much the same number as find subsistence over the corresponding area in Europe. But in China the bulk of this population is concentrated in the fertile lowlands of Eastern Szechuen, which province appears to be hopelessly congested with a population of sixty odd millions, while the two provinces of Kweichaw and Yunnan are credited with barely twenty millions between them. The much-needed migration does go forward to a small extent, but it is hindered by the want of roads and the reluctance of the Government to facilitate mining enterprise, except when organized as a purely official undertaking. Hence the settlement of these two provinces, which have been largely cleared of their original inhabitants during the past two decades, proceeds but slowly. The causes of these clearances were the well-known Panthè rebellion in Yunnan, which resulted in the practical extermination of its Mussulman population, and the insubordination of the "Miao-tse," the aboriginal population of Kweichaw, which has led to their being mostly killed off from the northern half of the province, scattered remnants having alone escaped to the more inaccessible regions in the south . . . It is estimated that, notwithstanding the difficulties of transit, one fifth of the woollen goods imported from Great Britain into North China *viâ* Shanghai go on to Szechuen, as well as one-tenth of the cottons.

'In regard to Yunnan, it is reported that Messrs. Davenport, Hosie, and Rocher, all describe the vast extent of terraced hills and of irrigation works, now abandoned, that cover the whole face of the province, as well as the seemingly ubiquitous mines of gold, silver, lead, iron, tin, zinc, and copper, besides jade, amber, sapphires, lapis-lazuli, turquoises, and agates. Mr. Davenport winds up by saying, in short, a volume would be required to point out all the mineral wealth of this richly-endowed province.'

In respect to Szechuen, the article says, 'All the products of the sub-tropical regions here flourish to perfection, with the exception of cotton, which is always at its best in plains by the sea. In addition to the staples of rice and wheat (this latter now largely supplanted by the poppy), the land is gay with crops of beans, barley, maize, buckwheat, pulse, sorghum, ground nuts, rape, the sugar-cane, hemp, potatoes (sweet and ordinary), the tobacco-plant, and the mulberry.'

As the Sonkoi river is navigable to a point

within the frontier of Yunnan, the trade of the eastern portion of that province naturally belongs to France, as it is dominated by her Tonquin settlement. That of the western part, however, comes within our sphere of influence. 'There is, after all,' as remarked by Mr. Baber, 'no necessity for Governments or merchants to be exercised about the special advantages of this or the other route. Given a certain trade, and well-devised regulations to encourage and protect it, the discovery of the easiest lines of communication may safely be left to the traders themselves.'

Mr. Grattan Geary's conclusions on a theme which has much interested various mercantile communities, as well as a not unimportant section of the general public, may, in the opinion of those imbued with sanguine expectations, be too highly coloured, but in that of others undoubtedly gauges the situation pretty correctly. 'A great Burmo-Chinese trade,' he declares, 'is not possible, and it is idle to calculate upon it. Whatever trade is to be looked for must depend on the natural development of the country itself.' *

The mineral wealth of Yunnan is proverbial; but during the Mahommedan rebellion the metal trade entirely disappeared, and has not yet had time to revive. With perhaps the exception of opium, the same may be said regarding other products, judging by recent consular reports. Mr. Baber, who passed through Yunnan with the Grosvenor Mission, when trade was completely paralysed

* 'Burma After Conquest.' London, 1886.

and agriculture was absolutely at a standstill after a calamitous civil war, was 'astounded at the extent of poppy cultivation both in Ssu-ch'-uan and Yunnan . . . In ascending the river, whereever cultivation existed we found numerous fields of poppy. Even the sandy banks were often planted with it down to the water's edge; but it was not until we had begun our land journey in Yunnan that we fairly realised the enormous extent of its production.

'With some fear of being discredited, but at the same time with a consciousness that I am underestimating the proportion, I estimate that the poppy-fields constitute a third of the whole cultivation of Yunnan. We saw the gradual process of its growth, from the appearance of the young spikelets above ground in January, or earlier, to the full luxuriance of the red, white, and purple flowers which were already falling in May. In that month the farmers were trying the juice; but we did not see the harvest gathered. We walked some hundreds of miles through poppies; we breakfasted among poppies; we shot wild ducks in the poppies. Even wretched little hovels in the mountains were generally attended by a poppy patch. The ducks,—called locally opium ducks,—which frequently supplied us with a meal, do really appear, as affirmed by the natives, to stupefy themselves by feeding on the narcotic vegetable. We could walk openly up to within twenty yards of them, and even then they rose very languidly. We are not, however, compelled to believe with the natives that the flesh of these birds is so impregnated with laudanum as to exercise a soporfic influence on the consumer.' Captain Gill also alludes to the pronounced extent of poppy cultivation in Yunnan, and the prevalence of opium-smoking in that province, which resolves itself into a Chinese proverb to the effect that an opium-pipe is found in every house in the province of Kweichaw, but one in every room in Yunnan.

An entirely novel, if not an alarming phase of the opium question, has developed in consequence of the meeting of Cathay with Farther India. It resolves itself into the grave responsibility not only of governing our own recently-acquired border tribes, who one and all are more or less addicted to opium consumption, but in guarding our old fellow-subjects from being demoralised by contact with a country almost entirely given up to the cultivation of the poppy, and where even the wild-fowl are subject to its narcotic influence.

The benevolent, well-meaning, but practically ignorant people in England, altogether biassed in favour of one side of the subject, refuse to listen to the other, and are in favour of the revolutionary proceeding of either ruining India by diminishing her annual revenue by five-and-a-half millions sterling, or taking this sum from the pocket of the British tax-payer, on the crotchety grounds that her opium traffic injures the morals of the Chinese. With the easy philosophy which insists on this high price being paid for rescuing the Celestials from the consequences of their own self-indulgence, it is hard to conjecture what these easy-going, irresponsible, and wilfully-ignorant people will say now that the wind has been taken out of their sails.

'It seems hardly possible,' as Sir James Stephen says, 'to suggest anything that can heighten the absurdity of destroying the cultivation of the opium in India for the purpose of preventing some millions of Chinese from smoking it, and that for no other reason than that the English think it bad for them; the Chinese themselves insisting on the habit.'* To cap this unwisdom, the only available course seems to be the submission of a humble petition to the Son of Heaven, praying His Imperial Majesty to destroy poppy cultivation in the Flowery Land, because they think it also demoralises our own people.'

We have now to reconcile ourselves to the indisputable geographical fact that the province of Yunnan lies immediately beyond our border, a country accredited with various natural resources, more or less undeveloped, excepting that of the poppy, which flourishes exceedingly. With non-enterprising inhabitants steeped to the lips in opium, and ready to dispose of their surplus stock on the one side, and our too-readily seduced people on the other, opium smuggling—which almost amounts to a science in the hands of the Celestials—will be vastly increased. The excise department will doubtless be put on its mettle, but may

* *Nineteenth Century.* June, 1891.

readily be trusted to exert itself to the utmost in the welfare of the people and the interests of good government, to abate what must be accepted as a necessary evil.

The opium question, so far as it affects our other border tribes, presents altogether a very different aspect—so much so that, far from being deleterious, opium, when used in moderation, poses as a real friend to various clans who exist and even flourish in areas deadly, in some seasons of the year, to other people.

As noted in an article of the *Times* of March 21st, 1892: 'The legitimate use of opium in India is determined by two sets of causes; by geographical or climatic necessities, and by needs arising out of the prohibitions of religion or the temperament of races. The latter are familiar to, and clearly understood by, all careful students of the question, and require but a brief comment. It is found, as a fact of past history and of present experience which it is impossible to struggle against, that, when an Indian race or population is rigidly precluded by religion or custom from the use of intoxicating liquors, it makes up for the prohibition by the use of narcotic or stimulating drugs . . . . To turn to the northern provinces, the populations which consume opium most largely are the two finest military races of India, the Rajputs and the Sikhs. The Rajputs have never been under direct British rule; the Sikhs are the Indian race which has most recently passed under British rule. But both of them are in a special manner precluded by religion and custom from the use of spirituous liquors, and both of them have always made amends for the deprivation by the use of narcotic or stimulating drugs, among which opium is, again, the most innocuous . . . . These, however, are facts familiar to everyone who has a practical acquaintance with the history and causes of the use of opium in India. The other set of causes, arising out of climatic or geographical conditions, has not hitherto been so generally recognised. It is broadly understood that opium has its value as a prophylactic. But only those who have made a careful study of the question are aware how widely opium is used as a daily article of consumption with a view to the maintenance of health, and as a defence against the diseases endemic in certain geographical areas. Such geographical areas include most of the great deltas of India and some of the most fertile river valleys . . . . The deltaic populations are not, however, the only populations in India to whom the moderate habitual consumption of opium is confined. The use of the drug in damp and hot river valleys, which reproduce in some degree the climatic conditions of a delta, has long formed a subject of administrative regulation.'

The remarks of the Excise Commissioner of Assam in reference to some of the wild clans in that province, *mutis mutandis* apply to the peoples we are now discussing. 'They themselves say that they would die from fevers if they did not use opium, and I have known medical men who have had much experience of the province hold the same view. These people are opium-eaters, but not of the class described in the [Anti-Opium Society's] papers. They are good agriculturists, good subjects, and good fathers of families. They take their opium just as a good Englishman would take his peg. We believe on moral grounds that any attempt to prohibit the present moderate use of opium would be fraught with harmful consequences to these Children of the Forest. The only result will be the substitution of some other form of stimulant or narcotic. Now, what are the alternative forms in India? There is, first, the use of spirits, and, second, the use of the Indian hemp in one form or another, practically of bhang. We have had sufficiently wide and sufficiently sad experience of what the first alternative means. The Aborigines Protection Society and similar philanthropic bodies can testify clearly as to the results of the introduction of spirituous liquors among tropical peoples unaccustomed to their use . . . . The other alternative, the habitual use of bhang, would be a cheaper one, but it would be infinitely more deleterious. The *cannabis Indica*, or Indian hemp, can be surreptitiously grown by the side of every ditch, on every dung-heap, and in every homestead garden throughout wide provinces of India, and with ease in all. It is difficult to regulate the use of preparations made from the plant; it would be impossible to stop it. Yet those preparations are more seductive, and infinitely more destructive to the mind and body, than opium. We believe we are right in stating that deaths from the use of opium are almost unknown in Indian hospitals, and that crimes from the abuse of opium are almost unknown in our Indian courts. But bhang, even used on a small scale, as at present, sends every month its batch of victims to the Indian lunatic asylums, and produces every year its tale of criminal insensates who run amuck in Sepoy regiments, and perpetrate tragedies in Indian village life.'

That opium is abused by some of the more enlightened races in Burma is unfortunately true, but its abuse is infinitely less common than the abuse of intoxicants in England. A man drunk with opium is never a public nuisance, as he often is under the influence of spirits. The former may doze away his time ignobly, but is never offensive; the latter, on the contrary, by too pronounced behaviour, may be decidedly objectionable.

The Christian missionary, with commendable zeal, distributes gratis his tracts far and wide—'casts his bread upon the waters'—in full assurance of the truth of the Biblical promise as to the saving of souls. The 'heathen Chinee,' meanwhile, itinerates throughout the country, and in every out-of-the-way village is to be found also distributing gratis, with 'a smile child-like and bland,' his vile opium, knowing that he will afterwards be recompensed for the outlay by the increased demand for the drug, though the people be ruined body and soul. The respectable members of the Lower Burma communities, apathetic though they may be as regards the administration of their country, have very decided opinions on this subject, and would welcome a law similar to that in force in Upper Burma, making it penal to indulge in opium.

This idea was scouted as grandmotherly legislation when, some twenty years ago, a Peguan Sir Wilfrid Lawson clamoured for 'local option,' and when it might have been practicable. Magistrates and police-officers of that period complained of the demoralisation of their people owing to the rapacity of the excise revenue laws, but they were not then encouraged to descant on unpalatable truths. Now that matters have come to a crisis, and the remedy amounts to the heroic, the Government of India are prepared to prohibit the possession to Burmans in Lower Burma as well as Upper Burma, provided that the Local Government can show (1) the evil to be as great as represented; (2) that the prohibition is practicable; (3) that it would not entail evils as great as those which it is desired to remove. 'It might perhaps be good,' as an ex-Chief Commissioner remarked, 'to prevent the use of opium in Burma, just as it would undoubtedly be useful to prevent the use of whisky in Scotland. But the two things are equally practicable.'

The accounts furnished by travellers who entered Burma from China, though fuller than those of the ill-starred missions from the Burmese side, were, to say the least, notably discouraging. The reiteration of remarks on the results of war, famine, and pestilence—recording the fact of once populous towns and villages having been dismantled or become ruinous heaps; heretofore highly cultivated fields and gardens, wildernesses; the quondam robust and well-to-do inhabitants, veritable 'scarecrows,'—is heartrending; while the frequency of information detailing the trouble of ascending steep mountains, only to descend them on the other side, becomes, as one of the narrators confesses, somewhat monotonous.

We derive, however, some encouragement from the able and interesting report submitted by Mr. Davenport on the capacity for trade of the country traversed by the Yunnan mission in 1875–76. Though Bhamó was handicapped, when he wrote, by being in the possession of the King of Burma, he was of opinion that, in spite of the then dreary outlook in Yunnan, the Bhamó trade might be materially increased at no distant date.

After enumerating at length the various natural products, including the enormous mineral wealth of Yunnan, he lays particular stress on the fact that the province funishes the most delicate tea in the Chinese Empire, the plants being found all over an extensive range of mountains in the district of Puerh. He further records that before the Mahommedan revolt a great deal of yellow silk and satin was exported to Burma, probably for priests' vestments; but, in the reckless destruction which characterises civil wars in China, the mulberry-trees have been destroyed. That this trade will be vigorously resumed, Mr. Davenport entertains no doubt, as the Chinese have a special aptitude for resuming ancient industries which have been abandoned under fortuitous circumstances. Suffice it to say, the South-Western provinces of China have much to give for much required, and it therefore behoves us to do our very best to revive and develop the trade which formerly existed.

To return to Captain Sprye. History repeats itself in regard to his project. The Blackburn Chamber of Commerce only lately returned to the charge, and pointed out to the Secretary of State for India that it is 'highly important, for the fostering of British trade and the spread of our industries, that the railway from Rangoon to Ssu-mau should be taken in hand and completed with the least possible delay.' This high functionary, as is his wont when identical injunctions are received periodically from other Chambers, assured his correspondent that the communication should be forwarded to the Viceroy of India for consideration. Railways have been successful in Burma, and the line so peremptorily demanded by English mercantile communities would doubtless also be so *in time*. The *crux* of the matter, however, depends on the words emphasised. A short line passing through a Salisbury plain fairly populated and productive, is a different thing to a very long line traversing a congeries of St. Gothard mountains, sparsely peopled with undeveloped resources. The fact that the one can recoup its promoters for their initial outlay in four or five years, and even begin to pay a respectable dividend, can as readily be conceived, without undue strain on one's credulity, as that a very long period must elapse before the same satisfactory result can be achieved in the case of the other. If the latter were made, it would, no doubt, be extremely beneficial to Burma, as it would encourage immigration thereto, and make the adjacent region productive instead of being comparatively barren. But the Government of India, encumbered by a heavy financial responsibility, is unlikely to sanction the necessary expenditure for a gigantic railway scheme of this kind, in the face of official reports received from its responsible officers on the spot. Her Majesty's Consul at Bangkok in September, 1891, forwarded to Lord Salisbury a copy of Mr. Assistant Archer's report on his recent journey in the Mehkong valley, informing his lordship at the same time that he had also sent copies thereof to the Government of India, the Commissioner of Burma, Her Majesty's Ministers at Pekin, and to others interested in the subject, believing that 'by giving it full publicity in the press and elsewhere much good would result in undeceiving those who have been led to form an undue estimate of the value and importance of the districts in question.'

According to Mr. Archer, Indo-China may appropriately be divided into three zones: 'the upper zone, or high mountainous region, comprising a country over two thousand feet above the level of the sea, and extending, roughly speaking, from Burma across the Shan States to near the delta of Tonkin, and from Yunnan, on the north, to about the twentieth degree of latitude southward; the middle zone, including all the hilly country above an elevation of five hundred feet; and the lower zone, comprising all the coast-line and the lower valleys of the Irawadi, Salwen, Mënam, Mehkong and Red River. Chiengsën may be described as the natural gateway from the upper zone of Central Indo-China with its high, open plateau, to the fertile and populous valleys of the middle zone. The best route from north to south and *vice versâ* must be through Chiengsën, where the Mehkong valley opens out and offers a natural passage.

'If Yunnan is to be reached by a railway from the south, it must, in my opinion, run up the valley of the Mehkong from Chiengsën. Not only would this route offer no great engineering difficulties, but it would pass through a comparatively populous and fertile country . . . It must, however, be borne in mind that the trade of the Yunnanese caravans that pass through Chiengmai is chiefly in imported goods for the markets of Kyaington, Chienghung, and other places on their route, and that but little is taken on to Yunnan. The goods they bring down from Yunnan, a little raw silk, salt, hats, shoes, walnuts, and other articles of little value, cannot pay their transport, so that the trade in the woollens and cottons of Moulmein on the return journey alone is profitable. Considering, therefore, that the export trade of Yunnan is poor and unprofitable, while the import trade is small, it is difficult to find sufficient grounds for the high hopes entertained of the commercial development of Yunnan.'

In detailing his personal experiences, Mr. Archer remarks: 'Besides bullocks and carriers, we also met a number of large Chinese caravans. The muleteers are generally Mahommedan Yunnanese or Hôs, but some are Chinese from the borders of Szechuen and Kweichaw. The local people distinguished them from the Mahommedans as 'Hô Luang,' or men of Greater China and pork-eaters. The leader of their long train of mules is much more ornamented than I have seen westward, having its head gaily decked with silver trappings, foxes' tails, peacocks' feathers, and even gaudy labels of foreign goods. These caravans come from either the Northern States of Chienghung or from Yunnan, but one was composed of Chinese of a different type from the Yunnanese, and came from as far as Szechuen. To show how little direct intercourse there is between China proper and the North of Siam, I may say that these Chinamen are the first I had met anywhere in or close to Siamese territory other than immigrants by way of Bangkok . . . The greater part of the trade of these regions is therefore comparatively local, and foreign goods have very little share in it.'

In a leading article in the *Times* of the 4th April, 1885, pointing out the futility of endeavouring to rouse the official world to appreciation of the importance of new railways, new markets, and new political relations, declaring it is the nature of officialism to go on like 'melancholy smooth Meander, gently purling in a round,' and bemoaning the defects of a parliamentary system that provides no motive power to force officialism into any more fruitful kind of activity, it is suggested that, if plans of this kind are good for British commerce, British merchants should take the initiative without relying on Government assistance. When projected lines to Far Cathay are destined to traverse regions more or less free from control by any responsible Government—such as the Burmo-Siam railway, involving conditions wherein the consideration of political elements are inevitable,—even the most reckless speculator might reasonably hesitate. But when they are wholly in British territory, and England and China prove that they are fully determined to act up to the spirit of Lord Rosebery's convention of 1886, by which both are bound to encourage trade between the Flowery Land and Burma, the British mercantile world will no longer have excuse for hanging back; indeed, it will be to blame, if it does not rise to the level of the situation. The same may be said as regards Chinese rulers, who, as already explained, in days long gone by were endowed with a very pronounced political as well as commercial sagacity, which fully recognised the great importance of free intercourse between the Middle Kingdom and India.

When the English obtained practical sway over the magnificent highways of the Brahmaputra and the Irawadi, and a glance at the map proved that the traditionally rich and densely populated South-Western provinces of China were far nearer British territory than the sea-coast of the Flowery Land, the desirability of tapping them in the interests of direct commerce was fully recognised. The various heroic attempts made from both countries to bring this idea to a practical issue have, after all, only brought home to us the sad and uncompromising fact that the object in view is not nearly so easy as it looks on the map. A similar remark is applicable in connection with the notable French expedition which culminated in a brilliant geographical but otherwise abortive exploit, wherein the disappointment was enhanced by the discovery that the Mehkong was by no means a second Irawadi. The subsequent failure by which, at vast cost of lives and treasure, it was found that the alternative route by the Sonkoi or Red River was also impracticable, is similarly a case in point.

It will be seen, from what we have already said, that the astute statesmen of the Flowery Land, in bygone days, considered the possession of Yunnan of paramount importance to the Empire, because it dominated the trade as well as political matters connected with the peoples of Farther India. Further, it will be noticed that, in spite of encountering great physical difficulties, large Chinese caravans have for centuries, at regular intervals, visited the Irawadi basin, without being encouraged by the least reciprocity. There is absolutely, therefore, no valid reason to imagine that Celestial statesmen of the present day will reverse the policy of their predecessors, or that the merchants of the South-Western provinces will not take advantage of any outlet for the produce of this region, which necessarily remains undeveloped owing to the serious difficulties of export. Our bounden duty is therefore obvious, and unless we prove ourselves equal to the occasion, we cannot with propriety denounce the alleged impracticability of the Chinese—as we are apt to do—when by our own *laches* our pet schemes have miscarried.

That the Chinese should go heart and soul with us is, of course, much to be desired, for by mutual co-operation great results may be expected; but even passive indifference or actual obstruction on the part of officials will not avail in the long-run. For if we, alive to our manifest duty, bring home to the minds of intending settlers that our territory is a safe, pleasant, and profitable country in which to reside, and in this way offer sufficient inducements to traders and agriculturists to emigrate to the Irawadi valley, they will come, and, if we would, we could not stop them; the more so if, by improving the communications between the two countries, we practically prove that the easiest and most convenient outlet for the pent-up trade of the South-Western provinces of the Middle Kingdom is through British territory. The Chinese Government at one time successfully managed to put an embargo on emigration; but this craze soon developed proportions which defied control. A like result is inevitable in reference to the development of the trade of, and emigration from, this region. When once they have been fairly started, even the ukase of the Son of Heaven will be as ineffectual to arrest their progress as was the bidding of King Canute in the case of the obstinate waves of the sea.

The natural forebodings in regard to the advent of Celestials, indulged in by white races, are untenable in the case of homogeneous peoples; and the supposed difficulty of governing the former,—which some say weighed so heavily with Lord Dalhousie when he elected to allow the Lord of the White Elephant to retain a portion of his kingdom as a buffer between our territory and China,—would indeed be a sorry plea for refusing to welcome people who, if properly managed, would before long justify us in referring to our possessions in Farther India by their old name of the Golden Chersonese. *Apropos* of these remarks, we would quote the opinion of an eminent authority:—

'The one thing needful,' he says, 'to make the Chinaman useful, is to govern him firmly and fairly. The traders, pure and simple, will probably not stay. The landholder will, if he is governed fairly, as I trust we shall govern; but, as the Straits Settlements have proved, he must also be governed firmly, or he will be troublesome. He is very clannish, and clan-feuds are petty wars. The Straits Settlements, it is true, are supplied mainly from the populations of the confines of Fuh-Kien and Kwang-Tung, who are eminently clannish and rebellious. Their land is the cradle of political affiliations. In Yunnan we have a different people—just now fearfully impoverished, and I cannot say what their temper may be.'

In the interests of our sparsely populated possessions, the pronounced proclivities of the Chinese in accommodating themselves to quasi-cognate races ought to be encouraged rather than checked; for experience proves that the mingling of Celestial blood with that of the Mongoloid races in the Golden Chersonese has been as satisfactory as like intercourse of Europeans and natives of India with the same people has been the reverse.

As the author of an able article in the *Times* of 28th December, 1886, truly remarked:

'When the road to China is open, there will be a rush of immigration, which appears likely to have a very marked effect on the indigenous population of the country. There is no hard-and-fast line of demarcation between the Burmese and Chinese races. Cognate alike in descent and religion, they will readily blend into one people; and the Chinese, as the more energetic and intelligent element, will absorb the Burmese.'

The prospect then is, he goes on to say, that

Burma 'will, in the not very remote future, be mainly populated by a sturdy race of Chino-Burmese origin—a vast improvement on the present inhabitants of the country.' That most mixed races in the East, inheriting the vices of both parents, constitute an ethnological failure, has long been accepted as a truism; but the Chino-Burman, markedly endowed with their good qualities, represents a decidedly improved type, and proves an exception to the rule.

The Chinese who come from the littoral districts of the Middle Kingdom are practically as much temporary sojourners as the English. Though very useful members of society, they cannot be rated as altogether satisfactory immigrants. They spend as little as possible in the country of their voluntary exile, hoarding nearly all their earnings to take back to their own land; and, inoculating the people with whom they sojourn with their vices of gaming and opium-smoking, leave these accomplishments only as a parting legacy—for even their bones, in case of death, are sent back to the Flowery Land. Most of them, being traders, do not affect the labour-market at all, and consequently do not give rise to the heartburnings so rife in other countries where they drive the whites out of the field. Baron Hubner remarks that 'the last war of England and France with China was of incalculable importance, because it destroyed the real "Great Chinese Wall," which from time immemorial had separated four hundred millions of souls from the rest of mankind,'—in other words, it gave an impetus to Chinese emigration, which has been progressing with enormous strides ever since, especially in the United States, Australia, and the Pacific States of America. 'With wonderful natural gifts"—he goes on to say—'the Chinese competes with the white man wherever he meets him, and is checking, conquering, and ousting him, not indeed by force, but with the weapons of labour and thrift.' It is no wonder, then, that a violent prejudice exists against Celestials in the minds of white men thus handicapped.

Antagonism of this kind neither exists now nor is likely to obtain in the Golden Chersonese, where they come in contact with homogeneous peoples; and therefore it is to be earnestly hoped that we may be able to attract men such as those who constructed the Pacific Railway, in order to obtain the requisite labour for utilising the vast areas of waste land which are eminently adapted for tea-cultivation, and as such offer promising investments for capital. For permanent residents, however, their compatriots, who have for ages been pressing towards the Irawadi valley, are a more important factor for consideration in the immigration problem. If the movement be discouraged, as some recommend, its satisfactory solution must be relegated to a very distant future.

Neither the Son of Heaven nor the general public of the Flowery Land encouraged prolixity in the matter of travellers' reports. A narrative describing an explorer's personal experiences by flood and field, his conclusions, however edifying, or even a highly imaginative description of a conversation between a Stanley and a pigmy would have been denounced by them as intolerable 'padding.' The oft-quoted traveller who, after a long sojourn in a newly-discovered country, summed up his experience of its inhabitants by simply stating that they had no manners and were distinguished by odious customs, must have been a Chinaman and not a Britisher, as generally supposed. The terseness of his report would appear, in fact, to betray his nationality, as it is in strict accord with the recognised Celestial pattern. The glories of Ormuz and the Ind, for instance, were described by the Imperial Commissioner Chang Kien as a region 'moist, flat, and very hot, with a civilised people accustomed to train elephants.'* Again, according to Mr. Baber, 'if a Chinese of average intelligence and education be asked what he knows of Yunnan, he will reply that it is rich in gold, silver, white copper, and precious stones; that it is a long way off; that travelling is very difficult throughout the province, as shown by the proverb "Ch'ih Yunnan-k'u" (to eat the bitterness of Yunnan); that it is a very unhealthy country; that the inhabitants speak a very unintelligible tongue; and that it is cool in summer.'

Allowing for the glamour that afflicted the otherwise matter-of-fact Purchas, Fitch, and other

* Yule's 'Cathay, and the Way Thither.'

BURMESE COMMANDER-IN-CHIEF.

travellers of the sixteenth century, when describing the glory, honour, riches, and power of the Burmese monarchs of their time, and the numerous kingdoms and peoples subject to their sway, as well as independent of their rule, the whole of Farther India must have been well if not densely populated. To take for example Purchas' narrative of the conquest of Siam by the King of Pegu. 'Sion was the Imperiall seat and a great Citie, but in the yeere of our Lord God 1567, it was taken by the King of Pegu, which King made a voyage, or came by land, foure moneths journey, with an Armie of men through his land, and the number of his Armie was a million and foure hundreth thousand men of Warre; when he came to the Citie, he gave assault to it and besieged it one and twenty moneths before he could winne it, with great losse of his people; this I know, for that I was in Pegu sixe moneths after his departure, and saw when that his Officers that were in Pegu sent five hundreth thousand men of warre to furnish the places of them that were slaine and lost in the assault; yet fore all this, if there had not beene Treason against the Citie, it had not beene lost.' He admits that the possibility of providing commissariat for such a vast army is open to grave doubt, but explains that 'he that knoweth the nature and qualitie of that people, will easily beleeve it. I have seene with mine eyes, that those people and Souldiers have eaten of all sorts of wild beasts that are on the earth, whether it be very filthie or otherwise all serveth for their mouthes; yea, I have seene them eate Scorpions and Serpents, also they feed of all kinde of herbes and grasse. So that if such a greate Armie want not Water and Salt, they will maintayne themselves a long time in a bush with rootes, flowers, and leaves of trees; they carry Rice with them for their voyage, and that serveth them in stead of Comfits, it is so dainty unto them.' Fitch also admits this difficulty, and explains it in similar fashion.

Purchas had certainly exalted notions regarding the Sovereign of the country, inasmuch as he was of opinion that 'there is not a King on the Earth that hath more power or strength than this King of Pegu, because he hath twenty and sixe crowned Kings at his command. He can make in his Campe a million and a halfe of men of warre in the field against the Enemies.' Without recapitulating his quaint details, suffice it to say Fitch corroborates Purchas in every way.

Nicholas Pimenta, who visited Burma at the close of the sixteenth century, contrasts the glories of the King referred to by these travellers with the fallen fortunes of his successor. Pegu, which was at the zenith of its fame during the reign of the former, dwindled into complete insignificance and abject misery under the rule of the latter, whose horrible cruelties estranged his subjects, and whose insane folly placed him at the mercy of his enemies. The King of Siam, perceiving that his rival's hands were full owing to complications with Ava, entered on Pegu territory, 'divulging a rumour that he came to ayde his Lord the King. This was much stomacked by the King of Pegu, who sent an armie against him, commanding the Generall to bringe him captive. But this armie disposed itself, and, neglecting the King's command, returned to their homes.' To bring the recalcitrant sovereign to his senses, the Pegu monarch sent another army against him of ninety thousand men. The Siamese, by 'faire offers,' staved off the assault till the river Meh-kong rose as usual in March, and, inundating the country, caused such havoc to the besieging army that scarcely seventy thousand men returned home, and these without horses and elephants.

In spite of this catastrophe, the Peguan King sent four other expeditions against Siam, gaining nothing tangible thereby, on each occasion losing half of his army, and in the last his son also. Maddened by these failures, he determined to make a supreme effort, enlisting every available male. But his people, mindful of the calamitous results of former expeditions, stubbornly resisted this levy. 'Some became Talapoies (Friers in their Ethnicisme), others hid themselves in Desarts and Woods, and many sold themselves for slaves. The King caused Ximibago, his Uncle, to search the publike Records, and to presse one halfe to the warres, he also proclaimed that all which in such a space had turned Talapoies should returne secular; the young should be compelled to the warres, the old to be exiled into the Region of the Bramas, whom after he also changed away for

Horses. He ordained also that all the Peguans should be branded in the right hand, that every man's name, countrie, and condition might be known. They, seeing themselves thus opprobriously branded, Talapoies forced to returne, Secular and old men exchanged for Horses, began to rebell.'*

By his exceedingly harsh policy, Prome, Martaban, and other important places were alienated, ruined, and made desolate. 'The next stage of his furie was the Kingdome of Ava, where hee commanded his sonne the Governour to bring them all into the Kingdome of Pegu, now so destitute of Inhabitants; but, the aire not agreeing, they broke out into pushes and diseases, which also infected the Natives, that some with impatience of the torture threw themselves into the river.' Finally, in 1600, the tables were turned on the King of Pegu by the sovereigns of Arakan and Toungoo, when he received the same measure that he had meted out to others. The results of this internecine warfare were indeed horrible, effacing the population so decidedly that the dire effects are still apparent after a lapse of three centuries. An eye-witness, writing to Purchas, thus describes the scene: 'It is a lamentable spectacle to see the bankes of the Rivers set with infinite fruit-bearing trees now overwhelmed with ruines of gilded Temples and noble edifices; the wayes and fields full of skulls and bones of wretched Peguans, killed or famished, and cast into the River, in such number that the multitude

* Purchas' 'Pilgrimes.' 1626.

of carkasses prohibiteth the way and passage of any ship; to omit the burnings and massacres committed by this the cruellest of Tyrants that ever breathed.' Nicholas Pimenta declares the people were reduced to such want that they resorted to cannibalism. A very unlikely story, as the horrible suggestion is not corroborated by other travellers, and flesh was by no means a necessity for vegetarians, who had always the bounteous jungle to fall back upon.

Though Purchas and other mediæval travellers in the East refer to the country between Pegu and Siam, the impression derived from their rather vapid narratives is somewhat vague, as it merely gives colour to the belief—as already suggested in connection with Farther India as a whole—that it was then a more populous and important region than it is now. Fitch is the only one, seemingly, who speaks of it from personal observation, and his description of Zimmé (Chengmai), bald though it be, is comparatively interesting, as it proves that it was then, as now, a notable trade *entrepot* between China and Burma, though it has decidedly dwindled into comparative obscurity since his time. 'Jamahey,' he tells us, 'was a very faire and greate Towne, with faire houses of stone, streetes very large and well-peopled . . . . Hither to Jamahey come many merchants out of China, and bring great store of Muske, Gold, Silver, and many other things of China worke . . . Heere is a great store of copper and Beniamen.'

We may be thankful, however, for these glimpses of a country which has, till within very recent times, been consigned to obscurity, if not oblivion. Lieutenant (afterwards General) W. C. M'Leod awoke new interest therein by the report of his journey in 1837 from Moulmein to Kiang-Hung, on the Chinese border. We have since had the benefit of explorations made by various travellers; so, as Sir H. Yule remarks, 'One thing we can safely prophesy, and that is, that the veil will never again descend on the geography of Indo-China, and that the game of conquest and politics in that region, the vicissitudes of which have been heretofore almost confined to the struggles of obscure States within its bounds, will henceforth be played by powers from afar, and will probably influence the future of old European Governments.'*

The value of the Burmese ruby is now so universally known and appreciated that it commands quite as high a price at its place of origin as it does in London or Paris. It is, therefore, interesting to learn that this beautiful and deservedly-esteemed precious stone was, comparatively speaking, little thought of and almost a drug in the market when Purchas visited Pegu. According to this traveller, it appears that four royal brokers had then the monopoly for the sale of rubies, men apparently the incarnation of all that is generous, benevolent, and kind, who would scorn to entrap the unwary—veritable Brothers Cheeryble rather than of the Ah Sin type. They had such a large stock on hand that they naturally were anxious to secure customers for them, even at 'most vile and base prices.' Yet, constrained by a commer-

* Sir H. Yule's Introduction to Gill's 'River of Golden Sand.'

cial probity highly commendable, they never dreamed of taking advantage of foreigners ignorant of the value of precious stones. So very punctilious were they, indeed, in respect to giving no occasion for the least scinticle of suspicion as to their fair dealing, that, after giving their customers every opportunity of carefully examining the rubies in their ware-rooms, they demanded only their fair market value; they also allowed them to take the selected articles to their own dwellings, in order to scrutinise them leisurely, and also to obtain the opinion of experts thereon. And, as if these concessions were not ample, they also allowed them the option of returning the goods if they repented of their bargains; though, according to Purchas, these 'honest heathens would have preferred a blow in the face than that this should be decided on.'*

Recent statistics prove that Burma, under the heads of Trade and Progress, is advancing by leaps and bounds. In twenty-five years, for instance, the total external trade rose in value from £4,860,000 to £22,460,000. In 1885–6, or year of annexation, the revenue of Lower Burma amounted to only £2,580,000, whereas in 1890–1 it had increased to £3,550,000. Thus, in a period of five years after the annexation, the increase in revenue was represented by the respectable total of £1,270,000, while the increase in expenditure came to only £330,000. Apparently the bulk of the surplus revenue went to India, but the figures on this point are not very clear. More recent

* Purchas' 'Pilgrimes.' 1626.

returns, however, indicating the amounts allotted to Burma as well as those reserved for imperial needs, are certainly open to the remark that the supreme government has treated this very deserving province with scant liberality. The more recently annexed territory does not yet pay for itself, but it is evident it will very soon do so.

Burma, though the most progressive of our Indian dependencies, is still, as it were, in her nonage, and only faintly indicates the glorious future that awaits her, if justice be done to her very great capacity for improvement. There is every reason for believing that, some three centuries ago, the whole of that part of Farther India now under the British flag was fairly, if not densely, populated. But it has never since recovered the result of the internecine wars of the sixteenth century, so graphically described by Purchas. The effect of recent anarchy in some parts of the region has been appalling; but as the benefits of settled rule have, in many ways, already become apparent, and as the country is remarkable for its fertility and the abundance of its natural resources, it is hoped it will soon make up leeway and revert to its former prosperity.

Handicapped by absence of land communication and sparseness of inhabitants, the really great capabilities of the country are not so well known and appreciated as they will be when quasi-cognate races, now pressing downwards from the upper fluviatile regions, shall have occupied a territory which history proves is capable of supporting a large population, and recent observers opine may become the great granary of the East. Some idea of this great bar to the progress of the country may be gauged by the fact that, even now, hundreds of villages are cut off from trade for eight months of the year, owing to the impracticability of the jungle roads for cart traffic from the effects of the monsoon.

Intersected as the Delta is by innumerable creeks, its requirements are more or less fully met by steamers and boats. The same may be said of the towns and villages on the banks of the Irawadi and other rivers. But, owing to the labour difficulty, and the scarcity of materials for metalling roads, Macadam's invention is still practically confined to the chief towns and head-quarter stations of the different districts. Only a very few years ago, the most enterprising engineer hardly dreamed of a railway in a country subject to an abnormal rainfall of such persistency as to cause broken bricks, their only available metalling, to succumb to the least pressure in the way of traffic, and eventually to revert to their original clay during the season Jupiter Pluvius reigns supreme. After numerous surveys and reports which came to nought, the line from Rangoon to Prome, one hundred and sixty miles in length, at last became an accomplished fact. Financially, it was so successful that another line was constructed to Toungoo, and eventually carried on to Mandalay after the annexation of Upper Burma. The latter, while proving an equally good investment, resulted in good government, prosperous content, and other adjuncts of civilisation, in lieu of anarchy, dissatisfaction, and semi-barbarism. This trunk line, which now has its terminus at the City of Gems, will, no doubt, be soon carried on to Bhamó, and in course of time connected with the Indian system on the other side of the Patkoi range, through which it will run. A branch line to the Shan States, from which equally happy results are anticipated, has already made good progress.

When the initial drawbacks to complete success have been removed, which may be expected in the near future, it is believed that Burma and its dependencies, with their easily accessible and very convenient ports in the Bay of Bengal, and with peoples who promise to be most excellent customers, offer for some time to come a more advantageous field to traders than the much vaunted but, comparatively speaking, inaccessible Hinterland, with its congested populations, who are by no means so susceptible of being taught new wants as our own subjects. The Burmese are lavish in their expenditure; on the other hand, Chinese thrift is proverbial. Sir William Hunter, judging by the average surplus of imported over exported treasure, proves that the Burmese can afford to spend a much larger portion of their income on luxuries, such as personal adornment, as well as on theatrical performances, pony and boat-races, and other amusements, indicating a much higher standard of comfort than is to be found in Indian households. From what travellers tell us of the peoples of South-Western China, a like comparison holds good. It would appear that the Celestials we are so desirous of exploiting, like their countrymen in other provinces of the Flowery Land, are by no means so ready to part with their spare cash as are the Burmese, especially for articles they consider superfluities, such as novelties, however ingenious, which are intended to supersede old-fashioned contrivances inherited from their ancestors. Thus, on the Burmo-Chinese frontier, Captain Gill found that the little machine for striking a light by means of compressed air, in use with the rudest tribes, held its own in competition with Bryant and May's matches, though, by a mercantile enterprise that deserved a better fate, the latter were procurable in the market at a price only a very little more than they fetch in the streets of London.

The same observant traveller informs us that 'a Chinaman may express the highest admiration for a pair of European candles, but, if they cost a trifle more than his filthy oil-lamp, he will rarely exchange the glimmer of his time-honoured institution for the brilliant light of a composite.' Again he tells us, a Chinaman, if he can, will grow his own grain, grind it or husk it, and cook it on his own premises. If possible, he will cultivate his little bit of cotton, and weave the cloth without assistance from beyond his own household; all his clothes are perhaps made by his wife and family; and thus he is almost independent of extraneous aid. The Burmese and Shans have intuitively learned that this is not the most economical way of doing things. They are apt, it is true, to substitute cheap and flimsy Manchester goods for the somewhat dearer but more durable products of their native looms; but it may be urged, after all, that this weakness has its compensating advantage in the interests of British commerce.

Matter-of-fact people are of opinion that, before we launch forth into unknown regions, we should thoroughly develop our own territory, which, for some time to come, will afford abundant scope for our best energies. Enthusiasts, however, declare the latter can wait, and in the meantime must be content with the humbler *rôle* of providing a road to the regions beyond; and, having fully made up their minds that they constitute a veritable El Dorado, they persistently endeavour to persuade their countrymen to take possession of the wealth provided by the gods before it is snapped up by others. Though their dreams, as Mercutio has it, may not be 'the children of an idle brain, begotten of nothing but vain phantasy,' they resolve themselves, after all, into an allegory. Like the valuable treasure bequeathed to his children by the man in the fable, which he assured them would be found three feet below the surface of his garden, and which really consisted in the extraordinary richness and fertility of the soil, by reason of digging and delving it to that depth, so the enormous gain to be secured by the exploitation of Far Cathay and Farther India consists rather in their gradual development by ordinary prosaic methods than in the *bonâ-fide* existence of treasure trove.

APPENDIX.

LETTER FROM THE KING OF BURMA TO THE QUEEN OF ENGLAND.

From his Great, Glorious, and Most Excellent Majesty, King of the Rising Sun, who reigns over Burma, to her Most Glorious and Most Excellent Majesty, Victoria, Queen of Great Britain and Ireland.

'MADAM, MY ROYAL SISTER,—Prompted by a desire to act in accordance with the duties incumbent on independent sovereigns, who rule over great countries, which leads them to establish friendly relations with each other, if they do not already exist, and to cement, strengthen, and confirm Royal friendships which have already been established, I have taken it into my most earnest, careful, and deliberate consideration the best means to cause the great friendship that exists between Burma and England to be placed on a secure, lasting, and firm basis; and, having also an earnest desire for the confidential intercourse which independent Sovereigns should have with each other, I have appointed an Embassy, consisting of Mengyee Maha Saythoo Kenwon Mengyee, Envoy Extraordinary and Minister Plenipotentiary; Maha Menlha Kyaw-den Paden Wondouk, Attaché; Maha Mengyaw Rajah Pangyet Wondouk, Attaché; Menhla Zayathoo Saraydawgyee, Secretary to the Embassy, and have entrusted them with a Royal letter to Your Most Gracious Majesty.

'On arrival in England, the Envoy will have an opportunity of bearing personal testimony to the feelings by which I am actuated in regard to the friendly relations which I am anxious to promote between the two countries.

'I pray to Almighty God that He will ward you from all that is evil, and that He will vouchsafe to shed His benign influence over Your Gracious Majesty, the Princes and Princesses (Your Majesty's sons and daughters), and other members of the Royal Family, as well as over Your Majesty's nobles and officers of Government.

'Given at the Royal Palace of Ratnâbon (Mandalay), in Burma, this eighth day of the Waxing Moon Taboung, 1233, Burmese Era; corresponding with the 5th of February, 1872, of the Christian Era.

'I am, Madam, my Royal Sister,
'Your Great and Most Glorious Majesty's
Good and Royal Brother,

(Signed) THEEREE PAWARA WEEZAYA NUNTA YATHA PUNDEETA MAHA DUMMA YAZADE YAZA,*
His Great, Glorious, and Most Excellent Majesty, King of the Rising Sun, who reigns over Burma.

PAGAN GYEE MYO-SA MENGYEE MAHA MENHLA SAYTHOO,
His Excellency the Prime Minister of Burma.

* It is said that this was the first occasion on which a King of Burma condescended to place the Royal sign-manual to a letter or document of any kind. The Ruler of Land and Sea hitherto relegated this duty to his Minister of Foreign Affairs.

HER MAJESTY'S REPLY.

'20th February, 1873.

'My Friend,—It is with the utmost gratification that I have received the marks of Your Majesty's friendship presented to me by Your Majesty's Minister Plenipotentiary, the Mengyee Maha Saythoo Kenwon Mengyee. I cordially reciprocate the sentiments which they express.

'It is, as Your Majesty truly observes, always conducive to the maintenance of peace between Empires, that the Ministers and subjects of one Sovereign should visit the territories of another, and that thus, by the extension of mutual knowledge, the bonds of friendship may be strengthened alike between rulers and between nations.

'It has afforded me great pleasure to receive Your Majesty's Envoys, and I have observed with much satisfaction the cordiality with which they have been welcomed by my people in all parts of my dominions which they have visited.

'I forward this letter by the hands of a trusted officer, who will deliver it to Your Majesty, together with a portrait of myself, as tokens of my friendship and esteem.

'With assurances of the interest which I feel in all that relates to Your Majesty's happiness and prosperity,

'I am, Your Majesty's sincere friend
and well-wisher,

'Victoria R.'

LETTER FROM THE KING OF BURMA TO THE PRINCE OF WALES.

From His Great, Glorious, and Most Excellent Majesty, King of the Rising Sun, who reigns over Burma, to His Royal Highness, Lord of the Eastern House and Heir-Apparent to the throne of Great Britain and Ireland,—Greeting,

'His Majesty has much pleasure and satisfaction in forwarding the accompanying Most Ancient and Honourable Order of the Golden Tsalway of Twenty-One Strands set with rubies—the privilege of wearing which belongs solely to the Heir-Apparent of the Burmese throne.

'His Majesty trusts that His Royal Highness will appreciate the honour that is intended to be conveyed thereby, and wear the decoration.

'Given at the Royal Palace of Rutânbon (Mandalay), in Burma, this eighth day of the Waxing Moon Taboung, 1233, Burmese Era; corresponding with the 5th of February, 1872, of the Christian Era.

THEERREE PAWARA WEEZAYA NUNTA YATHA PUNDEETA MAHA DUMMA YAZADEE YAZA,

His Great, Glorious, and most Excellent Majesty who reigns over Burma.

THE END.